THE 100 BEST JOB$ FOR THE 1990s & BEYOND

CAROL KLEIMAN

Dearborn
Financial Publishing, Inc.

D0814905

Dedication

To my sons, Robert Kleiman and Raymond Kleiman Jr.; my daughter, Catharine Bell, and my son-in-law, Kevin Bell: The future belongs to you.

While a great deal of care has been taken to provide accurate and current information, the ideas, suggestions, general principles and conclusions presented in this book are subject to local, state and federal laws and regulations, court cases and any revisions of same. The reader is thus urged to consult legal counsel regarding any points of law—this publication should not be used as a substitute for competent legal advice.

Publisher: Kathleen A. Welton
Associate Editor: Karen A. Christensen
Senior Project Editor: Jack L. Kiburz
Interior Design: Lucy Jenkins
Cover Design: Anthony C. Russo/The Complete Artworks
Photography: © 1992 by Catharine Bell

© 1992 by Carol Kleiman
Published by Dearborn Financial Publishing, Inc.

All rights reserved. The text of this publication, or any part thereof, may not be reproduced in any manner whatsoever without written permission from the publisher.

Printed in the United States of America

92 93 94 10 9 8 7 6 5 4 3 2 1

Library of Congress Cataloging-in-Publication Data

Kleiman, Carol
 The 100 best jobs for the 1990s and beyond / Carol Kleiman.
  p. cm.
 Includes bibliographical references and index.
 ISBN 0-79310-420-3 (paper)
  1. Job hunting—United States. 2. Labor market—United States.
  3. Vocational qualifications—United States. I. Title.
 HF5382.75.U6K54 1992   92–256
  331.7′02′0973—dc20   CIP

"Knowledge is power, and Carol Kleiman's writing is and always has been about empowering her readers. By providing forewarnings of workplace changes, specifics about the best jobs and uncommon sense on how to get them, *The 100 Best Jobs* becomes more than a book—it's an investment."
—Gloria Steinem, author,
Revolution from Within (Little, Brown)

"No one knows jobs better than Carol Kleiman. She sees career prospects in the year 2000 as clearly as she sees them today. This one-of-a-kind book is a must-have guide and lifeline for all job seekers and all job holders—whether your collar is white or blue."
—John Sibbald, executive recruiter
and author, *The Career Makers*

"Columnist Carol Kleiman combines technical analysis and expert interviews with years of real-world writing about emerging labor trends. If you need to know about jobs and the future—and what student, employer or employee doesn't—you should read this book."
—Ann McLaughlin, former U.S. Secretary of Labor

"*The 100 Best Jobs* is ammunition for those fighting for a place in the workforce of the future. Bulging with practical facts and advice, it is a handbook for counselors, a step-by-step guide for new labor market entrants, and a powerful refresher for the mid-career worker who is exploring new options. It would make the perfect graduation present!"
—Julianne Malveaux, PhD,
contributing editor, *Essence* Magazine;
economist/syndicated columnist,
San Francisco, California

"Carol Kleiman does not just describe *The 100 Best Jobs*—she tells you how to get them. Whether you're eager to find a job or just considering a move, you'll find her distilled wisdom, much of which is given in the form of 'inside tips,' profoundly useful."
 —Thomas R. Horton, chairman,
  American Management Association

"*The 100 Best Jobs* is the most comprehensive and practical collection of information and advice on employment opportunities and outlook. . . . It should be required reading for anyone interested in career growth, seasoned or entry level, but particularly for those who have been disenfranchised from the process of selecting and developing careers. . . . It is written with unparalleled compassion and understanding of the challenges and tribulations that we go through in our professional and career growth."
 —Irma Claudio, executive director,
  Hispanic Alliance for Career Enhancement,
  Chicago, Illinois

CONTENTS

THE 100 BEST JOBS
(Alphabetical Listing)

Accountant/Auditor
Actor/Director/Producer
Advertising and Marketing
  Account Supervisor
Agricultural Scientist
Aircraft Technician
Appliance/Power Tool
  Repairer
Architect
Arts Administrator
Automotive Mechanic
Bank Loan Officer
Bank Marketer
Biological Scientist
Carpenter
Chemist
Clerical Supervisor/Office
  Manager
Commercial and Graphic
  Artists
Computer Operator
Computer Programmer
Computer Service Technician
Computer Systems Analyst
Cook/Chef

Corporate Financial Analyst
Corporate Personnel Trainer
Corrections Officer/
  Guard/Jailer
Cosmetologist
Court Reporter
Database Manager
Dental Hygienist
Dentist
Dietitian
Drafter
Economist
Editor/Writer
Educational Administrator
Employment Interviewer
Engineer
Environmental Scientist
Farm Manager
Financial Planner
Firefighter
Flight Attendant
Flight Engineer
Food Scientist
Health Services
  Administrator

PREFACE

This book grew out of my realization in 1987 that the employment world of the 1990s and beyond would be radically different—and that most people were unaware of what was coming. I decided to make it my personal mission to fill the need for information, so that students, job seekers and career changers would not be aimlessly looking for jobs that no longer existed or training for fields that are dead ends.

What followed next were five years of intensive research into the new labor market and interviews with experts willing to forecast employment trends in the coming decade. Much of my expertise in the area is based on the two nationally syndicated columns I write for *The Chicago Tribune:* "Jobs," which I've written since 1983, and "Women at Work," which I've done since 1981. Additional information came from "Open for Discussion," a freelance column I wrote for the *Tribune* from 1986 to 1989 that often focused on employment issues. From all of these sources, I found vital facts to help workers in a rapidly changing technological age.

This book is unique, because in addition to important statistical background and projections it has information not available anywhere else—a listing of the 100 best jobs for the 1990s and beyond. I chose the jobs based on my own intense research, years of being on the cutting edge of change in covering the employment beat for the *Tribune*, information from the U.S. Department of Labor and interviews with career counselors, directors of professional associations, economists, human resources/ managers and people actually doing the jobs I was researching. The list of 100 jobs combines facts and tips that no other career book offers: salary projections for the year 2000, specific job requirements and the inside track to moving ahead.

This book is for you—to help you find a job with a future, to switch careers, to get promoted and to reach your goals. It will give you the information and strategies you need to make the right decisions about what you want to do and where you want to work. It is for those searching for new jobs and new careers, for managers who want to know what the future holds and for employers who want to hire and retain the best qualified workers.

Job hunting, career changing and moving up the corporate ladder can be overwhelming, especially if you don't have the facts. But employment opportunities don't have to be a maze of confusion and frustration. This book will help you cut a clear path through the modern-day jungle of a high-tech society, a multicultural workforce, constantly changing job requirements, demanding career strategies and a competitive global economy. It will help you develop skills to keep up in a rapidly changing workplace. It will help you move up in a down economy.

Your success is what this book is about.

ACKNOWLEDGMENTS

Researching what will happen in the future is a difficult assignment that requires a certain amount of courage and a lot of expert advice. So many people have helped me it is impossible to list all their names, but I especially want to thank the following friends and colleagues for their insights, information and support: Bob Zachariasiewicz (I put Bob first because alphabetically he is usually last), Carole Ashkinaze, Jeff Bierig, Terry Brown, Dick Ciccone, Laurie Cohen, Koky Dishon, Wayne Faulkner, Terry Fencl, Sandra K. Finley, Mitchell Fromstein, Jack Fuller, Joan Giangrasse, Octavia Harriston, Bob Howe, John Jansson, Mary Jane Johnson, Howard R. Kaufman, Sheila King, Rick Kogan, Anne Ladky, Connie Lauerman, Rochelle Lefkowitz, Sherren Leigh, Victor Lindquist, Maureen Markham, Pat Matsumoto, Ann McLaughlin, John Mellott, Dorothy and Wayne Merritt, Brad Mitchell, Rocky Mosele, Lois Orr, Mike Royko, John R. Sibbald, Marge Simonson, Diann Smith, Gloria Steinem, Darlene Gavron Stevens, Charles Storch, Mary Suh, Karen Thomas, Larry Townsend, Howard Tyner, Fran Victor and Owen Youngman.

I am deeply grateful to my agents Teresa Cavanaugh and Jean Naggar for encouragement and frequent hand-holding dating back to 1987, when I decided to write this book. I also am grateful—and awed—by the expertise and professionalism of my publisher, Kathleen A. Welton; Bobbye Middendorf, Dearborn's senior marketing manager; and the entire Dearborn staff. I also want to thank Pat Stahl for her expert copyediting of this manuscript.

In particular, I want to thank *The Chicago Tribune* for its kind permission to use material from my "Jobs" and "Women at Work" columns. I also am indebted to the hundreds of people I've interviewed over the years for this book for their time, patience and expertise.

And a very special thanks to Terry Savage, financial author and friend, for her powerful example of how networking really works.

INTRODUCTION

It takes hard work to find work and to plan for your job future. This is true under the best of circumstances, whether you are entering the labor market for the first time, are a recent college graduate or have been working for a while and are looking for a change. It's true in the worst of times, too, whether you have been fired, laid off or are a victim of a merger, downsizing or takeover. It's true if you're a blue-collar or office worker replaced by jobs going overseas or by automation, or if you're a mid-level manager or executive stuck in place. And it's true whether the economy is booming to new heights, moving sideways, slowing down or in a full-scale recession.

There will always be good jobs available; it's just a matter of knowing how to find them. With a U.S. labor force of 126 million workers, competition is fierce for the top jobs that offer good salaries, career advancement and excellent benefits. Those who are trained and skilled in the professions that are expected to grow in the 1990s will have the best shot at positioning themselves for rewarding careers. But how do you know which professions are "hot"?

In this age of instant communication, knowledge of the job market is a powerful tool because the economy is changing rapidly from the production of goods to the production of services. While the future is not written in stone, much of it is being cast right now by technology. And now is the time to start thinking about careers that will be marketable in a society dramatically different from today, a society that is almost upon us. By the year 2000, the computer, television set and telephone will be one object tied together by fiber optics. Ultrasonics, eddy currents, lasers and thermal-wave imaging will be as familiar to us as microwaves and camcorders are today. This book will help you get ready for employment in the brave new world of the next 25 years by showing you how many of the professions that are popular today will be reshaped and redefined by the new technology—and how some will diminish and even disappear.

THE TRENDS

Many of the trends that will impact on your job in the 1990s already are in place. Here are some of them:

- By the 21st century, 90 percent of the 21 million jobs expected to be created will be in the service-producing sector of the economy, a dramatic shift that began in the 1970s away from the preponderance of manufacturing jobs in the United States.
- Two divisions of the service-producing sector— services and retail trade—will create 75 percent of the 21 million new jobs. The dominance of service jobs already is here: Of the 12 million new jobs added to the economy between 1985 and 1990, fewer than 1 million were in manufacturing; the rest were in the service-producing sector.

- Service jobs will not pay as well as the blue-collar jobs they're replacing, which means annual incomes and the standard of living of U.S. workers will, on the average, decrease. And because many formerly well-paid blue-collar workers will not be able to make the switch to high-tech jobs, the number of so-called "dislocated" workers—workers whose jobs have become obsolete and who do not have the skills to perform the new jobs being created—will, unfortunately, increase.
- In an economy driven by automation and high-tech inventions, engineers, scientists and mathematicians will be the professionals most in demand. They will be sought after by manufacturing, business, government and academia. Though the work of U.S. scientists is respected worldwide for precision instruments used in medical procedures and communications, and though concern about the environment is widespread, there remains a serious shortage of U.S. scientists.
- A college degree or technical or vocational training—credentials beyond high school—will be basic requirements for most of the jobs with a future. The service-producing sector of the economy will need workers who have specialized skills, are computer literate, intelligent and good communicators.
- Specialty niche occupations, such as those of bookkeepers, stenographers, word processors and administrative assistants, will give way to jobs with far greater responsibilities, including self-scheduling and management.
- American job seekers will be competing with workers from all over the world to create the best goods and services in a global economy that will become more international every day. But the United States will suffer from a critical lack of skilled employees

and will actively recruit trained workers from all over the world.

- Only 15 percent of the net new entrants to the work force will be white men, as the nation's demographics shift and present day minorities and women become the majority of entry-level workers.
- Flexible hours, child care, job sharing, working from home and cafeteria benefits will be a way of life in a corporate America eager to recruit and retain qualified workers.
- By the year 2000, three out of every four workers currently employed will need retraining for the new jobs of the next century.
- U.S. workers will change professions three times over their work lives and will change jobs six times—sometimes by choice, sometimes at the employer's request and sometimes because of new technology that makes their jobs obsolete or radically restructured.

WHAT MAKES YOU ATTRACTIVE

In the long run, the basic question you'll have to answer about your career potential in the 1990s will be whether you have the education, training, experience and inside information to make you attractive to would-be employers.

These questions are the ones I research daily as a writer for *The Chicago Tribune.* I've written my nationally syndicated Jobs column since 1983, and I realized early on that even job seekers with extensive schooling in their field are not prepared to find a job in it, despite their enormous investment of time and money to become employable. Many educational institutions and vocational and technical schools charge a high tuition to teach the tools of the trade, but very few professors or administrators ever bring up the subject of where to apply those skills. Every day I get letters and phone calls from new graduates, career changers and other job seekers asking about the prospects for their chosen profession, because no one has ever discussed employment trends with them. Another frequent query is, "What do employers want?" The answers to these questions might surprise you. And they should also help you find your niche in the exciting labor market of the 1990s.

MAKING THE RIGHT MOVES

Ignorance of the job market can be painful. Just ask a 35-year-old man who was a purchasing manager for a small manufacturing company in Pennsylvania. Concerned that he might lose his job because of drastic reductions in staff—the company eventually went bankrupt—he went to technical school to learn tool and die design.

"I felt that part of my problem in finding a new job would be that I had no technical background," he wrote me. "I wanted to do something about that."

Shortly after he completed the course, the company went under, but he wasn't worried: He had prepared for exactly this situation. "But when I looked for jobs in tool and die design, there weren't any," he wrote. "The making of tool and die machinery has gone overseas, but nobody told me, certainly not any of my instructors. I'm devastated. I wasted my time and money at that school. What do I do next?"

Fortunately, his training wasn't completely wasted because he was also qualified to repair tool and die machinery, a well-paying trade that, unlike design, has not gone overseas. Repairing doesn't pay as well, it's not as prestigious, but it's one of the jobs that will continue to grow in the next century.

Another reader, age 19, bolstered her high school diploma and experience as a clerical worker by earning a certificate in stenography at a business school. She worked days and went to school at night.

"The school told me their graduates got jobs immediately, but when I finished the program, I couldn't find a job anywhere," she said. "No one wants stenographers, they want secretaries who are computer literate and have management skills. I'm still looking for a new job—and now I have a student loan to repay."

I suggested the clerk consider working for a temporary agency. I had two things in mind: Temporary agencies are projected to have a large job spurt in the next century, and the big ones, such as Kelly Services and Manpower, also give new hires free training and updating in office skills.

She made the switch and sounds much happier these days. "I'm finally computer literate!" she said. "And I like working for this agency so much I'm staying on. In a few months, they're going to let me supervise a group of temporary clerical workers, so I'm finally on a career track."

Even if you've been highly successful, you have to cushion yourself for changing times. A frantic New York stockbroker, age 47, called me on his car phone to complain that after five years of making big bucks, he was out on the street—and it wasn't Wall Street.

"I went back to school a few years ago to get my MBA because I wanted to run my own firm," he said. "Now, I don't even have a job. What do I do next?"

I told him what he already knew: For the present at least, the party generally is over for wheeler-dealers, financial hotshots and deal makers. But the good news is that jobs on Wall Street are cyclical and, just as there are downswings, there will be upswings. I told him that unless he wanted to take a trading job at a much lower salary or for commission only, or to switch to the technical side of the business and research market trends—he might have to wait until the investment industry is back on track.

I suggested he look for a job in other financial services, such as banks, and at governmental regulatory agencies, such as the Resolution Trust Corporation. He ultimately got a fairly high-paying job as vice president of marketing for a small community bank. He plans to stay there until he can make his move back to Wall Street. He's naturally disappointed, but he was wise to get his MBA while things were going well: It was his ticket, he says, to his job at the bank.

THE RIGHT INFORMATION

The problems faced by the former purchasing manager, clerk and stockbroker are not unique, and this book is filled with information that will help you avoid the mistakes commonly made by job seekers. When I was a visiting lecturer at Harold Washington College in Chicago, I taught a course on jobs in the year 2000. Since the school is a community college and my course was given at night, I had expected the class to reflect the college's typical students: young adults earning their associate degrees at night while working full time during the day. Instead, the majority of my students already had degrees from four-year colleges. Five had master's degrees. Three had MBAs. And almost all worked full time. They ranged in age from 21 to 60 years, were bright, eager and articulate. And they were attending my lectures because they were in jobs they had prepared well for but hated or couldn't advance in—and they didn't know what to do about it.

In the class sessions, they learned about future employment trends, analyzed what they really wanted to do, met with human resources executives in growing fields and discussed what additional training they would need to meet their new career goals. Many commented that if they had known about the dramatic changes in the U.S. labor market that are expected to peak in 2000, they probably would have chosen different fields in the first place. But, after taking the course, they finally felt they were moving in the right direction.

In doing research for my column and traveling the country giving talks to clubs, businesses, professional associations and networks, I've discovered that most people—despite the fact that they will work for almost 40 years—make career plans almost blindly, without a clue about job trends. This book will help you avoid that pitfall.

A PERSONAL INTEREST

I have personal as well as professional concerns about employment in the next century. All three of my children have their own service businesses: Catharine Bell is a photographer and writer, owner of Catharine Bell Creative Services; Raymond Kleiman, Jr., is a filmmaker and co-owner of The Runman Company; and Robert Kleiman is co-owner and vice president of Smart-Text, Inc., a market research firm.

Robbie is the youngest, and his career path is perhaps the prototype for succeeding in the 21st century. He was 15 years old when he started scooping ice cream for the Ravinia Festival Association, a popular summer outdoor theater in suburban Chicago run by The Levy Organization, a high-powered restaurant and real estate company. Over several summers, he became a steward, moved up to handling inventory for Ravinia's seven restaurants—and fell in love with the food services industry. Between his junior and senior years at Lake Forest College, Robbie served as a beverage intern at Ravinia and got credit for it toward his degree. As I remember, he even invented a few delightful drinks. While in college, he worked as a waiter, checker and host at other Levy restaurants and for noted restauranteur Gordon Sinclair, learning the business from the bottom up.

At Lake Forest, a liberal arts college, Robbie majored in business—a wise combination of technical and humanities courses. He studied economics, marketing, computer programming and word processing. He learned to do payroll and inventory control. And he also studied psychology, languages and sociology. The latter are assets in the new business world where communications and understanding of colleagues and other cultures are vital underpinnings of success. After he earned his bachelor of arts degree, Robbie enrolled in a three-month course at the Echols International Travel and Hotel Schools. Evelyn Echols, its founder, recruited him by pointing out the hospitality business is a growth profession throughout most of the world, and that a hotel would be the place for him to apply his food services and managerial skills. She also showed him her school's placement rate: 97 percent.

When Robbie completed the hotel training course, he compiled a resume with help from a professional resume service that emphasized his background in food services and the variety of experience he had accumulated in the field. Echols arranged an interview for him with a new international hotel opening in Chicago, and on his first try Robbie was hired as assistant food service supervisor, an hourly job with commission. After 18 months there, he was hired as a food and beverage manager at the world-class Ritz Carlton Hotel—a quantum leap to management and to salary and commission. His promotion to hospitality manager came one year later. In 1991, he left the Ritz-Carlton and started his own market research firm that specializes in content analysis, consumer response measurement and customer satisfaction.

HOW TO USE THIS BOOK

Part I of this book gives more insights into work in the coming century. Chapter 1 presents information on the new demographics of the U.S. labor force and on the impact of a global economy on the U.S. workforce. The next three chapters describe the future workplace, the fastest-growing fields and the best jobs to train for now and in the next century. Chapters 5 and 6 explain how to get and keep a job with a future and how to change jobs or start your own business. Chapter 7 is a reality check to determine if you're moving in the right direction—with advice about the right moves to make.

Part II of the book takes a closer look at the top 100 jobs, graphed by industry—educational and skill requirements, industry outlook, career paths, current salaries, salary projections and inside tips. A glossary at the end of the book defines terms ranging from *career, job* and *profession* to *cafeteria benefits* and *global economy.*

Your job is one of the most important parts of your life. It determines your life-style, your quality of life, your professional status and much of your personal satisfaction. You will be working for the rest of your life, by choice or necessity, and the best of all possible worlds is to spend the coming decades doing something you enjoy, in a career in which you can advance.

The 100 Best Jobs for the 1990s and Beyond will help you master the complexities of the job market in the 1990s. My hope is that you will find in these pages opportunities and suggestions that will allow you to succeed, to contribute to society and—above all—to be happy.

PART I

The Changing Workplace

1

THE NEW DEMOGRAPHICS

When you open the door to your office in the next century, you probably won't be too surprised when you see a vast array of high-tech, sophisticated, computer-driven equipment. But you will be surprised when you see your coworkers: Radical changes in the composition of the U.S. workforce are projected to be in place by the year 2000, the result of current demographic trends that most people, including employers, are not aware of.

According to projections by the U.S. Department of Labor,[1] here's how the workforce will look:

- White men, for decades the majority of workers, will make up only 45 percent of the total workforce and, even more significantly, only 15 percent of net new entrants.
- Women, minorities and immigrants will account for 80 percent of the U.S. labor force growth. Women will make up 47 percent of all workers and will be hired for 64 percent of all new jobs. Minorities and immigrants will fill 57 percent of the jobs that will be created. By the year 2000, there will be

3.7 million additional Black workers, 6 million Hispanics and 2.4 million more Asian Americans.

- Though 141 million people will be in the labor force in 2000, it will grow slowly—by only 1.2 percent a year compared to an annual growth rate of 2.6 percent in the 1970s. The reason: a "birth dearth" of entry-level workers. In 1995, the number of Americans 18 to 24 years will bottom out at a little under 24 million, compared with a peak of 30 million in 1980.
- One out of three people will be 50 or over by the turn of the century. The average age of the U.S. worker will be 39 years, compared to 36 in 1990. And the country's 76 million baby boomers will be in their 50s. The largest age group of workers will be those who are 35 to 54 years old.

WHAT THE CHANGES MEAN

The many demographic changes that are going to affect the U.S. labor market are known as "the new diversity" or "the diverse workplace," terms that refer to the fact that by the end of the century employment will open up to anyone who is qualified. "When you're growing at 500 percent a year, you grab whoever walks in the door who can get the work done," said Sandra Gunn of Lotus Development Corporation, who started and staffed two new divisions in the first four years with the high-tech firm.[2]

Though all the changes are important, perhaps the most dramatic projection is that the white male will no longer be the typical new American employee. It means that previously underutilized segments of the labor force, such as women, minorities, immigrants, elderly, disabled and retired workers, will be actively recruited and retained by business and industry—instead of being last hired and first fired. The middle-aged, interracial workforce will be a stable, reliable and productive pool of employees, serious about their careers and job futures. As one mature minority woman puts it: "We'll finally be popular!"

Due to projected labor shortages, the United States will become a land of opportunity for skilled workers, regardless of age, sex, race or national origin. Despite the continuing debate over affirmative action—which opened the doors for women and minorities—employers in coming years will emphasize equal employment as a recruitment tool instead of fighting the idea. "Economic necessity means that women, minorities and the disabled will be swept up [by employers]," says a human resources representative of Shawmut National, a Boston-based bank holding company.[3] The ramifications of the new demographics were apparent to Ann McLaughlin in 1989 when she was U.S. secretary of labor. She told a meeting of the AFL-CIO that by the end of the century, the United States would be able "to deliver on a promise that has never been made to the American people before: We can offer a job to everyone who wants one, provided they have the skills, education and training for the 21st century workplace."[4] And, though employers will still prefer to hire a worker who is already qualified, in order to fill job openings they will be forced to teach new employees everything from reading and writing to highly sophisticated computer skills—in the workplace and on company time.

THE IMPACT ON JOBS
AND LIFE-STYLES

Demographic changes, as marketing experts will tell you, trigger the development of products and services to meet new consumer demand, and that in turn precipitates the creation of new jobs and the elimination of some existing ones. The aging or "graying" of America is a statistical change in the U.S. profile that will have a strong impact on what the new jobs will be. In the 1990s, people will be living productive lives well into their 80s due to advances in medical technology. As a result, jobs in the health care industry are beginning to expand right now, with excellent career opportunities for registered nurses with specialties in geriatrics and for occupational and physical therapists, opticians and optometrists, mental health workers, audiologists and radiologic technicians.

Workers will live better in the coming century. According to the Hudson Institute's *Report on the Year 2000: Work and Workers for the 21st Century,* the average standard of living will rise for the millions of new entrants to the workforce. Since women and men will be working longer hours because of the projected labor shortage and growing emphasis on increased productivity of individual workers, there will be less leisure time. That means less time for household chores and home maintenance. Janitors will be the number-one unskilled worker in demand in the 1990s. Housecleaning services, lawn care, child and elder care and personal shopping services also will grow.

Because of the influx of foreign workers and the need to upgrade the skills of all workers, employment opportunities for management and training consultants will increase. The need for a better-educated, more technically trained workforce will be apparent at every level. There will be a severe shortage of professionals such as scientists, English teachers, librarians, managers and sociologists with doctorate degrees. Those who have PhDs will be vigorously recruited by colleges and universities to fill faculty slots and by business and industry to work in research, quality control and employee training. (See Chapter 3.)

WOMEN AT WORK

The influx of women into the paid labor market goes hand in hand with the decline in numbers of white men as new hires. The number of employed women will surge to 66 million by the year 2000 from 57 million in 1990—a revolution that will continue to have a far-reaching impact on both the home and workplace. The issues that concern women now will be exacerbated in the 1990s by their greater numbers in the workforce: child care, elder care, flexible hours, on-the-job training, job sharing, paid maternity and parental leaves with guaranteed jobs on return, pay equity, sexual harassment, nontraditional jobs and opportunities to advance. One of the challenges in the 1990s for businesses that want to be successful will be how they accommodate the needs of their female employees. (See Chapter 2.)

"By the 21st century, we will have so much proof of women's capabilities and our successes will be so frequent that any nagging doubts about our abilities should be removed," says Eileen P. Scudder, a certified public accountant and partner with Touche Ross & Co. "The reality of more women in the workplace who have been professionally trained and who are moving up will force management to include more women. . . . I find there are many men today in their 40s and 50s who realize that their daughters are about to face these issues. And they want their daughters to have every opportunity."[5]

Though by sheer numbers women in the 1990s should have far more job equality, it won't happen by itself. "Training is the issue, through government programs and partnerships with industry," said Gloria M. Portela, an attorney and member of the federal commission on workforce quality and labor market efficiency. "Training is the difference to women between being employable and unemployable." The Women's Bureau of the U.S. Department of Labor forecasts that the "most exciting reality of the 21st century" will be that women, who are projected to change careers four to seven times during their work lives, will be into every kind of job across the board.[6] Virtually all of the new jobs women will hold will be in the service sector. The bureau predicts most of those jobs will be in career fields with a future and good pay, such as finance, transportation, telecommunications and real estate.

However, the Women Employed Institute, a national advocacy and research organization, disagrees. "Although women will account for the majority of the workforce growth, they will still have a disproportionate share of the lowest paying jobs," says Anne Ladky, its director. And Linda Dorian of the National Federation of Business and Professional Women's Clubs warns that "unless women learn the skills the burgeoning service sector demands—communications, mathematics, information processing and computer literacy—an underclass will emerge. Women will be the underclass."[7]

Segregation by Gender

Projections indicate that in the 1990s jobs across the board will open to women, a welcome change from today, when 52 percent of all women who work full-time are clerical and service workers and 40 percent are concentrated in only ten occupations with salaries below $20,000 a year. By contrast, men are spread across the remaining 500 job classifications of the U.S. Labor Department with average salaries above $20,000 a year. This form of job discrimination is called *occupational segregation*. But gender, it is hoped, will not be important in a labor market in dire need of skilled workers or in a world where most jobs will be done by pressing the right sequence of buttons on the computer to activate office or factory equipment around the world. In far greater numbers than they are today, women will be carpenters, truck drivers, plumbers, astronauts, engineers, police officers, auto technicians, radiologic technicians and chief executive officers. They will be highly visible in computer technology, which is new and open to everyone, rather than only in word processing, which is a dead-end job where they now predominate.

The women who now are breaking down barriers in the building trades, engineering, technical fields and other formerly all-male professions are laying the groundwork for equal opportunity for all women. "I love flying," says Christine Gardner, who became a pilot for United Airlines in 1989 at the age of 27.[8] In college, she majored in engineering psychology and, after being around airplanes on school projects, decided she wanted to learn to fly. "I earned my private pilot's license and met female flight instructors," says Gardner. "And that's when I realized I could advance and become a commercial pilot myself. Everyone was fair and decent, but there's always the element that since you're a woman, you have to prove your ability. . . .But once you have confidence, you can do anything."

OLDER WORKERS NEEDED

The "graying of America" means age will no longer be a serious handicap for qualified job seekers. Diann DeWeese Smith was 63 years old when she resigned as vice president of a major Chicago hospital. Despite her years of experience, her impressive credentials in public relations and fund raising, and her high visibility in the community because of her numerous volunteer activities, Smith told me she was worried. I assured her she would have no trouble finding a job in the booming health care industry and that she was protected by federal age discrimination laws. But her deep concern was that despite her achievements no one would hire her with her gray hair. Smith, who has custody of her two teenage grand-daughters and plans to work full-time for at least another decade to put them through college, also was worried that it would take a long time for her to find another job. She had been a well-paid, highly ranked executive, and it usually takes those jobs seekers—even the younger ones—at least a year to be placed in comparable positions. But Smith, who is respected in the health care community, found there were many people who wanted to hire her, gray hair and all. Within six months, she accepted a job comparable to her previous one and now is executive director of the Foundation for Hearing and Speech Rehabilitation and is a national consultant on health care and communications issues.

Her success—and the foundation's, too, because it has an extremely capable director—is an indication that barriers are beginning to fall for older, qualified workers. Workers age 50 and over, and some much younger, call or write me almost daily to report age discrimination they encounter when job hunting. I know their stories are true, but slowly the picture is changing. "Older workers soon will undergo a radical and welcome change in status," predicts economist Jane Bryant Quinn. "Instead of being shown the door to make room for the young, they'll be courted by companies seeking their strong work ethic and special skills. The slow 'discovery' of older workers will correspond with dropping numbers of the young."[9]

An Encore for Older Workers

During the massive layoffs in the 1980s because of downsizing, mergers and acquisitions, mature workers, especially middle managers, were hit the hardest. Now, retired workers are being asked to come back as consultants or as part-timers by major corporations in need of mature, experienced workers. The Travelers Corporation, IBM, General Electric, McDonald's, General Dynamics, Grumman, Digital Equipment and Harris Trust & Savings Bank have job banks—lists of former employees who want to work—to keep retirees active on a part-time basis, filling important job slots.[10] Federal studies show that more than 50 percent of Americans 65 and over work part-time, and David N. Gamse of the American Association of Retired Persons reports that "out of 30 million members of our association, 10 million are working and another 10 million wish they were."

Kelly Services, a national temporary firm based in Troy, Michigan, gives free training to workers 55 and older who sign up with the firm. Its program is called Encore: The Kelly Services Program for Mature Workers. "We're asking older workers to put their lifetime experience back to work because they have the skills and education that are needed," said Irene Adams, a Kelly senior vice president who founded the program. "Our mature workers are doing a fabulous job. We know they have talents, and we need their talents and want to put them to work."[11]

Lillian A. Wallin, who is in her 80s, is a temporary Kelly Services office worker. The agency taught her word processing. "Work is good for you," says Wallin, who was forced to retire from her job as a licensed insurance broker. "Otherwise, you get sick and, perhaps, die."

DISABLED BUT ABLE

The shift to an economy that needs brains from one that depended in many instances on brawn alone will open up job opportunities for disabled Americans in the coming century. Increasingly, people with disabilities—a term that includes those who are blind, visually or hearing impaired, mentally ill or paralyzed—are demanding their rights to equal job opportunity and to physical access to the workplace. There are an estimated 35 million disabled people in the United States, and 27 million are between the ages of 16 and 64—the normal working age group.[12] About 25 percent of that age group, or close to 7 million, work full-time; 10 percent work part-time; approximately 60 percent want to work but have no jobs. The federal Rehabilitation Act of 1973 prohibits discrimination in hiring of disabled workers and gives a tax benefit to their employers. The federal Americans with Disabilities Act of 1990 mandates workplaces must be made accessible to handicapped employees. It is not charity to hire the disabled: A survey by Louis Harris & Associates shows that a great majority of employers rate the performance of disabled workers as good to excellent. Other studies reveal that disabled workers have lower absenteeism and a turnover rate almost five times lower than that of nondisabled workers.

Paul L. Scher, a manager with Sears' Merchandise Group, doesn't think of himself as blind. "I think of myself as Paul Scher, who is extremely inconvenienced at times," says Scher, a *cum laude* graduate of Harvard University who also has a master's degree and a doctorate. "It's no big deal. I function with the equipment I have and take a back seat to no one." He urges employers to "give us a chance and evaluate our performance on the same basis as that of any other applicant. Treat disabled people as you would like to be treated."

A MAJOR PROBLEM: ILLITERACY

Though many previously excluded groups of workers will thrive in a service society, illiterate workers will be at risk. As much as 30 percent of the present workforce is illiterate, and the harsh reality of so many people who cannot read or write on an eighth grade level and who have meager skills that do not match the needs of the coming century is a disturbing demographic trend. The high percentage of workers lacking basic skills is particularly disquieting in view of the fact that occupations requiring the most education and training will have the highest growth rate in the 1990s, according to the Bureau of Labor Statistics. Almost half of all new jobs will fall into the highest skilled groups: managers, technicians and professionals. In particular demand will be engineers, lawyers, paralegals, health care specialists, environmental scientists, social workers, corrections officers and computer programmers and analysts—all jobs requiring advanced training. By contrast, there will be fewer opportunities for laborers, file and shipping clerks, messengers, typists and word processors—all jobs requiring little preparation. (See Chapter 3.)

NECESSARY SKILLS

A study conducted by Allstate Insurance Company shows the growing need for skilled workers—and the lack of them. Among the findings:

- Fifty percent of all new jobs created in the 1990s will require some education beyond high school, and almost one-third will be for college graduates only. Today, only 22 percent of all occupations require a college diploma.
- Sixty-one percent of companies surveyed report they already have trouble finding qualified people to fill professional and technical positions. And two-thirds report the current pool of applicants for entry-level jobs "lack basic skills such as reading, writing, mathematics, problem solving and communications."[13]

"After decades of having surplus entry-level workers, America's employers are now going to experience a steady decline," says David Pearce Snyder, a consulting futurist with the Snyder Family Enterprise in Bethesda, Maryland.[14] "Employers will be forced to pay premium wages for new recruits so inept that they'll have to send them to remedial training simply to bring them up to basic performance standards." Former Xerox Corporation chief executive officer David T. Kearns observes that "the American work force is in grave jeopardy. We're running out of qualified people." And Eastman Kodak Company estimates 10,000 of its employees do not have the basic skills needed to implement necessary changes to make the company more competitive in 2000.[15]

Personnel experts are worried, too. More than one-half of human resources executives surveyed by Towers Perrin report they are "very concerned" about the skills gaps. And many industries, such as hotels, fast-food chains and commercial banking, are beginning to do something about it. The American Society for Training and Development says corporations are spending $240 million of an estimated $210 billion training budget to teach workers the basic skills they should have learned in school. "The new worker will be expected to have skills that were previously required only of supervisors and management," said Anthony P. Carnevale, chief economist of the association. Carnevale points out that in a high-tech workplace, all employees must be able to think creatively, solve problems and plan ahead.[16]

ADVANCED ON-THE-JOB TRAINING

Though more attention is being paid to training unskilled workers, employers will continue to do what they've always done: offer programs to upgrade the skills and broaden the horizons of qualified, capable workers with potentially bright futures in the company. The rest of the $210 billion corporate training funds goes to keeping workers informed of rapidly changing technological skills and management techniques. Motorola and IBM, for instance, maintain their competitive edge by keeping their employees up to date in state-of-the-art automation.

New graduates are prime targets for advanced training. More than one million college seniors are graduated each year with bachelor's degrees, and many of them need additional training in their first job in order to move laterally to other departments, to move upward to positions with more responsibilities or simply to keep current. Corporate America has long provided programs for "the best and the brightest." But because of the shortage of skilled workers, corporate classrooms in the 1990s will also include new hires who have switched jobs or careers, retired persons working part-time in new fields and long-time employees.

THE HUDDLED MASSES

The shortage of U.S. workers will cause some employers to turn to immigrants to fill jobs, and landmark federal legislation anticipates this demographic change. Since 1965, the federal government has been extremely reluctant to grant temporary visas to foreigners to work in any job that could possibly be filled by a U.S. citizen. In the main, immigrants have been allowed to work in jobs requiring low skills and little education, to fill slots in fields that have high turnover and where employers are desperate for workers. Many of the jobs they filled have been those U.S. citizens don't want: They became domestic workers, janitors, cooks and hotel and restaurant workers. Few were allowed to work in the professions, but now that is changing because the United States is facing a severe labor shortage. To keep America competitive, the restrictive immigration law had to be changed.

The Immigration Act of 1990 raises total legal immigration levels from 540,000 in 1989 to 700,000 a year until 1993.[17] In 1994, it will go down to 675,000. The increase in total numbers of immigrants—465,000 will be relatives of current U.S. citizens—means there will be a larger pool of workers for the worker-hungry labor market. The most significant change is the granting of 140,000 of the total visas for highly skilled professionals and business investors:

- Forty thousand of the 140,000 new visas are earmarked for "priority workers" and those with "extraordinary ability" in arts, sciences, education, business or athletics.
- Forty thousand visas will go to immigrants with advanced degrees or "exceptional ability."
- Forty thousand visas are for college graduates with skills needed by U.S. industry.
- Ten thousand visas are for "special immigrants" such as ministers and religious workers.
- Ten thousand visas are for immigrants who invest $1 million in the U.S. economy and create at least ten jobs.

Despite the law's radical changes, by 2000 immigrants will make up only 3 to 5 percent of new entrants to the U.S. labor market, according to Malcolm Cohen, director of the University of Michigan's Institute of Labor and Industrial Relations. Cohen, acknowledging that employers already are suffering from a shortage of U.S. citizens with professional skills, believes that despite the relatively low percentage of new immigrants the 1990 legislation "can make a difference" to the U.S. economy, especially in a global marketplace where there will be international competition for skilled workers.[18]

THE GLOBAL ECONOMY

Cohen's point is well taken: Economies of the world affect each other by their exports and imports. This vast, new international development is encapsulated in the term *global economy*. It refers to the erosion of geographic boundaries for business activities, and job seekers throughout the world are affected by it. New York Life Insurance, for instance, sends its claims to a post office box in Kennedy Airport. They are then sent by overnight courier to Dublin, Ireland, where they are keyed into a computer in a small town 60 miles away. The next day they are transmitted by computer back to the insurance company in the United States. "In this way, the Irish have become part of the U.S. labor force," said economist Richard B. McKenzie, adjunct fellow at the Center for the Study of American Business at Washington University in St. Louis. In the scenario McKenzie describes, a job that can be done by Americans has gone overseas, but the global economy also brings jobs to qualified U.S. workers. Though Japan has taken away much of the American auto, steel, and consumer electronics markets, the highly competitive Asian country lacks scientists to do basic computer research—a U.S. specialty and one of the few electronic areas in which Americans still have the edge over Japan.[19] With the global society eradicating national boundaries, Japanese computer and electronic manufacturers are opening research labs in the United States near universities and hiring away prominent theoretical computer scientists to work for them.

The global "job bank" began to appear, with good news and bad news, as a serious factor in U.S. employment in the 1980s. The Urban Institute reports that one in six manufacturing jobs created in the United States during 1989 was due directly or indirectly to trade in exports. At the same time, the federal General Accounting Office says the manufacture of Japanese cars in the

United States cost Americans 36,000 jobs in 1988 and 1989 because of high-tech manufacturing techniques requiring fewer workers.[20] Welcome to the world marketplace!

A Small World

The global economy is spreading rapidly with the unification of Germany, the alliance of powerful European countries into the "borderless" European Economic Community of 12 million people and the reemergence of market economies in Eastern Europe and in the various Soviet republics. Already established as major players— as you know from your cars, clothes, shoes and appliances—are Japan, China, Singapore, Hong Kong, Taiwan, Korea and Mexico. Over the past two decades, the American share of total world exports has remained at a healthy 17 percent, and in the 1990s, the economic strength of the rest of the world will be a major business stimulant for U.S. entrepreneurs. World trade is a fact of economic life, and decisions by the General Agreement on Tariffs and Trade (GATT), a Geneva-based forum where trade disputes are negotiated, have a ripple effect throughout the world, directly affecting U.S. workers who make auto parts to be shipped to German car makers, as well as Taiwanese workers who manufacture consumer goods to be shipped to the Commonwealth of Independent States, formerly the Soviet Union.

Futurists say early recognition of the coming global economy will position U.S. business and industry— among them food chains, law firms, manufacturers and educators—to be successful in one world of work. The world marketplace will be a door of opportunity for U.S. businesses that have the courage to open it. Financial institutions and investors will be literally "on top of the world," creating multinational companies with international boards of directors.

What about the U.S. Worker?

In the excitement of rising to the challenge of fierce global competition, one aspect of the international marketplace has largely been ignored: What will the global economy mean to U.S. workers in the 1990s?[21] Will there be another surge in massive job losses from imports and outsourcing that already have occurred in the steel, auto, textile, electronics and shoe manufacturing industries? Will U.S. workers be competing with lower-paid employees overseas and with immigrants at home? Lynn R. Williams, president of the United Steelworkers of America, told a conference on the global economy held at Washington University in St. Louis that workers are concerned about what he calls "the lowest common denominator." The term, he says, refers to "the idea that employers seek out somewhere in the world the lowest common denominator of wages or of safety, health or environmental provisions as a basis from which to produce goods. They then ship those goods back to the United States, forcing our workers to be in competition with the poorest and the worst...in the world." Williams voices the concerns of Americans who fear their jobs and standard of living will slip away in the future because of immigrant workers. But other experts are more optimistic.

Effect on Jobs

"The movement to global economy occurring now means a very harsh, competitive environment—and that will have a profound effect on jobs," said Roger E. Levien, vice president of strategy for Xerox Corporation in Stamford, Connecticut. Xerox is a $13 billion document processing and financial services company with 100,000 employees worldwide. More than 50 percent of its copier and duplicating business is done overseas. "Today, we can move people to jobs or jobs to people," said Levien, who previously headed a think tank in Vienna established by the United States and the former Soviet Union to brainstorm global industry. "Most jobs are portable because of technology and transportation." His advice to workers: "A degree of worry is legitimate, but not if you have world-class skills. You will be competing against Chinese, Russians, Poles, English, Brazilians and Kenyans. You will have to do a better job and raise your skills." Robert Eisner, professor of economics at Northwestern University, says, "U.S. exporters of Idaho wheat, Iowa corn, Hollywood movies and Boeing planes are affected by what's happening elsewhere. If the rest of the world is more prosperous, that's better for us—it means we will have more jobs here."

World Standards

Washington University's McKenzie insists Americans will not lose jobs in the first decade of the 21st century when the global economy reaches its peak. "From 1980 to 1989, we gained approximately 18 million jobs, an increase of 20 percent," said McKenzie, also professor of economics at the University of Mississippi in Oxford. "And 10 million Americans are connected with foreign firms operating in the U.S.—3 million of them working directly for the firms." Because of the "full integration of national economies," McKenzie says "all workers must be on their competitive toes, to match not local but world standards. Otherwise, the jobs will go elsewhere—to those places that offer the highest quality at the lowest prices."

In 1976, Mitchell S. Fromstein took over Manpower, Inc., a temporary personnel service headquartered in Milwaukee. At the time, it did $300 million in sales and was operating in 20 countries. Now the firm, which was based in London from 1987 to 1990, is back in Wisconsin and does more than $3 billion in sales in 33 countries. Fifty-five percent of its business is outside the United States. "I think fear of being overcome by a unified Western Europe or by Eastern Europeans is overdone," says Fromstein, who early on recognized and became an important player in the global economy. "Excess labor in Eastern Europe will have a greater impact on Western Europe than on us. Don't worry so much about it: U.S. companies will come out strong as world competitors—and that will create jobs here."

Not All Jobs Affected

Not all jobs can be relocated or exchanged internationally, even in a vigorous global and high-tech economy. The shortage of truck drivers in Japan and of long-haul drivers in the United States will not be solved by an international marketplace. Selling real estate, most medical care delivery, laundry and cleaning services and government and law protection jobs are among those that cannot be transported overseas. "The fact that there will be increasingly competitive markets for many goods and services does not affect everything," said Ronald E. Kutscher, associate commissioner of the U.S. Bureau of Labor Statistics. "Multiple factors are at work, however, and when foreign investment comes here, American workers are employed. But, at the same time, when there are products that are internationally traded that we cannot make in the U.S. at a competitive price, there will be a serious risk that those jobs will be lost to us some time in the future. They will go overseas."

Best in the World

Businesses and workers in the United States must accept the fact that the new labor force will be culturally diverse and will have a strong international flavor. The projected demographic changes indicate expanded employment opportunities and the promise of new vigor and cooperation. "We believe these changes are going to affect profoundly [in a positive way] the competitive abilities of American business in the global marketplace," said Jill Kanin-Lovers, vice president of the consulting firm of Towers, Perrin and head of its "Workforce 2000" taskforce. The new demographics of the U.S. workforce add a special spin to career opportunities in the 1990s. Futurists emphasize that a global society means you will be competing directly or indirectly with job seekers from all over the world. Being the best and the brightest in the United States right now puts you on track for many of the top job opportunities, but in the near future you will have to be the best and the brightest in the world.

2

THE WORKPLACE OF THE 21ST CENTURY

The scarcity of skilled workers discussed in Chapter 1 and the new technology of "smart" machines—computers that do much of the work, respond to voice commands and link you instantly with sophisticated data from all over the world—will precipitate changes in traditional ways work has been done in the past and in management's elitist attitude toward employees.

Some of the changes:

- There no longer will be a "typical" workplace. Many of the people who now work at your side, in one location, will be working out of their homes or from offices or plants throughout the world, linked by automation and instant telecommunications.
- Instead of the traditional "military" way of management in which the boss (the "general") gives orders and the workers (the "troops") obediently follow them, the emphasis will be on skilled, educated workers making important decisions for themselves about their work priorities and schedules. The present managerial attitude that executives know all the answers and workers know very little will be

replaced by a mutual respect for the important contributions of each.

- The current erosion of middle managers will accelerate as those who actually perform the work add
managerial responsibilities to their job descriptions. And teamwork, slowly being introduced in
the 1990s, will be widespread with worker-
managers planning projects in a collaborative
rather than competitive environment, working in
offices and plants with top executives to set corporate agendas.

- In an information society, continuing education
will be one of the most important factors in professional advancement. Throughout their careers,
workers will be asked to upgrade their computer,
mathematical and technical skills; to develop communication and interpersonal techniques; and to
appreciate the cultures of clients and colleagues in
the global marketplace. They will be required to
take courses both at the workplace and in outside
educational settings.

- Liberal arts majors will be vigorously recruited by
employers who previously went after business majors. MBAs (master of business administration) will
still be in demand, but those with a strong background in the humanities will be preferred.

- The "old boy" network in which white males share
inside information and power only with other
white males will be challenged by the influx into
the workplace of women, minorities and immigrants. The result will be more parity in hiring,
wages, training and advancement for all qualified
employees.

- Flexible hours will replace many of today's traditional 9-to-5 jobs because of the numbers of women
in the workforce. By the 21st century, the so-called
Yuppie emphasis on "the quality of life" and "per-

sonal life-styles" will blend into an overriding concern about having enough time for both work and family. However, even though work hours and work days will be negotiable, some estimates are that worker-managers will be on the job an average of 60 hours a week.

- The coming demographic "crunch" and high cost of recruiting and training qualified workers will force employers to offer a large array of flexible benefits in addition to traditional health and retirement protections. Child care, elder care, job sharing, voluntary part-time work, family and medical leave, and fitness and "wellness" programs will be commonplace. They will be offered out of bottom-line, financial necessity by businesses and industries that for most of the 20th century have insisted that employees' family matters are none of their business. For example, Aetna Life & Casualty Co. estimates it saved $2 million in 1991 because of its family leave policy.
- Unions, the traditional organizers of industrial workers, are expected to diminish in importance as the nation's industrial base erodes and the service sector of the economy increases. Only 16 percent of workers were union members in 1990, continuing a steady drop from more than 30 percent in 1970. Manufacturing employees, once the mainstay of the union movement, made up only 13 percent of union workers in 1990. Union membership, however, is expected to increase among local, state and federal government workers and among clerical and support staff in banks, colleges and universities. But even a shortage of skilled workers may not be enough protection for nonunion employees, and worker-managers may form independent, unaffiliated bargaining units to equalize the power relationship.

FLEXIBLE SCHEDULING

In the 1970s, the influx of women into the paid labor market raised the issue of flextime and created the demand for "customized" schedules that allow employees to meet their responsibilities at work and home. In the 1980s, employers began to investigate the need to break away from strictly scheduled 9-to-5 workdays. By the early 1990s, more than half of the nation's biggest companies, aware of the coming demographic changes, offered some form of flextime. A study of 450 employers by the consulting firm of Hewitt Associates shows that flexible scheduling arrangements were in place at 54 percent of the companies. The two most common arrangements were flextime, provided by 76 percent of the employers, and voluntary part-time employment, by 65 percent. Job sharing was allowed at 31 percent of the firms; compressed time (working only at peak hours), 23 percent; work at home, 15 percent; and individual scheduling and summer hours, 4 percent.[1]

"Corporations are making changes [in flexible hours], but it's not a revolution, it's an evolution," said Ellen Galinksy, co-president of Families and Work Institute in New York.[2] And Charles S. Rodgers of Work/Family Directions in Boston says "mainstream corporations are sensitized to the problem—and that's progress." He says businesses are reevaluating "basic assumptions of the corporate culture about how people work and how careers are developed." The acceptance of flextime is expected to be in place by the 21st century for bottom-line reasons. "Employers will have to be open to alternate work schedules to attract and to retain top employees," said Karen A. Batenic, director of corporate human resources for Sara Lee Corporation. "Flextime is a way for employers to show concern and commitment to employees." Batenic takes advantage of her firm's flextime by coming in at 8:15 A.M. and leaving at 4:45 P.M. "The time difference seems small, but it allows me to get an express train in and brings me home 45 minutes earlier," said the director, who lives in the suburbs and has three small children.

OTHER WORK ALTERNATIVES

One of the most highly touted work schedules of the 1980s was the four-day workweek of 32 hours instead of the five-day workweek of 40 hours. In 1978, four days of work was described as the "new standard for U.S. industry," and the U.S. Chamber of Commerce predicted it would be common by the 21st century.[3] Instead, downsizing, layoffs and mergers of the 1980s and early 1990s led to fewer people doing more work, and the move toward a 32-hour week has been replaced by working even longer hours. The pattern emerging is one of working fewer hours in the office but more hours from home.

The Electronics Industries Association reports that in 1991 an "astonishing" 30 million households were part of the "explosive phenomenon" known as the home office.[4] It projects that in the coming decade, millions more Americans will work full-time, do after-hours work from home and start their own cottage businesses. "Sophisticated home office products will allow people to work faster and smarter at home and, ultimately, be more productive," said Gary J. Shapiro, vice president of the association's consumer electronics group. He notes that, "The computer may be the brains of the home office communications network, but the telephone, facsimile machine and telephone answering device are the nerves."

Some employers resist the inevitability of staff members' working outside the office beyond hands-on supervision, but this attitude, too, will change with the ultimate breakdown of the military approach to management. And an important aspect of home work is that it is not solely a woman's issue: A 1989 survey of 521 of the nation's largest companies showed that 40 percent of their employees who worked from home were men—and 8 percent were managers.[5]

FAMILY BENEFITS

Millions of people are expected to work at home for some part of the day, but the bulk of employees will continue to work at offices and plants. Almost everyone will be at work, so corporations—whether they want to or not—will have to become involved in child and elder care, family and medical leave and other family benefits. More and more corporations will move to "cafeteria" benefits, in which employees choose and help pay for only the benefits most helpful to them and their families. As they did with the slow introduction of flextime, most companies are moving toward these essential benefits in a manner that can be best compared to the way porcupines make love: very carefully. More than half of women with children under the age of one are in the paid labor force, but only 2 percent of U.S. companies have on-site or near-site child care.[6] Pioneers such as Stride Rite, a leading marketer of children's shoes, opened the first on-site child care center in 1971 at its Cambridge headquarters and in 1990 was the first to open an on-site intergenerational day care center for employees' children and elderly dependents. However, most companies are taking other helpful but relatively tiny steps.

Among them:

- *Employee workshops.* These are available to employees who need help handling stress or balancing work and family responsibilities.

- *Child care and elder care information and referral networks.* Employers pay the consulting agency that makes the referral; employees pay for the child or elder care.
- *Dependent care spending accounts.* These are set up by employers to allow employees to set aside up to $5,000 in pretax income to cover child care expenses and to save money by paying lower taxes. Employers also save money by paying lower payroll taxes.
- *Family and medical leave.* This is usually unpaid leave for both women and men after the birth or adoption of a child or to care for a family member. Benefits are continued throughout the leave and employees have a guaranteed job on return. A few corporations, states and municipalities now offer employees this benefit. Advocates of the proposed federal Family and Medical Leave Act, which requires U.S. employers to offer ten weeks of unpaid leave, consider its passage essential, but businesses are concerned about its cost.
- *Financial assistance.* This is a financial subsidy in the form of cash payments to help employees meet child care expenses.
- *Sick child care.* Emergency sitter service is provided for employees who need help at home for a few days. Companies make arrangements with hospitals that offer the service or with private caregivers who come to the home.

OTHER IMPORTANT BENEFITS

By the year 2000, employers will likely emphasize not only family benefits, but also attractive pension, health, life insurance and wellness programs. According to a

1990 study by the Employee Benefit Research Institute, 84 percent of employees surveyed say these benefits are very important in deciding whether or not to accept a job. "If given a choice between two identical jobs—only one of which offered these benefits—respondents said they would require a median amount of $10,000 in additional pay to accept the job without benefits." The Research Institute says 61 percent of Americans regard health insurance as their most important benefit, a percentage certain to rise as private insurance becomes more expensive and less available to individual workers. Forty-one percent said they would not accept a job that does not provide a pension, another figure certain to rise as Americans question the ability of Social Security to meet the needs of the flood of baby boomers reaching retirement age in the next century.[7]

To combat rising health care costs for current and retired employees, companies are educating their work forces on how to stay well as a long-term cost containment method. "In 1980, 'wellness' was unheard of," says Ed Stasica, a health care management consultant active in the National Wellness Council. "By 1990, it had attained California fad status. Now it is here to stay."[8] Workshops on staying fit, proper nutrition, stopping smoking and exercise and aerobics are offered at the worksite and on company time by firms such as Amoco, DuPont, Navistar International and IBM. By 2000, corporate wellness programs will be commonplace and smoke-free workplaces will be almost universal. Employees will benefit by being healthier, and employers by reducing their health and fire insurance premiums. However, there is concern by job applicants and present employees that the multitude of pre-employment tests and wellness programs may constitute an invasion of privacy, especially in the areas of tests for AIDS, psychological problems, drugs, alcohol, weight, genetics and smoking.

COMPUTER LITERACY

No matter what your present job is, it will be revolutionized by new technology. Automated methods of performing work once done by hand or by massive machinery have invaded business and industry. The emphasis on technology is the reason brains will be so much more important than brawn. Even garbage collection, a job once viewed as requiring only a truck driver's license and a strong back, will be upgraded into higher tech and higher skills. "Garbage collectors will need computer skills because one-person collection trucks will be completely automated," says George Vander Velde, vice president of science and technology for Chemical Waste Management, the research and development division of Waste Management, Inc. "Trucks will have on-board computers that sense where the container is, pick it up, read its contents, evaluate its weight and determine the billing."

Martin L. Bariff, associate professor of information resources management at Illinois Institute of Technology, urges people in the job market to remember that "in one way or another, information technology is going to touch the professional—as well as personal—life of every individual, no matter where you are in the organization. You will be a personal information manager." Dr. Bariff says that means "you are going to have to know how to store information within a computerized network, access information within that network, perform computer analyses of work related to your job, and know how to work with and communicate with other computers in the system. . . . The new technology will surround you 360 degrees."

You do not have to be a computer genius; you just have to learn the basics that help you do your job. "You don't have to understand how computers are put together," observes John M. Lusa, editor in chief of *Networking Management,* a magazine for sophisticates in the new technology who run voice and data computer networks for large companies and government agencies. "After all, you don't have to know how to design a car to drive one, but it is important to understand how it operates." You probably already know word processing, but you'll need to learn how to use the computer as more than a typewriter and printer.

A short course, often only one or two days, in programming and how to access databases—which your employer might offer on-site or be willing to pay for when you take it off-site—will prepare you for success in the 1990s and beyond. And, if you become interested in computers, you can go as far with the new technology as you want. The skills you acquire will pay off in getting better jobs and promotions during your professional life.

THE IMPORTANCE OF TRAINING AND EDUCATION

In a workplace driven by technology, a college degree is the number one requisite for the best jobs. Next in importance are associate degrees or certificates from community colleges and vocational and trade schools. "We are entering a new employment era...where a postsecondary education is a must," says Michael Acquaviva of the Pennsylvania Department of Labor and Industry.[9] Many companies will pay for additional training and education because they are eager to upgrade employee skills and can deduct tuition reimbursement to employees of up to $5,250 a year.

Apprenticeship programs, in which you earn while you learn, are also expanding. Though 70 percent of more than 300,000 apprentices registered with the Labor Department's Bureau of Apprenticeship and Training are in construction, the U.S. apprenticeship system is expanding to include service jobs such as child care provider, computer programmer, veterinary technician, chef, health care worker, bank teller, paramedic, audio-video repairer, laboratory technician, commercial designer and customer service representative.[10]

Skilled workers have leverage in career and work location choices and generally earn more. Patricia Rojek wisely prepared herself for the workplace of the 21st century. She had been out of the labor market for five years raising children when she began to think about going back to work. Married, with two children, her last job had been as a grocery store cashier, despite the fact that she had a degree in theology from the University of Dallas. Rojek told me she wanted to do something different when she returned to paid employment, something that would last into the next century. She subsequently enrolled in a college technical and professional communications certificate program, which she attended part-time at night. "I knew I had to learn about computers," Rojek says. "I didn't even know how to turn one on." And learn she did: word processing, programming, desktop publishing, databases, spread sheets and graphics. Today, Rojek is a technical writer for a large insurance company. "I earn a good salary, far more than I got as a cashier, and I have a job with a future," she says.[11]

Geoffrey K. Holloway was graduated in 1989 from the University of California at Berkeley with a bachelor's degree in mechanical engineering and also has prepared well for a future in a field he loves. "I'm attracted to this type of work because I want to be in an environment where there are machines and dials and gadgets," says Holloway, whose first job was working as a technical staff systems engineer for a nuclear generating station of a public power company. "I work on some of the mechanical and electrical systems that create the power that's produced here. I can see, hear, smell and touch the whole plant environment—and that's what I like to do."[12]

Another advantage of being trained in a growth field you enjoy is that the more you learn, the more you earn: Workers with more education earn more and are less likely to be unemployed.[13] Government studies show that in 1986 workers with four or more years of college had average annual earnings of $33,443 and had an unemployment rate of 2.1 percent. Those with one to three years of college earned $10,000 less and had an unemployment rate of 2.3 percent. High school graduates earned $19,844 and their unemployment rate of 4.8 percent was double that of college graduates. Workers with less than four years of high school, the people who previously were able to enter skilled trades and make excellent salaries, averaged only $16,606 annually. Not surprisingly, they had the highest unemployment rate of all: 6.8 percent.

A Liberal Arts Degree

Though corporations once vigorously recruited college graduates with business degrees, in the eyes of more and more employers a bachelor of arts is becoming the degree of choice. "A good liberal arts education produces generalists who can think critically and creatively, exercise judgment, sort through complexities, tolerate ambiguity, communicate effectively and adapt to change," says a man who should know: Stanley Gault, head of Rubbermaid Inc., a major producer of rubber and plastic products.[14] The management progress and management continuity study, funded by AT&T, which tracks liberal arts majors in the Bell System, reports that what is most telling, in terms of management skills and advancement, is their majors." Ann Howard and Douglas Bray, industrial psychologists in charge of the study, which they began in 1977, observe that "managers who majored in the humanities and the social sciences are the strongest in performance, and a greater proportion are apt to be promoted to higher levels within the organization."[15]

One of the best ways to prepare for corporate careers is to mix business courses with liberal arts, a well-rounded approach that is appropriate for the 1990s. My son Robbie, who majored in business at Lake Forest College, a liberal arts school, made a fortuitous choice. Businesses competing in a global economy and operating within the framework of a shrinking labor force need employees with backgrounds in literature, language, history, sociology, physics, chemistry, biology, ethics and psychology—as well as in traditional business courses.

Because of the corporate focus on humanities, the liberal arts graduate who majored in English also is becoming a prime job candidate. Remember the old joke?

Personnel Officer: "What did you study in college?"
Job Applicant: "Nothing."
Personnel Officer: "Oh, you majored in English."

Traditionally, English majors found low-paying jobs in publishing. Those with master's degrees or doctorates became teachers and professors. But few jobs in business were offered to them. Now, English majors are recruited by computer software companies; advertising agencies; banks and law, consulting, technical, public relations, sales and brokerage firms. English majors are finding career opportunities in the entertainment field, where they work both nationally and internationally as managers, corporate executives and directors. Jacob Adler, professor of English at Purdue University in West Lafayette, Indiana, says "majoring in English is an extremely promising road to employment."

A sophomore at the University of California at Santa Barbara wrote me that he switched from majoring in business to liberal arts with a major in English. "I spent a summer as an intern at a brokerage firm, and it hit me that what I need are communications skills and a background in international politics," he said. "I plan to major in English and minor in political science. I think that will be my entree—believe it or not—into corporate America." I believe it, I told him.

Graduate Degrees

A master's degree is an important tool for professional advancement of social workers, librarians, accountants, managers, engineers, human resources personnel, journalists, architects, landscapers and business and financial executives. A new master's degree is being offered in liberal studies, an outgrowth of the growing importance of the humanities in the business world. Once again, the combination of business and liberal arts subjects works well for the future workplace. A former Houston real estate agent told me he had been worried for several years about declining real estate sales. "I didn't like what I saw," he wrote, "so I prepared for a worst-case scenario with a view to getting out of the business. I stayed in for the two years it took me to complete my master's degree in marketing, which I thought would work well with my undergraduate degree in business science. And then I got out of real estate—just in time. I now have a good job and a relatively secure future as marketing manager for a food chain. I took a chance, but without my master's degree, I probably would be unemployed for a long time."

The MBA Degree

The most talked-about degree in the 1980s was the MBA. People had a love-hate relationship with it. Holders of the degree were envied for their high salaries but blamed for the leveraged buyouts, mergers and takeovers that put so many people out of jobs. Columnist Mike Royko put it this way: "First, we have the MBAs, especially the Harvard MBA, who came along after World War II and took over American industry. With their bottom-line approach, MBAs did such a brilliant job that the Japanese may soon buy the whole country and evict us." In the 1990s, demand for MBAs slackened somewhat, though it increased among those with backgrounds in the humanities.

Royko notwithstanding, an MBA degree continues to be an important educational credential and a ticket to high-paying jobs in the future workplace. But much of its glamour will be gone. "The contemporary wisdom that the MBA degree leads to a corner office with a large salary no longer holds," says Roger Jenkins, associate dean of graduate business programs at the University of Tennessee in Knoxville. "Instead, today the MBA is an investment that yields returns over time and permits MBA graduates to track faster than bachelor's degree holders."[16]

Still, starting salaries for MBA graduates of the top graduate business schools remain high at $50,000—it just takes longer to get a job. "The MBA is more in style than ever," according to Richard J. Thain of the Graduate School of Business at the University of Chicago. "In fact, my feeling about the future is that they, and other graduates with master's degrees but particularly MBAs, are in what I would call the 'catbird seat.' " Dean Thain says that projections indicate shortages in the number of graduate students. "More and more companies will regard recruiting of MBAs as a form of marketing," he said. "They know it's going to be hard to get good people. Manufacturing is a good example: Manufacturers used to get the cheapest person they could find, often an engineer out of college, and exploit that person. They've paid the price for that and are starting to realize they need the best talent to run their companies in a global economy: the MBA."

On the lighter side, in addition to almost certain financial success, another irrefutable reason to be the possessor of an MBA was suggested in *Newsweek* magazine. It reported on a survey finding that MBAs have the most satisfying sex lives of any other married professionals![17]

Doctorate Degrees

A PhD (doctor of philosophy) is the icing on the educational cake, and its payoff may be enormous. Professionals with doctorates, especially in science or engineering, will be in so much demand they could become a privileged class in the 1990s.[18] Though PhDs are entering the business world, most of them are professors, and there is a projected shortfall of PhDs because of the high number of retirements expected among aging college faculty in the coming decade. A 1989 survey of 465 schools by the Association of American Universities indicates that by 2000 there will be a shortage of 7,500 natural scientists and engineers with doctorates.[19] Shortages of PhDs in the humanities and social sciences are occurring now.

A doctorate makes the difference in professional advancement for psychologists, chemists, social workers, architects, economists, educational administrators, pharmacists, personnel trainers, statisticians, anthropologists, speech pathologists and researchers in any field. Of course, physicians, lawyers, dentists and veterinarians are among those who cannot be licensed to practice without a doctorate. David Gries, head of the computer science department of Cornell University in Ithaca, New York, points out that if you want job security in the next century, "A PhD in either engineering or computer science is a fail-safe career. The job placement rate is 100 percent."

Continuing Education

Nearly one in four major companies—double the number in 1982—requires upper-middle and senior executives to participate in continuing education programs, according to a study by Pennsylvania State University.[20] But top managers aren't the only ones who understand that knowledge is the key to survival in the future workplace. That's why so many people, on their own time and at their own expense, are flocking to classrooms in high school adult education programs, private trade and vocational schools, community colleges, colleges and universities. They're buying books and tapes to learn a foreign language, especially Spanish, French, Japanese, Russian, Arabic and Korean. They're studying communications, business practices and finance. They're updating their computer skills. Other popular continuing education courses include international affairs, management, self-motivation and assertiveness, marketing, human resources, tax law and quality control of production. People are investing time and money because they know it will pay off in the future, and it will.

Vocational Schools

Technical and trade schools provide important job skills and give a jump start for a myriad of jobs such as mechanics, repairers, cosmetologists, computer programmers, aircraft technicians, drafters, travel agents and hotel personnel. Tuition is expensive, so it's important to know as much about the schools as you can before signing a contract: Who are the teachers? What are their credentials? What is the school's placement rate? Do they return all or a portion of your money if you withdraw?

There are many excellent trade schools, such as the Echols International Hotel and Travel Training Schools. But beware of the sleazy ones that, according to financial columnist Jane Bryant Quinn "are bleeding millions of dollars from the federal program for guaranteed student loans. . . . They sign up poorly educated, unqualified students by promising them brilliant futures. . . . Students take loans to pay for their 'education,' but soon discover they can't do the work. . . so they drop out, with nothing to show for their hopes and efforts but a debt they can't pay back. The school keeps the money, or part of it. The bank is reimbursed by the federal government—that is, you and me."[21] Still, vocational training is an important option; you must first carefully investigate it.

Even the best-educated person cannot just walk into an office or plant and get a job without appropriate training. That means you have to know what fields to prepare for, the ones that will expand and grow in the 1990s, the ones that will have the best job opportunities. In the next chapter, you'll learn which are the fastest-growing industries and professions to prepare for.

3

THE FASTEST-GROWING FIELDS

The switch to a service-producing economy in the United States is shown in the fields projected to grow the fastest in the 1990s. The new fields have endless possibilities—and they are all in the service sector. A list of six of these promising categories, compiled by the U.S. Bureau of Labor Statistics, shows graphically how technological inventions will affect the way you earn your living:[1]

- *Health care.* Technology will create new opportunities for medical practitioners and technologists. New imaging machines that provide instant color pictures of the interior of the human body and lasers that make surgery unnecessary are breakthroughs that will revolutionize the health care field. In addition to increased opportunities for nurses and other support staff, jobs will be created in the design, manufacture and repair of new medical equipment.
- *Robotics.* Though the use of artificial intelligence in the manufacturing of products such as automobiles is moving slowly in the United States, it is

growing rapidly in Japan. Both countries, however, are creating robotic devices to do some of the detail work now done by humans, such as quality control and chemical analysis. The projected creation of complex, thinking robots that can see, hear, feel and obey will precipitate the need for highly skilled professionals who can build, service and market them. Demand for engineers, technicians, electronic designers and robot installers and repairers will increase.

- *Computer graphics.* Technological progress also will make computer-aided design/computer-aided manufacturing (CAD/CAM) and computer-aided imagery (CAI) two of the fastest-growing fields in the next century. Both are used to automate the design and manufacturing of products from industrial design to fashion. New opportunities will arise as computer simulations do away with drawing boards and prototypes. CAI, which gives objects a three-dimensional form, will revolutionize entertainment, especially movies and videos.

- *Information technology.* Because of the new international reliance on the latest information, demand for workers capable of manipulating and analyzing data will rise. Advances in microelectronics, fiber optics and digital technology will create jobs in storage, retrieval, analysis and transmittal of information. Telecommunications, which includes the telephone, electronic mail, cable TV, computer networks and satellites, will be one of the fastest-growing fields in the 1990s.

- *Biotechnology.* The application of biological systems to technical and industrial products and to solving medical mysteries will be the new frontier of the next century. Jobs in genetic engineering will be plentiful, as biologists and other scientists work to understand and prevent human and animal diseases, to produce better drugs, to create disease-resistant crops, to neutralize pollutants and even to devise microorganisms to extract oil.

- *Lasers.* There will be a strong demand for medical staff trained in the delicate microsurgery of laser medicine and for laser specialists to work in communications and manufacturing. Lasers will be used in a variety of ways—to speed up communication through fiber optics, to cut diamonds, to align underground pipes and sewers and to speed up the publishing process. Job opportunities will be plentiful for engineers, physicists, optical technologists, computer scientists and technical and production workers.

THE VARIOUS JOB SECTORS

Though most of the jobs described above are highly technical, most of the fields that will show the greatest growth are "old-fashioned" ones. Jobs will be plentiful for building custodians, paralegals, cashiers, secretaries, registered nurses, mechanics, salespeople, truck drivers and teachers. To understand which fields have the most potential, it's necessary first to understand how the U.S. economy is structured.

As explained in the introduction to this book, the economy is divided into two sectors: service producing and goods producing. The service-producing sector, which will create four out of five of all new jobs by 2000, includes transportation, communications, public utilities, wholesale trade, retail trade, finance, insurance, real estate, government and services. The latter—the services division of the service-producing sector—includes business, personal, automotive, legal, educational, health and social services. The goods-producing sector is made up of agriculture, forestry, fishing, mining, manufacturing and construction. It will decrease to 27.6 million jobs by 2000 from 27.9 million in 1986. Only one industry in the goods-producing sector is expected to have a significant expansion in job opportunities: Construction is projected to increase to 5.8 million jobs by 2000 from 4.9 million in 1986.[2] Manufacturing industries in the goods-producing sector that are expected to show some gains are exports in general and miscellaneous plastic products, office and accounting machines, commercial printing, business forms, newspapers, chemicals and commercial aircraft.

The Good News and the Bad

Valerie A. Personick, economist in the U.S. Labor Department's Office of Economic Growth and Employment Projections, has created a chart depicting the industries whose production is expected to increase by 2000 and those expected to slow down or decrease.[3] Her projections have direct bearing on where the jobs will be:

Fastest-growing industries (in alphabetical order): amusement and recreational services, arrangement of passenger transportation, computer and data processing services, day-care services, electronic computing equipment, electronic home entertainment equipment, human resources management, management consulting services, medical instruments and supplies, miscellaneous electronic components, nursing, office furniture and fixtures, offices of physicians and osteopaths, oil and gas field services, optical and ophthalmic products, outpatient and health services and facilities, partitions and fixtures, pharmaceuticals, radio and television communication equipment, residential care, retail, semiconductors and related devices, telephone and telegraph apparatus, temporary personnel services, X-ray and other electromedical apparatus.

Slowest-growing industries: blast furnaces and basic steel products; crude petroleum; electrical and electronic assemblers; footwear, except rubber and plastic; iron and steel foundries; silverware and plated ware; new nonbuilding facilities; luggage, handbags and leather products; metal mining; miscellaneous primary and secondary metals; mobile homes; natural gas and gas liquids. Also: new farm housing, alterations and additions; new gas utility and pipeline facilities; new local transit facilities; new nonfarm housing; new conservation and development facilities; private households; railroad equipment, ship and boat building and repairing; tobacco manufacturing; watch, clock, jewelry and furniture repair.

The Labor Department also gives some specific numbers of job openings: Retail trade, which includes food and beverage services, will hire an additional 1.8 million workers in the 1990s; miscellaneous business services will add 1,342,000; public and private education, 971,000; offices of physicians and osteopaths, 886,000; nursing and personal care facilities, 847,000; temporary personnel services, 834,000; wholesale trade, machinery and equipment, 614,000; computer and data processing services, 612,000; supermarkets and grocery stores, 598,000; and legal services, 519,000. However, there will be decreases in jobs for railroad workers, telephone installers and repairers, stenographers, statistical clerks, textile machine operators, directory assistance operators and compositors and typesetters.

As you read these lists, you can see what has happened and will continue to happen to the American economy: Most of the growth industries are computer, technical or electronic related. Most of the decline is in manufacturing. However, when you look at various industries for job potential, don't automatically rule out manufacturing. It will provide more than 18 million wage and salary jobs in the 1990s. The job openings will be for top managers, especially for operations executives with strong financial backgrounds. (See Chapter 15.) "Manufacturing still is an honorable profession with good job opportunities, but we need people with different types of skills," says Richard F. Teerlink, president and chief executive officer of the $800 million Harley-Davidson, Inc., who has a degree in accounting and an MBA.[4]

THE PROFESSIONAL
MOST IN DEMAND

The brain drain of many of the nation's brightest students from mathematics and science to the financial sector in the 1980s has led to a projected shortage of engineers. Engineers lead the list of professionals who will be most in demand in the next century. (See Chapter 11.) Though a slow economy in the late 1980s and early 1990s affected everyone in the labor market, including engineers, the shortage of these professionals already is here: Engineering jobs represented 33 percent of the hardest-to-fill positions in 1991, according to a recent national survey of human resources recruiters.[5] In the 1990s, the demand will be highest for electrical, electronics, mechanical, product design, manufacturing, tool, test, process and production engineers. An estimated 192,000 additional electrical and electronics engineers alone will be needed by the 21st century. Job opportunities will be plentiful for engineers and other technicians skilled in data processing and system, hardware and software analysis. And the engineer who figures out how to recycle plastic products will be very rich.

THE SEMIPROFESSIONAL
MOST IN DEMAND

Paralegals are the semiprofessionals who will be most in demand in the 1990s. (See Chapter 9.) While the demand for lawyers is expected to grow by 71 percent in the 1990s, jobs for paralegals are expected to balloon by 104 percent in the same time period. What's significant about this is that "para" anything will be in demand because these workers are technicians, and technicians in every category will be sought after. They are the people who take detail work from professionals and free them up to do their thing—in other words, to make big bucks. Other semiprofessional jobs with a good future outlook include dental technicians, ophthalmic technicians, medical assistants, physical therapy aides, medical records technicians, administrative aides, library technicians, home health aides, surgical technicians, teacher aides and educational assistants.

THE BLUE-COLLAR WORKER MOST IN DEMAND

Though the category of blue-collar worker is being phased out by the U.S. Department of Labor and regrouped under service workers, it generally refers to unskilled or semiskilled jobs. The blue-collar worker most in demand in the 1990s will be the janitor, one of the few fast-growing occupations that doesn't require advanced training or even a high school diploma. In 1988, there were 2.89 million janitors and cleaners; by 2000, there will be an estimated 3.45 million—a leap of 555,000. "We're running out of janitors," says Ronald E. Goerne, president of Professional Cleaning Systems, Inc.[6] Unless you plan to open your own cleaning services business, janitorial work, despite the use of high-powered, automated machinery, is not a career with a future. It's a low-end job characterized by poor salaries, few benefits and high turnover. However, a janitor's job, like that of a waiter or waitress, will always be available if you're not prepared to enter the more satisfying and rewarding industries in the 1990s and beyond.

DON'T FORGET UNCLE SAM!

Though it doesn't have a specific "industrial" category of its own, the federal government is America's largest employer. With a civilian workforce of 3 million, the government hires more than 300,000 employees each year in some 200 different occupations. Almost 98 percent work in the executive branch, the rest in the legislative and judicial branches. Eighty percent hold white-collar or service jobs, a trend that is on the upswing in the federal government as it is for the rest of the economy. Half of all federal employees work for the Department of Defense. Many people erroneously assume that if you're a federal employee, you must work in Washington, but only 14 percent of the workforce is located there.[7] After more than a decade of budget cutbacks in personnel, reductions in force, massive switching of full-time jobs to part-time ones and the use of temporary workers, local, state and federal governments will be in a hiring mode by the 21st century. Job opportunities are expected to grow by 9.7 percent. Hiring by governmental bodies—not including schools, universities or hospitals—is projected to account for 811,000 new jobs, according to the Department of Labor.[8]

At the federal level, the United States will increase its hiring just to keep a stable work force, says Len R. Klein, acting associate for career entry and development for the U.S. Office of Personnel Management. The personnel office does all hiring for federal agencies, except for the U.S. Postal Service, which is a quasi-governmental agency.[9] Agencies that will be hiring include federal administrative offices, hospitals, educational institutions, government operations and electric utilities. "We feel we're on the cutting edge of change," says Klein, who spent 22 years with the Navy as a civilian employee before joining the personnel office. "There's a certain thrill working on matters of national importance. After all, there's only one National Aeronautics and Space Administration and one

Center for Communicable Diseases." The personnel manager adds, however, that "if you're driven by bucks, this is not the place to come. Our salaries for professionals are low at the entry level compared with the private sector, though we do catch up within four years. But we cannot match the salaries executives get."

State and municipal governments will be hiring service workers such as police officers, firefighters and prison guards, mostly as replacements for retired workers and turnover. They will also add employees in passenger transit, electric utilities and administrative agencies.

Many of the people who go into government work are well aware that advancement is quicker and salaries higher in the public sector. But they are motivated by the need to make a positive contribution to society, to help others, to give something back. These are also important considerations when job hunting.

THE NOT-FOR-PROFIT INDUSTRY

The kind of satisfaction that comes from working for your city, state or federal government is similar to the positive feeling many people get from working for private, nonprofit agencies. "The nonprofit sector is a magnet for cause people—dreamers, doers, idealists, entrepreneurs and community activists," says Lilly Cohen, director of development of the Port Washington, New York, Public Library and coauthor with Dennis Young of *Careers for Dreamers and Doers* (The Foundation Center).

According to The Foundation Center, a publisher specializing in information about nonprofit organizations, there are more than 1 million nonprofit agencies in the United States concerned with health, education, social welfare, religion, unions, arts, culture, community activism, social and fraternal organizations and foundations. One of the fastest-growing sectors of the service economy, with more than 8 million employees in 1991, non-profit agencies are projected to continue to grow into the next century. There are nonprofit agencies for almost every cause or interest, from the Abbott and Costello Fan Club to Zonta International. The *Encyclopedia of Associations* has 885 pages of listings—only a handful of all nonprofit groups.

My daughter Cathy's first job as editor and staff photographer at The Lincoln Park Zoological Society gave her the chance to combine her love for journalism, the community, wildlife and the environment. She was especially attracted by the fact that the Lincoln Park Zoo is one of the few zoos in the world that charges no admission. Her concern about ecology is widespread among her generation of women and men born in the 1960s. Devising ways to develop land without endangering wildlife, to save rain forests, control pollution and radiation and to dispose of waste are environmental industries that are prospering in the for-profit sector, but the momentum—and the humanitarian ideals—come from nonprofit organizations. Public concerns about the greenhouse effect, wildlife extinction, oil spills, acid rain and the deterioration of the ozone layer have caused environmentally oriented jobs to grow. "Efforts to preserve the environment are expected to result in growth of jobs in that area in the 1990s," reports the U.S. Department of Labor's *Occupational Outlook Handbook*. " . . . We are part of a biological web and cannot stand alone—we need other living things," says Constance E. Hunt, environmentalist with the Army Corps of Engineers.[10]

The growth of environmental jobs shows a desire among students, job seekers and job switchers to do work that is personally gratifying and has a good future. With a better idea of which fields will be expanding, you will be able to decide where you would like to be. To help you in making important career decisions, Part II of this book will zero in on the 100 best jobs in the 1990s and beyond.

4

FUTURISTIC JOBS

Employment experts look to the 21st century and warn: "Don't wait for the future to happen. Start getting ready now!" But futuristic jobs, by definition, don't exist yet. They have no exact educational nor skills requirements. No one can estimate what their salaries will be nor the best career paths to take. But there are glimmerings of what these jobs will be in the dramatic technological, scientific and communications discoveries that are being developed so rapidly.

Futurists paint a world that will in many ways resemble the technology depicted in *Star Wars* and other science fiction works. But this will be real: Tomorrow's information infrastructures will revolutionize the way we make contact with one another, both visually and by audio. This one fact alone will profoundly affect the creation of jobs and how they will be performed. By 2020, scientists predict the widespread use of optical fibers, the somewhat magical use of light beams to carry information over glass fibers smaller than a human hair and capable of printing the entire *Encyclopaedia Britannica* in a few seconds. At the same time, the new "killer technology" of photonics, which will supplant electronics in the next century by using networks of telephones linked to computers to process information, will bring us instant data.[1] In the next century, interconnected telecommunications networks will mean more people will work from home—and their employers will be scattered throughout the globe.

Doctors will make house calls without leaving the office. Hand-held telephones will connect a caller anywhere in the world directly to satellites. Televisions, computers, fax machines, telephones and audio and video equipment will be part of one seamless system.[2] Artificial reality, also called *cyberspace*, will use computer technology to create digital "worlds" into which humans can actually "climb": You will be able to see, feel, hear and smell an alternative three-dimensional environment generated and controlled by machines.[3] Nanotechnology, a theoretical process by which you will be able to build food, homes, computers and anything else out of individual atoms of such substances as carbon, hydrogen, nitrogen and oxygen, will revolutionize human existence, predicts Gary Knight, technology analyst with Microelectronics and Computer Technology Corporation, a research and development consortium in Austin, Texas. "There would be this machine," Knight says. "You'd stand there and say, 'I'd like a ham and cheese on rye,' and click, click, click—you have a ham and cheese on rye."[4] Nanotechnology will not only provide ham and cheese sandwiches, it will also turn upside down the way we work and what we do.

Underlying the extraordinary changes on this planet will be the continued penetration by humans of outer space. The highly developed countries of the world will inhabit space colonies powered by solar satellites, predicts Gregg Maryniak, executive vice president of the Space Studies Institute in Princeton, New Jersey. "It's possible there are children today who are going to grow up in a world where there will be more people living off Earth than on it," he says.[5]

FUTURISTIC INDUSTRIES

In the 21st century, occupational categories will remain pretty much the same: Most of the jobs listed in Chapter 8 as having exceptional potential for the 1990s have familiar titles, though the education and training required and the way jobs will be performed will be radically different. "There will be more similarities than differences in jobs in the next decade because things move slowly," says John B. Mahaffie, associate with J.F. Coates, a Washington consulting firm that does research on the future.[6] But there definitely will be differences in jobs of the future, particularly those created in the following industries, some of which overlap.

- *Biotechnology and genetics.* The advent of genetic engineering will affect everything from medical therapies, especially cancer, to new foods and food products. Biotech pharmaceutical companies that manufacture new lines of drugs that offer gene therapies will face fierce competition in the global marketplace.
- *Communications and entertainment.* The consumer electronics industry, with upgraded versions of compact disc players, VCRs, camcorders and televisions, will compete with fiber optics technology to bring the world the latest in communications and entertainment. The new standard for high-definition television (HDTV), digital audiotape players (DAT), the use of holograms that recognize images or

speech, and global and satellite-based cellular phone systems will make instant communication a reality and put access to entertainment at your fingertips.

- *Computers.* Giant national networks of information—an information infrastructure—will transport billions of bits of data per second. Radio frequencies—wireless transmission of information—will be set aside to allow personal computers to receive and transmit information. Computers will be activated by the user's voice. "Smart" computers will link utilities to customers' appliances, opening up a new range of services. Computer software will move into classrooms and teach many of the lessons.

- *Fuels.* Alternative fuels such as liquid hydrogen, ethanol, methanol, compressed natural gas, propane and electricity—which create little pollution—will change the petroleum and automotive industries.

- *Lasers.* Computer-guided lasers will speed up manufacturing, especially of automobiles, heavy equipment and furniture. They will change medical care, in particular surgery, and will make dentistry truly painless by replacing the drill.

- *Marketing.* Laser scanners, personal magnetic cards, bar code technology and electronic coupons will give stores and marketing consultants a database of who is buying what. Adding to the collection of more in-depth information will be marketing surveys analyzed by computer programs that react to the human voice. Junk mail will go high-tech, using computer diskettes, videotapes and catalogues that play catchy tunes and commercials. Videos with commercials will market products in medical waiting rooms and business reception areas.

- *Medical technology.* High-magnetic fields, the technology that powers nuclear magnetic resonance machines in hospital radiology departments, will change the way diagnoses are made. The electronic images revealed will be printed on film with instant black-and-white photographs. Optical fiber technology, tiny video cameras and miniature surgical instruments will be used to perform pinpoint surgery. Research will focus on the brain—the ultimate computer.
- *Robotics.* These automated "workers" will be used to measure ingredients, milk cows, handle radioactive material, pick merchandise off shelves and do housework.
- *Science and superconductors.* Atom smashers, such as the $600 million Supercollider, will explain what mass is and will count, describe and measure the energy of subatomic particles. Scientists will analyze ultraviolet light from outer space objects, getting data on their temperatures, densities, chemical compositions and velocities. Electrically charged atoms will paint metal coatings on ceramic surfaces. Recycling of scrap materials, particularly plastic, will be a major scientific area.

JOBS OF THE FUTURE

Only the futurists, the people who make their living predicting what the world will be like decades from now, will hazard guesses about specific job titles. But futurists who have compiled such data have come up with some very interesting occupations. A list of future jobs collected by Washington consultant Norman Feingold includes some "far-out" ones: aquaculturist, asteroid/lunar miner, bionic medical technician, crytologist (preserves people through the ages), laser medicine practitioner, neutrino astronomer (deals with subatomic particles), planetary engineer, pollution botanist, robot trainer, selenologist (studies the moon as a geologist studies the earth), space trainer, thanotologist (counsels the terminally ill) and underwater archeologist.[7]

Futurist Mahaffie, coauthor of "Future Work" (Jossey-Bass), predicts "combinations of jobs and skills that will result in unique occupations such as lawyer-scientist, engineer-interpersonal relations specialist, engineer-salesperson and engineer-financial planner."[8] Clement Bezold, executive director of the Institute for Alternative Futures in Alexandria, Virginia, says there will be "expert high-tech systems in virtually all industries and service professions. Through computers, professionals will have the instant expertise of the best specialists in the world in any field at their fingertips. Almost any job involving knowledge will be affected." Bezold, coauthor of *The Future of Work and Health* (Auburn House), predicts ". . . machinery and artificial intelligence will increase productivity—and there may not be enough work for everyone." But John S. Mayo, senior vice president in charge of network systems and services at AT&T Bell Laboratories in Murray Hill, New Jersey, disagrees. "Go back 100 years and everyone worked on a farm," says Mayo. "Those jobs disappeared when the steam engine was invented, but that same technology created scores of new industries with new jobs of higher quality. Maybe robots will serve hamburgers, but new jobs will be created that are information-based, require advanced skills and don't depend on your being anywhere."

INDUSTRY LEADERS
AND THE FUTURE

Mayo, who has a doctorate in electrical engineering, is at the cutting edge of change. It is essential for him and other top-ranking business executives to have a handle on what's coming next in the job market. Mayo sees "major thrusts in telecommunications that include continued expansion of telemarketing and working at home or from wherever you are—the job will not know whether you're at one place or another." The technical combination of voice and data means, he says, "you will be able to talk on the phone and at the same time read the information you need on the screen. If you're an insurance agent, for instance, it means you don't have to be in the office. You can be anywhere in the world." The engineer predicts the need for mobility will have a "tremendous impact" on the way business is conducted and on productivity. "The increased use of cordless telephones and facsimilies, personal computers and video machines installed in cars will turn what has been idle commuting into productive time," Mayo says.

Environmental concerns and waste disposal are emerging as major industries of the 21st century. "I don't see a radical dislocation of workers, but I do see a general upgrading of jobs into higher tech and higher skills," says George Vander Velde, vice president of science and technology for Chemical Waste Management in Oak Brook, Illinois, an affiliate of Waste Management, Inc. Vander Velde, who has a doctorate in biophysics, says, "We'll see analytical methodology for separation of waste change to automation from manual techniques. There will be robots in the laboratory doing analytical measurements previously done by human technicians." The biophysicist also predicts that "the development of smaller microinstruments means we will be able to do more analysis in the field, on site. Right now, because of the heavier equipment involved, it's more efficient to do analysis on a centralized basis." He also believes there will be a major shift from emphasis on recycling alone to "looking at what the materials are" and what goes into them in the first place that create environmental problems. Biologically or chemically produced materials that are more readily recyclable will be created. The need for these new materials, he says, will open up jobs for microbiologists.

Another group of workers whose jobs will change are office workers. "Support staff will have different duties," says Roger Levien, vice president of strategy for Xerox Corporation in Stamford, Connecticut. He sees "an enriching of job content through computer use that will enable support staff to add more value to final products." Levien, who has a doctorate in applied mathematics and computer sciences, predicts that "a lot of the functions secretaries do now will be done through automation. A secretary's job will be more of a personal assistant, managing time and responsibilities of a group of people through information tools." Because of computers, the strategist says, workers will have more autonomy and authority, better automated equipment to work with and will be integral parts of team efforts. "The next stage is more teamwork," says Levien. "Everyone will be connected through personal computers, and you may be working on a project with someone in Tokyo or London. But more frequently, you will be communicating with people in your own building through new computerized electronic 'hallways' that will allow you to sit at your own desk and still interact closely with colleagues—just as you did in the past over the water cooler."

THE NEW FRONTIER: THE BRAIN

"With all the information that will be available, what is the new frontier?" asks Leon M. Lederman, Nobel laureate professor of physics at the University of Chicago and director emeritus of the Fermi National Accelerator Laboratory near Batavia, Illinois. "It's the human brain, so I predict that science and education will be intertwined, and education will be a big business, in addition to creating a science-literate workforce." Lederman, president of the American Association for the Advancement of Science, specializes in particle physics, currently a highly individualized study. But he predicts such research "will become a team effort. There will be groups of scientists working with students and engineers." The world-reknowned physicist sees "vast deployments of superconducting devices, such as floating trains two or three times faster than the bullet train, that will ride one foot above the rail, creating a magnetic field with no friction—at over 300 miles per hour. It will be the transition between rolling and flying." Lederman also believes physicists of the future will create "enormous, city-size water purification systems, reduce the cost of health care and raise the standard of living—without further messing up the environment."

Human reasoning will be a "powerful" part of jobs in the future, says Sanjaya Addanki, manager of artificial intelligence at IBM in Hawthorne, New York. He works on such things as intelligence accelerators, robotics, computer vision and computer voice recognition. Intelligence accelerators, says the scientist, who has a doctorate in computer science, "will allow you to offload the grunge part of your work to the system so you can concentrate on your work. The computer will be programmed to make educated guesses about what you want to know or do, and that will increase productivity." Dr. Addanki says instead of typing information to a computer display screen that stands upright, information workers will indicate what they want by pointing with a stylus to a flat panel screen built into their desks. "At IBM, we're involved in building technologies that will change the way people do their jobs," he said. "My personal view of 2050, for instance, is that everyone is going to become an information worker. The worker in the office and the worker in the factory, on the shop floor, will need more information to do their jobs and therefore will have to have more authority. Businesses will not be able to afford the deep management hierarchy we now have."

By 2000, Dr. Addanki predicts, "layers of middle management will be gone, and companies will get rid of the people who work on strategic management. I'm a middle manager, and I'll be out of work."

THE NEXT CHALLENGE: ADAPTABILITY

The world of work the futurists and strategists describe are mind-boggling. Are you ready to use computer technology to create your own world, print out entire books in a few minutes or talk to your computer? How do you feel about working for an employer and customers halfway around the world, seeing them on your video screen but never in person? Are you comfortable with the idea of working underwater to grow fish and sea products or as an asteroid/lunar miner in outer space? Can you adjust to the isolation of working from home or even in an office where meetings and conferences are held via personal computers? Will you be able to handle the stress of being expected to keep in constant communication through high-tech devices with supervisors, colleagues and clients even while driving a car? And most important of all, are you prepared for the many unforeseen changes that will surely occur and that certainly will affect your job and the way you perform it? Are you willing to be a student throughout your entire professional life, learning new ways to do things and then learning the new ways replacing what you have just learned?

Though many of the dramatic changes predicted in the workplace are years away, it is obvious that the key to survival in the coming high-tech, information society is flexibility, being able to accept new ways of doing things and the new skills requirements of your chosen profession. In the future, more than ever, you will have to adjust to technologies that will alter the way you work or possibly eliminate your job as it is currently defined. Flexibility is a key ingredient in getting the best job and moving ahead in the 1990s and beyond. And there are other important, practical guidelines to follow to position yourself for the future employment market. You will find these helpful "inside tips" in the next chapter.

5

INSIDE TIPS FOR GETTING THE BEST JOB AND MOVING AHEAD

Elliott Gordon had a good job working for a small, regional executive search firm, but he wanted to move into the big leagues. That was in 1981, a time of economic recession and high unemployment, but Gordon was determined to get the best job possible.[1] "I began calling all the major search firms, and the first six times Lester Korn (head of Korn/Ferry International, a prestigious executive search firm) didn't return my calls," Gordon says. "So I gave up on that and physically went to each of the prominent search firms, right to their offices, without an appointment. A lot of times it didn't work, but sometimes I got in because the top people were willing to spend 15 minutes with a guy who had the guts to come to the door."

Showing up cold in executive offices and asking for a job is a gutsy move, but it takes a certain amount of daring to get the job you want. Gordon was willing to take a chance—and it worked. In one of his interviews, he made contact with an executive who was leaving his firm to open a new branch for Korn/Ferry in Orange, California. He offered Gordon a job as managing associate. Today, Gordon is vice president of Korn/Ferry in Newport Beach.

"When you know where you want to work, you have to push a little harder and go that extra mile," says Gordon, who earned his MBA through Korn/Ferry's tuition reimbursement plan. "You have to get yourself in there, somehow. If you know what you want, go after it any way possible."

The executive's advice is an inside tip, a job-hunting tool not included in the usual litany of suggested techniques. Whether you're looking for your first job, switching careers or jobs, whether you've been fired or are on the losing end of a merger or takeover, inside tips may make the difference in whether or not you get a job. Conventional suggestions on how to get a job cannot be disregarded: It's still important to serve internships, answer ads, keep your resume current, network with friends and colleagues, follow up leads and learn how to negotiate a verbal or written employment contract. Gordon did all the basics, but he is successful because he went that extra mile and got a leg up on his competitors.

✦ **Inside Tip:** Don't be afraid to take risks.

THE HARSH REALITIES

Even though the coming shortage of skilled employees will work in your favor, looking for employment is a full-time job. That means making phone calls every day, sending out resumes and meeting with contacts.[2] You might have to spend money, too: Phone calls, new stationery, professional resume services, an answering machine or service and additional training cost money. And the more you earned in your previous job or currently are making, the longer it will take to find a new one. You can get a minimum wage job immediately, but if you are a serious career person, experts estimate in good times it will take at least three months to get an entry-level job. For those in the higher brackets, especially middle managers, it could take a year or more. The advantage higher wage earners who have been laid off or fired have, however, is that the big firms often supply outplacement services at company expense. But you are your own best resource: You will have to bite the bullet and do the hard work that finding a job requires. Those who are determined will be the most successful. You have to know what you want and be driven enough to keep working at it.

✦ **Inside Tip:** The secret to getting the best job is persistence, persistence, persistence.

A JOB YOU LIKE—OR LOVE

Though job hunting is an emotionally draining task, there is a positive side to it, too. It can be an occasion to fantasize a bit about the job of your dreams. The demographics of the 21st century workforce with its deep pockets of shortages of qualified personnel will give you a chance to do something you love and that you feel is socially valuable, a choice that can range from devising a system to monitor children at home from the office to designing new luxuries for a Porsche. The need to feel fulfilled is universal, and the smart job seeker will look for work that is rewarding emotionally as well as financially.

"Our top college seniors are looking for experience, the opportunity to explore, to be involved in something significant," says Barbara-Jan Wilson, director of career planning at Weslyan University in Middletown, Connecticut.[3] Wilson reports that when she ran a career options workshop for financial analysts at an investment brokerage firm, most of the questions from the group were about how to get into teaching and the Peace Corps and what jobs there are related to saving the environment. The rising interest in employment in nonprofit organizations is symbolic of the new demand for work that combines professionalism and self-satisfaction. (See Chapter 3.)

The quality of the job—that is, how much you enjoy doing it—is as important as the job itself. Knowing in advance that you probably will change careers four or five times in your life, it makes sense to groom yourself for a job you will really like in a profession that also has growth potential. Leslie Hurtig, a recent graduate of the University of Pennsylvania, followed her heart to her first job as an executive assistant at Pro-Media, a New York public relations firm run by Rochelle Lefkowitz. Pro-Media's fine reputation for handling accounts involved with the environment, economics and women's issues attracted Hurtig. "I was thinking of going into arts administration or small theater," says Hurtig, whose bachelor of arts degree is in English. "I had been exposed to career planning and knew my choices, but I didn't really know how my skills would translate to the work world: I'm good with people, but that never got me an A in any course I ever took." After she graduated, a friend told her about the opening at Pro-Media and Hurtig immediately saw the fit between her educational training and personal interests. "I saw the job as an opportunity to work for issues I believe in strongly and for developing my writing skills," she says. "I'm very happy here."[4]

✦ **Inside Tip:** If you have the choice, take the job that appeals to you, the one you fall in love with.

COLLEGE PLACEMENT SERVICES

If you are currently enrolled in school, the first day of class is none too soon to stop in at the career placement office. Help in finding the right profession and the right job are part of what you pay for with tuition. You'll be competing with job seekers whose career counselors give them job guidance, help place them in internships, set up on-campus recruitment and prepare them for job interviews.

✦ **Inside Tip:** Even if you were graduated from college 25 years ago, go to your school's career counselor for help.

Northwestern University's placement center is an example of the kind of help you can get—at no cost. Run by dean Victor R. Lindquist, it gives Northwestern graduates an advantage in seeking jobs by working with them as early as their freshman year, testing their personality and skills, informing them about the job market and training them in resume-writing and job-getting techniques. "Job seekers have a frightful lack of information about the responsibilities and skills required in getting a job," says Lindquist. "People approach the job market the same way they do blind dates: If it doesn't work out, there'll be another one along." That means getting a job by default and not by design. And that's not the way to do it."

✦ **Inside Tip:** If your college has a course in how to get a job, take it. It's as important as studies in your major.

COOPERATIVE EDUCATION

If you are currently enrolled in a postsecondary education curriculum, check with your school's placement center for information about cooperative education. Co-op education links your classroom work with on-the-job experience by allowing you to study part of the day and to work in a paid job in your field. Your school must tailor an academic program that fits your needs and set up a work program with a local employer. You'll get training, extra income and experience. "Many students make career decisions with little practical experience, and that's why co-op education is a powerful idea," says Dr. James Wilson, director of the Cooperative Education Research Center at Northeastern University in Boston. "It offers an education with long-term career implications."[5] When they graduate, many students get references and contacts in the field of their choice. Cooperative education students also find out, while there's plenty of time to make a change, whether or not they're in the right field.

✦ **Inside Tip:** Investigate cooperative education.

DOING YOUR HOMEWORK

Smart job seekers do their homework. That means spending a few hours hitting the books and the computer databases in your public or school library. Whether you're looking for your first job or a new one, want to switch careers, start your own business or simply update yourself on the current job market, the information is literally at your fingertips in the library. It's the place to get copies of annual reports of companies you may want to work for, to read books on job-hunting and resume-writing techniques and to get hands-on help from well-trained business librarians. Some 200 public libraries nationwide also have special educational information centers, one-stop job information areas, many of them funded by the W. K. Kellogg Foundation. They offer career guidance via computer programs, and their staffs work with you on an individual basis. In the private sector, college and university libraries are available only to students and alumni. Corporate libraries usually are open only to employees.

✦ **Inside Tip:** Go to a library and do your homework about your chosen field or potential employer.

Homework Assignment: Everything I Wanted To Know about ARCO

I recently decided to see firsthand what libraries have to offer the job seeker. With special permission, I was allowed to use the Career Information Center of DePaul University in Chicago, which is open only to students and alumni. The library is a small gem with 500 reference books, 10 computers, 20 videos, scores of magazines and newspapers and a staff of five librarians who are career specialists.[6] I decided to look into marketing as a possible profession. First, I studied the *Occupational Outlook Handbook.* It said that increased competition worldwide means companies will need more marketing professionals to survive in a global economy. It predicted that marketing will have faster than average job growth in the 1990s and beyond. Using a computer database the librarian directed me to, I searched out job possibilities in Los Angeles, where my son Ray then lived. I found 17 publicly owned companies in Los Angeles that have good-sized marketing staffs. Among the largest is Atlantic Richfield Company (ARCO). I also called up a computer software program that listed the company's top officers, annual reports and insider information.

◆ **Inside Tip:** Learn all you can about the financial condition of the company you want to work for.

Switching to another computer with a database of 800 periodicals on business and management, I found 83 articles relating to ARCO. Through them, I learned something about ARCO's compensation, equal opportunity and flexible benefits programs. I also learned it gives regular performance appraisals and has excellent communications with employees.

◆ **Inside Tip:** The earmark of a company that is good to work for and that will be successful in the 21st century is one with good human resources programs.

Next, I called up on the computer corporate and industry research reports by investment analysts. *Moody's Industrial Manual* gave a full history of the company. *Hoover's Handbook* also gave detailed information and was easier to understand. In Standard & Poor's "Corporate Records," I found the name of ARCO's employee relations director. Next, I studied books on resumes, on developing a marketing plan for my job hunt and on getting ready for a job interview. I watched a 20-minute video the librarian recommended called "Selling Yourself in an Interview." I checked out salaries in *Sales and Marketing* magazine.

Armed with printouts and copious notes, I was ready to ask for an interview with ARCO's personnel director— at least theoretically. And if we did meet, I could say with authority and confidence: "I read in *Forbes* that you are one of the best-managed major oil companies. You have a high percentage profit margin and an astute balance among production, refining and marketing." And if that wouldn't be enough to show I had done my homework, I could coolly add: "After sitting in front of a computer and studying 'Compact Disclosure,' a compact disc that lists information about some 12,000 public companies, I see that on the marketing front your company's low price/high volume strategy has produced substantial market share gains and enhanced your marketing profits in your integrated West Coast refining and marketing system."

◆ **Inside Tip:** Learn to speak the language of the profession you're interested in.

EVEN YOUR HAIRSTYLIST KNOWS

After you've done your homework, tell everyone that you're job hunting. Tell your friends, hairstylist, barber, car mechanic, doctor, lawyer, banker, insurance broker, mail carrier, dentist, golf or tennis pro, accountant, carpenter, parking lot attendant and everyone you know or do business with. Join professional associations, clubs, networks, community organizations and business groups, and let them know you're looking.

◆ **Inside Tip:** If your direct contacts don't have any leads, ask them for names of people who do—and follow up on them.

EVERYONE'S FAVORITE CRUTCH: THE RESUME

A good way to start job hunting is to send out your resume, but it's important to understand that while resumes can sometimes get you a interview or job lead, they cannot get you a job. Too many job applicants regard the resume as a sacred piece of paper that will deliver them of unemployment, but in our high-tech society, the traditional resume—a two-page chronological listing of work experience—is being replaced by videos.

◆ **Inside Tip:** Videotaped resumes are the coming wave, but keep them short and professional.

It will take a few years to wean job seekers and personnel officers away from the printed resume, so in the interim, there are important guidelines to follow in using a printed resume. Most can be applied to videos, too.

✦ **Inside Tip:** Don't send out general resumes. Be user-specific. Gear each resume to a particular company and send it to a contact within it. Or bring your resume, tailored to that company, to your job interview.

✦ **Inside Tip:** I am frequently asked if it is okay to lie on your resume. The answer is no. Companies do check facts. They don't want any expensive surprises.

Resume Options

The chronological resume is the most popular form. "Conservative companies want to see your work history clearly stated, starting with the present and working backward year by year," says Marsh Brill, owner of a resume preparation firm. But many job seekers find that another form, the functional resume, allows them to present themselves in a more positive light. Instead of listing the jobs you've held, you separate your work experience into categories of expertise. A third form is a biographical letter, which adapts well to audio and video resume tapes. In it, you describe your work experience and interests in a conversational manner.

One of Brill's clients, who had a poor work history, wanted to turn over a new leaf. He now was mature, goal-oriented and going to school at night to complete a degree in accounting. These were the important facts about him, he felt—not that he had been justifiably fired from his last two jobs. Brill helped him draft a biographical letter that said he was a new person, and it worked—he got an entry-level job at an accounting firm.

An informal approach also worked well for a recent college graduate who had a biographical resume, with name, address and phone number, printed on the front of an extra-large, shocking pink T-shirt. An honors graduate in journalism from the University of Missouri, she had an impressive list of credentials. The back of the shirt read: "Fit Guaranteed." She mailed out scores of them to newspaper editors and got an excellent response.

✦ **Inside Tip:** Don't be afraid to be creative to get an employer's attention. But also be neat, clear and concise.

Computerized resume databases are growing in popularity. A wide range of employers turn to them when they have job openings because the service is inexpensive compared to traditional employee searches and offers them names of prescreened applicants. The fee for job seekers to join varies, but before you pay to enter your resume, ask for names of people who actually found jobs through the service.

WHAT ACTUALLY GETS YOU A JOB LEAD

As mentioned earlier, networking—telling everyone that you're job hunting—is the best way to get a job. According to the placement firm Manchester, Inc., 60 percent of 351 clients surveyed over 18 months got jobs by networking.[7] Only 17 percent used an employment agency, and 15 percent answered or ran an ad. Other ways to find jobs are through executive search consultants, job fairs, alumni placement officers, professional associations, state employment offices, consulting firms and self-help organizations.

✦ **Inside Tip:** Job hunting is a numbers game. The odds on obtaining a new position increase in proportion to every contact you make.

Job clubs help you get a handle on the local employment market and give you emotional support at little or no cost. The formal ones are sponsored by a local government agency, community college, private association or religious group; the informal, but equally effective, job clubs are sponsored by a group of unemployed people themselves. A job club, usually composed of 15 to 20 people, keeps you motivated and gets you through the ordeal of job hunting. The formal ones are led by a qualified job counselor, but many informal clubs are successfully run by the members. Each member must make a commitment to stay in it till the last person gets a job.

In the 1980s, I helped a group of unemployed women form the network of Employable Women in Communications. It stuck together for six months, until everyone had a job, and still meets. "It's hard to job hunt," a network member said, "but the group pressed me to follow a specific routine each day. I also learned from the others to be nice to myself while going through this stressful time: I ate a lot of hot fudge sundaes!"

✦ **Inside Tip:** Invite headhunters and personnel directors to speak at your meetings.

HUNTING THE HEADHUNTERS

There are a variety of professional employment resources to tap. Each operates in a different way, so the credibility of each and what it can do for you has to be analyzed carefully. John R. Sibbald, a veteran human resources professional and president of the executive search firm that bears his name, helped define the categories discussed below:[8]

Executive recruiters. The most important thing to remember about these headhunters is they do not work for you, the job seeker. They work for the corporations and businesses that hire and pay them to find key managers and executives to fill job openings. Recruiters who work on a retainer are paid a portion of their fee—usually 33 percent of the starting salary for the job that needs to be filled—by the employer when they are hired to do the search. They usually find candidates for jobs paying $50,000 and up. Contingency recruiters are paid by the employer only when their candidate is hired. Most of the salaries contingency firms handle are less than $50,000.

◆ **Inside Tip:** Even though executive recruiters don't represent you, send your resume to those who are specialists in your profession.[9] There's no guarantee they will shop your resume around, but they sit on top of most of the best jobs in the country. Each year, hundreds of people get jobs by sending resumes to executive search firms that never heard of them before.

Employment agencies. These job placement firms also do not work for you. They work for the businesses that ask them to fill positions, most of them clerical and entry-level jobs paying less than $40,000. Like the contingency search firms, most are paid only when their candidate is hired. Make sure you use an agency where the employer foots the bill.

◆ **Inside Tip:** Never pay for a job.

Outplacement firms. These consultants are hired by employers to help their fired employees conduct a job search. They do not get you interviews or find you a job, but they provide office space, secretarial staff and job consulting while you search.

◆ **Inside Tip:** Some outplacement firms will work for you directly. That means you pay the fee for their services.

Career counselors. These consultants work for you directly and are paid by you. Most are psychologists. They do not place you in jobs; instead, they evaluate your skills and help you plan job strategies. They usually charge by the hour. Check out their credentials in advance and ask for references. The American Association for Counseling and Development in Washington certifies counselors. There also are career counseling firms that charge thousands of dollars up front and promise to tap you into the "hidden" job market. They do not get you a job, though many of their clients, desperate to find work, believe they will. Before signing a contract with them or turning over any money whatsoever, check them out with the state attorney general's office, your city's office of consumer fraud and the Better Business Bureau.

◆ **Inside Tip:** Before spending thousands of dollars for a career counselor's job list, check with Stuart Alan Rado, the Ralph Nader of the career counseling industry. He keeps tabs on who actually helps clients get jobs and who rips them off. For information, send a self-addressed, stamped envelope to Rado at 1500 W. 23d St., Sunset Island, #3, Miami Beach, FL 33140. Phone: 305-532-2607.

BIG VERSUS SMALL FIRMS

Once you've found out where the jobs are, the next step is to decide what size firm you'd like to work for: A small company has 100 employees or less; medium, 100 to 500; large, more than 500. Do your homework at the library and find out how many employees work for the firms you are interested in. There are pluses and minuses in big versus small.

Studies consistently show that employees of smaller firms are more satisfied with their jobs than those of large firms.[10] "Workers in small firms are satisfied because they know everyone else, have a sense of comradeship, of working together as a team for the good of the organization and have more control over their work environment," says John C. Gardner, president of National Small Business United, a trade association.

On the other hand, satisfaction isn't important to some job seekers. They want "big bucks," and those are usually offered only by large companies. According to a study by Linda S. Leighton and David S. Evans, economists at Fordham Law School in New York, workers employed by large firms earn 6 to 15 percent more than employees in comparable jobs at smaller firms. Larger firms also have far better benefits: The U.S. Bureau of Labor Statistics reports that 92 percent of larger firms offer medical care to full-time employees compared to 69 percent of firms with 100 or fewer employees. The known gap also applies to all other benefits, with even wider discrepancies between large and small firms in the areas of insurance, retirement plans and maternity leave. Larger firms also offer the best internships and on-the-job training, have more resources and offer employees more mobility.

Smaller firms, however, offer flexibility, a chance to learn the entire business and a more direct concern for the happiness of their employees. It's also much easier to rise to the top in a smaller firm. Employees of smaller firms feel more secure in their jobs than those who work for bigger businesses. And there's another advantage of smaller firms: While large corporations will continue to pare their staffs to rock bottom, most of the new employment in the United States in the 1990s will be generated by businesses with fewer than 50 employees. "Large firms may become traps, where you go in one end and never come out," warns Ann Markusen, economist and professor of urban affairs and policy development at Rutgers University in New Brunswick, New Jersey. "They tend to put you in a specialty, and you might become obsolete or stuck in place."

✦ **Inside Tip:** Don't limit your job search to the Fortune 500 companies. That isn't where the new jobs will be.

ON THE MOVE

Where is the best place to work? In a global economy, you have to consider the entire world. Let's take the United States first. Large metropolitan areas, by sheer numbers alone, will continue to offer the most jobs in the 1990s. But in an age of high-tech, smaller cities—like smaller companies—will also have excellent opportunities. Corporations are learning they can take their telephones, fax machines, computer networks and corporate jets to anywhere in the U.S. and set up business. They no longer have to be located near their customers or suppliers. New York City, long considered the most prestigious location, has lost some of its major corporations to less-congested cities. Exxon Corporation is one of the big businesses that have moved their central offices to Dallas, which has lower taxes and an ample labor force. This geographical trend is expected to continue among established firms, and new companies also are projected to set up business in less-expensive locales.

✦ **Inside Tip:** If the geographical location of your job is important to you, remember that the company may one day relocate.

Job openings in the United States are a changing mosaic of high unemployment in some areas and labor shortages in others. But by the end of the century, current projections indicate one of every six jobs created in the United States will be located in California. Other states with good job forecasts are Florida, Illinois, New York and Texas. Seven sunbelt metropolitan areas—Orlando,

Florida; Phoenix, Arizona; Riverside, California; Sacramento and San Diego, California; Tampa and West Palm Beach, Florida—will have the fastest economic growth between now and the end of the century, according to the U.S. Commerce Department. "Each of these areas has a good quality of life," says Mark Zandi, an economist with Regional Financial Associates in Westchester, Pennsylvania.[11] The six slowest cities for jobs will be New Orleans; New York; Rochester, New York; Pittsburgh; Cleveland; and Detroit.

✦ **Inside Tip:** Your freedom to relocate may be the key factor in getting the job of your choice.

Overseas employment sounds romantic, but the dream of living and working in a foreign country is often difficult to realize, especially for entry-level workers. Most countries give their own people first chance at the best jobs and severely ration work permits for foreigners. The best hope is to work for a multinational U.S. company—and their numbers will continue to grow. Once on board, request to be sent overseas.[12]

✦ **Inside Tip:** You can't just walk in and be sent overseas. The top people are nurtured locally and then sent abroad.

Despite the difficulties, there are millions of U.S. citizens, excluding the military, employed overseas by the U.S. government and businesses. Most jobs abroad are for those technically qualified, usually at the managerial level, in health care, international development, civil engineering, small businesses, information management, computers and English language instruction.

✦ **Inside Tip:** You must be prepared and heavily credentialed in your field—and have a job before going overseas.

So many people want to work overseas that many job seekers end up victims of scams. Beware of job-matching crooks who promise to get you jobs for cash up front—some as much as $1,000—and then don't deliver. There are safe routes to take to find jobs overseas:

- Contact your local state employment service, which lists jobs overseas.
- Apply for an internship to be a foreign service officer with the U.S. Agency for International Development. Write to the agency's Recruitment Division, Office of Personnel, Room 242 SA-1, Washington, D.C. 20523.
- Subscribe to the *International Employment Hotline,* a highly respected newsletter published by overseas employment expert Will Cantrell. Write to Cantrell at P.O. Box 3030, Oakton, VA 22124. Phone: 703-620-1972.

THE JOB INTERVIEW

All your efforts have paid off and now you have a job interview with a company you want to work for. No matter how nervous the thought makes you, a major part of landing a job is the interview. Traditional advice about this critical moment in your job search includes doing your homework on the company, organizing background material about yourself, dressing appropriately, making a good impression and trying to ascertain at the end of the interview where you stand and what will happen next. In a tight labor market, all the power is in the hands of the employer, but that shifts as the shortage of skilled workers increases. "Employers in the past have been like Procrustes, a Greek robber baron," relates Richard Thain of the University of Chicago's Graduate School of Business. "Procrustes had a bed, and when he captured people he put them on it. If they were too long for it, he cut off their heads or feet. If they were too short, he stretched them. In a sense, employers have done the same thing. But in the coming decade, employers will have to cut down or stretch the bed to fit the job seeker."

◆ **Inside Tip:** Talent and education are a powerful leverage in job interviews.

Selling Yourself

What happens in the initial job interview can determine whether or not you get the job. "The most important thing is to get the attention of the person interviewing you," says Lynn Bignell, cofounder of Gilbert Tweed Associates, a New York-based executive search firm.[13] "Let the interviewer know you as an individual as well as a job candidate." She advises asking insightful questions about the company, sharing an observation about something personal, such as your family, and trying to create a bond between you and the interviewer.

◆ **Inside Tip:** Employers will hire you if they feel the chemistry is right.

Personality traits may be just as important as your skills in a job interview. Energy, friendliness, confidence, a tiny dose of humility and the ability to speak well are the components of a good first impression. Human resources officers always cite failure to communicate effectively as the major reason their company did not make a job offer to a candidate. Bernadette Anderson, a speech pathologist, says there are three secrets to a successful job interview: "Speak well, speak well, speak well.[14]

◆ **Inside Tip:** The old arts of writing, speaking and listening are still important in a job interview—even in a high-tech society.

Employers are specific about what they want from applicants in a job interview. I constantly query employment managers in representative industries about their hiring desires and find they don't dwell on education or specific degrees. They expect you to have the proper credentials for the position you seek and to be able to communicate well.[15] Instead, they look for general traits such as good grooming, dependability, loyalty and work experience. Some employers are more specific: A small suburban accounting firm, Sklar & Sawyers in Lincolnwood, Illinois, wants you to have helped pay for your education because it shows a "sense of commitment"; the firm also prefers employees who live nearby because it is concerned about the stress of commuting. Smith Hanley Associates, a New York investment banking recruiting firm, prefers Ivy League graduates "who have done well in liberal arts, have a neat, clean appearance and can speak with confidence." Clorox of Oakland, California, a national manufacturing firm, wants you to know what you want. Service orientation is foremost at the Four Seasons Hotels, an international hotel chain. "A caring attitude" is what counts at Walgreen, a national drugstore chain, and teamwork is stressed by General Motors.

◆ **Inside Tip:** Before you go to your job interview, try to find out from current or past employees what the company culture is; in other words, what qualities does it really want in its employees?

The Job Offer

The hope of a job interview, of course, is that it will end with the right offer from the right employer. When that happens, step back and take a long, serious look at what you are doing. Even the most confident job seekers often accept the first job offered. They are relieved that the trauma of job hunting is over and immediately say yes. While it's certainly all right to take the first position offered, you may find you have doubts later on if you haven't explored enough other opportunities.

✦ **Inside Tip:** Grabbing the first job you can get may be a hollow victory. And taking the wrong job may deter you by several years in your climb up the corporate ladder.

Before that final handshake, take time to look inward and make sure you're not embarking on something that might make you unhappy. If you're an engineer who is concerned about ecology, or if you're a peace activist, for instance, you might be very unhappy working for a nuclear power plant. Next, look outward and examine your employer, your colleagues and the corporate culture. Make sure you can fit in. Go back to the library and look up financial reports on the company to make sure it's not ripe for a takeover or in serious financial difficulty.

✦ **Inside Tip:** Don't be afraid to ask hard questions once the job offer is made. The company has indicated it wants to hire you, and that gives you the leverage to find out all you need to know to resolve any doubts. Remember, if you don't do this and things do not work out, you shortly will be back where you started out: job hunting.

THE FINISHING TOUCH

Salary negotiations often are the most frustrating part of accepting a new job because you rarely have sufficient information to make an intelligent deal. Most employers are very circumspect about salary information, and that puts you at a tremendous disadvantage. But there are ways to break through the barriers of secrecy and obfuscation:

- Check the library for professional publications in your field. They list salary ranges of their membership at least once a year.
- Call your college placement office or the department you were graduated from and ask for salary information.
- Contact your local office of the U.S. Department of Labor Statistics, which issues salary scales nationally and locally.
- Talk to colleagues in your field. If they are reluctant to tell you their exact salaries, ask them to give you a range, such as between $25,000 and $35,000 a year.
- For a guideline of current and projected wages, study the 1991 and 2000 salaries for the top 100 jobs listed in Chapter 8. In addition to specific information about your profession, they will give you an overall idea of what employers are paying for a variety of jobs.

Having some idea of what you should be paid helps in your salary negotiation, though employers have a clear advantage because they know exactly what the job is worth to them, what competitors pay and whether applicants for it are plentiful or scarce. Most companies also have specific job descriptions and categories that determine your salary range; that range will determine your wages.

✦ **Inside Tip:** In most situations, the only leverage you realistically have is to negotiate for the most money you can get within your salary range.

If the job is the one you want, it might be smart to accept the salary offered without too much fuss, even if it's less than you think you deserve. After you position yourself at the firm and have had a chance to find out more about salaries, you can then negotiate with far more information and confidence. But state right up front that you'll be back soon to ask for more money.

✦ **Inside Tip:** Wait till you've been on the job at least six months to one year before asking for more money. That's how long it will take you to poke around and ascertain what the salary picture is.

Salary isn't your only financial compensation. Benefits are of utmost importance, especially for health care. I get calls daily from job seekers who are more concerned about getting health and pension benefits than a high starting salary. With soaring costs of health care, you would be wise to examine a company's benefit plan before signing on. In addition to the basics of health care, pension, disability, paid vacation and credit unions, companies in the year 2000 also will offer child care, elder care, employee stock plans, family leave and guaranteed jobs with seniority upon return to work after family leave or illness.

✦ **Inside Tip:** Ask for a severance agreement spelling out what benefits you will receive if, through no fault of your own, you are fired or laid off. Many new employees are asking for six months' to two years' severance pay, guaranteed outplacement and choice of outplacement firm.

There's another aspect of a job: the physical. Not only must you be in good health to be hired, but you must also be drug-free. If you are a smoker, you may be turned down. Corporations get large reductions in health, life and fire insurance if they have a smoke-free workplace and smoke-free workers. And, some firms won't hire you if you are overweight.

✦ **Inside Tip:** After you've passed the physical and other pre-employment tests and are hired, get every aspect of your new job—its description, whom you report to, benefits and promises made—in writing.

A TEMPORARY SOLUTION

If you need to earn money while conducting a job search and want hands-on information about your field of choice, consider a temporary job at any level in the profession or industry you want to get into. Temporary agencies are one of the fastest-growing industries in the United States, providing work not just for those between jobs but also for thousands of qualified personnel who do not want to or cannot work full time.

✦ **Inside Tip:** All job seekers, but especially new college graduates, should explore nontraditional opportunities when looking for a job—and temporary work is an excellent one.

"The growth of our economy will be fueled by new jobs at smaller companies, and secretarial and administrative assistant positions on a temporary basis at these smaller companies can offer tremendous opportunities for aggressive college graduates," says Walter W. McCauley, president and CEO of Adia Personnel Services headquartered in Menlo Park, California. Though placement of office support staff and factory workers is the bulk of temporary agencies' business, their range is widening to include the professional temporary: doctor, nurse, lawyer, accountant, librarian, pharmacist, security guard, paralegal, product demonstrator, physician's assistant, graphic artist, computer programmer, data processor, word processor, engineer, computer technician and—the newest entry—executive, also known as "boss for a day." Recent studies by the National Association of Temporary Services shows 54 percent of temps are hired to stay on the job full-time.

◆ **Inside Tip:** Temporary work is an excellent way to make important contacts in your field and to get references.

MOVING AHEAD

When you do get a permanent job, the one you want, you naturally will be interested in how you can move up the career ladder. A career is more than a job because it implies a long-term commitment to success. But a career does not move forward by itself. You have to make good things happen by monitoring and steering your progress.

◆ **Inside Tip:** Getting ahead is up to you: Nobody else cares.

There are many routes to success. Ambitious workers on the move continue to educate themselves by attending seminars, talks and workshops. They work toward advanced degrees. They're informed about what's going on in the job market in general and their own field in particular. They know the salary they should be making and the job assignments that should be theirs. They try to keep a high profile in the office by volunteering for special projects and taskforces. They do their present job well.

✦ **Inside Tip:** If it's your first job, you don't have to like everything about it. What's important is getting experience in the work world and establishing a good work record with all the basics—good attendance, willingness to pitch in, flexibility and some skill or knowledge in the field.

"In a very broad way, I planned my career by developing my talents and working for companies that utilized them," says Ellenmae Long, vice president of a successful marketing and communications company. "I can't say that every day I've been specifically concerned about my immediate career plans," she says, "but every single day I do think how I can do better, what I can learn, what I can give. But I'm no Pollyanna—I want a lot in return."

✦ **Inside Tip:** Do your best always, but keep a written record of your job achievements, including special assignments and volunteer work. It will come in handy at performance appraisal time.

A Zigzag Course

The route to success is no longer straight up. "Internal promotion paths have broken down as fewer and fewer companies hire for life," says Robert Jones of the U.S. Department of Labor. The traditional career path of starting with a firm and staying forever, moving up in tiny increments over the years, no longer is the way to go. "Tomorrow's typical career will be neither linear nor continuous, nor will it always be upward," says Thomas Horton of the American Management Association. "Instead, your work life will take more of a zigzag course. Those who prepare themselves for change and growth will have the highest probability of success." Though it's still important to find what you want to do and stick with it, it's shortsighted to focus on tailoring your skills and experience to satisfy the needs of one particular company. The key to success in moving from one employer to another is to continue to have "movable" credentials. I know of a corporate lawyer who was distraught when he lost his job in a corporate downsizing, but after he evaluated his skills he transferred them to what he has always wanted to do: He now works for a film production company. That was a major "zigzag" for him!

Because of the depletion of the ranks of middle managers, forward progress will be slow for many future workers. They may have to make lateral moves, which in the past have been viewed as close to demotions. But in the 1990s, a lateral move might serve you well: In football, a lateral pass, in which the ball is thrown to the side rather than forward, can set in motion an advance toward the goal. In business, lateral moves will be important rungs on your career ladder, giving you new experiences and skills, and sometimes leading to traditional promotions and raises.[16] Helen E. R. Sayles, vice president and manager of human resources at Liberty Mutual Insurance Group in Boston, made a lateral move and became a writer in the corporate human resources division. She had been training coordinator in the information systems department. Her goal was to get experience and to position herself in human resources, where she really wanted to be—and it worked. "It's obviously better to be promoted, but to suggest the traditional corporate expectation of moving only onward and upward is the only way would be a disservice," Sayles says. "A lateral move is often a good idea."

✦ **Inside Tip:** A lateral or sideways move inside a large company or to a similar job at another company can be beneficial if it adds to your portfolio. Companies look for people with broad-based experience.

SECRETS OF SECURITY

If you're in a job you like and want to keep it, you can make your job secure even during economic downturns by being the best possible person in it and by having a high performance level. "In my first job, when I worked for AT&T as an operator in Philadelphia, I insured job security the very first day by finding out what was expected of me—and then doing more," says Florine Robinson, president of Robinson & Associates, a management consulting firm that also does individual career consulting. Robinson worked two switchboards at the same time instead of only one. "I was a telephone operator with a strategy," she says. "I wanted to move into management, so I dressed the way supervisors dressed and became a supervisor within two years." Her dedication helped her to be promoted to the human resources department, which had always been her goal. And she was safe in her new job when high technology and divestiture of the telephone company drastically reduced the number of telephone operators. In 1984, Robinson fulfilled another dream: She opened her own consulting firm, using the experience she gained in personnel at AT&T.

✦ **Inside Tip:** Make yourself indispensable. Find out what part of the job your boss likes least and take it over. Learn to do it well and like it.

In *Macbeth*, Shakespeare warns that "security is mortal's chiefest enemy," so don't be lulled to sleep by the fact that you have a job and nothing can happen to it. It can.

✦ **Inside Tip:** A job is not forever. The only people you can count on not to throw you out are your own family.

PITFALLS ON THE JOB

In order to get ahead, you have to keep your job and, as crude as it sounds, that means protecting your flank at all times. No matter how you feel about office politics, you have to use them in order to survive and move ahead.

The Office Grapevine

It's through the grapevine—now more likely to be the message queue of your personal computer than whispered conversations over the water cooler—that you can find out instantly what's happening in the office, who's doing battle with whom, who's leaving, who's been hired and what rumors are going around, including those about you. It's the best and fastest way to find out what jobs are opening up and what new projects are on the horizon. Being part of the grapevine doesn't mean you should participate in malicious rumors. Look at the grapevine, instead, as a living newspaper filled with vital facts published just for you. You don't have to be cutthroat, but being active in the grapevine shows you care about your job, know where you want to go and have a plan to get there.

✦ **Inside Tip:** Use office politics to build a power base among your colleagues. The office grapevine is the communication tool of office politics. If you aren't part of it, you may not survive on the job.

Conflict in the Office

If you want to move up the corporate ladder, your technical skills will have to include how to handle a nasty boss, the office bully and colleagues who are overly aggressive or manipulative. If you are naive about these matters, you will be the victim of "office violence," says Andra Medea, who has been teaching defense against street violence and physical assault since 1970.[17] Now she's transferred to the office setting her nonviolent methods of resolving conflict. "Of the two, street fighting is cleaner," Medea says. "It's all a power struggle. When people try to intimidate you and you break down the pieces of how they accomplish that, it's the same in business as in the streets. You have to understand the pattern of what someone is doing and then disrupt it." Medea, who did some of her research by watching the activities of apes and gorillas in zoos, says one of the most frequent forms of bullying is "posturing." That's when people thunder at you, clench their fists, pound the table and create a scene.

◆ **Inside Tip:** When people try to intimidate you on the job, don't look frightened or upset because things will get worse. Stay calm and unimpressed, and they'll stop.

"Vanishing" is another problem that can seriously injure your career. That's when people, particularly women, make a suggestion and no one listens. It's as if you're not there.

◆ **Inside Tip:** Repeat your suggestion several times and then memo everyone on it later, says Medea. You can't get a bonus for an idea that never existed.

Medea's advice is an important strategy for success, which you cannot achieve if you're constantly harassed.

But there is a caveat, warns sociologist Arlene Kaplan Daniel.

✦ **Inside Tip:** "Be careful when combatting those in power because they have all the cards," says Daniel.

Treating everyone professionally is a healthy and positive way to behave. The cliche that you meet the same people going up as you will going down is true. Or, as poet Dorothy Parker put it: " . . . I know that every foe is faithful till I die."

✦ **Inside Tip:** Don't let yourself be pushed around, but fight back wisely.

Office Romance

Love is far more pleasant to think about than conflict, but when sex rears its attractive head at work, careers may suffer. In the 1990s, U.S. employees will work long hours, and it is natural that your social life will derive from work, where you spend the most time. But love and romance between two consenting employees doesn't always work out.

The spectre of the Mary Cunningham–Bill Agee love affair that rocketed through Bendix Corporation is an example of what can happen. Agee was the CEO and Cunningham a top executive who worked directly for him when rumors of a romance, which both denied, spread through the company. The couple is now married, yet at Bendix, where neither any longer works, their relationship is remembered with bitterness. "It tore the place apart," a former employee recalls.

Invariably, when employers do not like romance or marriage among its employees, it is the woman who is fired or who resigns. Title 7 of the U.S. Civil Rights Act protects women in that situation because it is a form of sex discrimination, and some states have passed legislation that makes banning marriage among employees or hiring spouses illegal. A 1990 ruling by the U.S. District Court in New Jersey invalidated the antispouse rule of the state's court system.[18] In a decision that minced no words, federal judge Nicholas H. Politan stated: "No law, regardless of intent, should have a chilling effect upon marriage. To the contrary, it should embrace marriage as a legitimate societal goal." And Vilma Bell, director of employee relations at S&C Electric Company, who has been married since 1966 to M. James Bell, senior vice president of the manufacturing division, says she's "biased toward hiring qualified family members, because I've seen it work well over and over again." Her firm has 40 married couples out of 1,000 employees. Nonetheless, office romances, even those that lead to marriage, can be disruptive.

◆ **Inside Tip:** If you want to move ahead in your career, think twice before you fall in love with someone you work with. And if you're a woman, think three times.

THE VIEW FROM THE TOP

Smart employees who know what to do to move ahead and what to avoid so they don't self-destruct during the climb are legitimate contenders for the top prize in the corporation: running the show. If you have your eye on being the president, chief executive officer or chair of the board, you will have to position yourself carefully within the company every step of the way. But the path to the top will be different for executives in the 1990s because it will require different skills and attributes.

✦ **Inside Tip:** In the 1990s and beyond, CEOs will need a global perspective. They'll no longer be able to say, "My only competition is in Bridgeport or Milwaukee. They'll have to say, "What's going on with the Four Tigers—Singapore, Hong Kong, South Korea and Taiwan?"

In the 1990s, CEOs and other managers will have to know several languages, finance, international economics, history and human resources. Their workforce and their client base worldwide will be multicultural, and they will have to be able to deal with diversity.

✦ **Inside Tip:** The CEO of the 21st century will be well traveled, fluent in French, German, Japanese and Russian and knowledgeable about fine art.

Much of the future executives' time will be spent dealing with something businesses have long ignored: their employees' family problems. "They'll have to be adept at resolving a whole rash of social issues, such as child care and the environment," says Robert L. Witt, chair and CEO of Hexcel Corporation, a multimillion-dollar firm headquartered in San Francisco that makes structural materials for the aerospace industry.[19]

✦ **Inside Tip:** If you want to run a company, you will need an international business and financial background —and the ability to nurture people.

Becoming president or chief executive officer of a company is a goal most people dream of but never achieve. In fact, many workers are frustrated because they see no promotions or challenging assignments in their future. In Chapter 6 we'll discuss what to do if your career is at a standstill.

6

CHANGING JOBS, SWITCHING CAREERS OR STARTING YOUR OWN BUSINESS

Achieving success in your job, moving ahead, reaching your goals exactly as planned—these are career dreams, and for some people they do come true. But if you are not one of those lucky people for whom everything works out perfectly on the first try, don't despair. You don't have to remain stuck in a dead-end job or career. In the 1990s, it will be much easier to move around or start your own business. Robert Jones, 32, has been a bank vice president for five years. Despite large-scale reductions in force at his bank, Jones's job seems fairly secure, but he is dissatisfied. "For the past three years, my raises have been small. I haven't been assigned to any interesting projects, and I feel burned out," Jones says. "It must be time for me to look for a new job." Robert Jones is not his real name but his situation is real. He's in a dead-end job, and he had better find a new one before inertia overtakes him or he's fired.

Changing jobs is as American as apple pie, and often just as tart. It's not done without a lot of hard work and even some anguish, yet U.S. workers change jobs and professions frequently. The ease with which you can change your job depends on the demand for professionals in your field, on the current economic climate and on the amount of risk you're willing to take. In 1987, before the last major recession began, and when qualified workers were sought after throughout the country, 31 million Americans were in their present jobs for only one year or less. They had little trouble finding their new jobs.[1] Compare this with the first nine months of 1990, when U.S. employers, at the height of the recession, trimmed 30,000 people a month from their payrolls, many of them filling the ranks of the unemployed for long periods of time.[2] But even in a sluggish job market—which is not predicted for 2000 because of the projected shortage of skilled labor— you have to take action when you feel stymied on the job.

THE GLASS CEILING

Women who want to move ahead professionally experience far more frustration in fulfilling their potential than men, particularly white men. By the year 2000, women will make up nearly 50 percent of the labor force, but it won't be the top half.[3] In a 1990 study of 799 public companies, *Fortune* magazine found only 19 women listed as the highest-paid officers and directors of their companies, less than one-half of one percent. The *glass ceiling* is a term that describes discriminatory practices that effectively keep qualified women from rising to the top job, no matter what their education, experience or years with the firm. "There appears to be a glass ceiling for women," Elizabeth Dole told me when she was U.S. secretary of labor. ". . . Nothing has changed. It has taken longer than we thought for women and minorities to move ahead."[4] Adrienne Hall, vice chair of Eisaman, Johns & Laws advertising agency in Los Angeles, one of the top ranking women in her field, warns women: "If you want to be president or chief executive officer, I would say lessen your expectations or you'll be disappointed. There are few women at the top."[5] Though it's important to keep trying to crack the glass ceiling, Jane Evans, president and chief executive officer of InterPacific Retail Group, a privately held investment company based in San Francisco, says, "I rarely give up. But if the situation is no longer right for me, I don't hesitate to look elsewhere."

The ceiling that keeps women in dead-end jobs and at low wages is made of glass, so perhaps it can be shattered. Lynn Martin, U.S. secretary of labor, also made the glass ceiling a top priority.

Many women crowded into the pipelines of middle management today are modern pioneers. The U.S. Department of Labor reports that women make up 40 percent of managers and administrators. Optimists, many of them these women, believe they will eventually get a fair shot at top jobs, hopefully by 2000. "Women should do their homework and join companies that are gender blind," says Jeanette Sarkisian Wagner, president of Estée Lauder International, headquartered in New York, the largest division of the $2 billion cosmetics firm. "After that, performance is what it's all about."

SEXUAL HARASSMENT: A BARRIER TO WOMEN

In 1991, one of the work world's most disgraceful secrets—sexual harassment of female employees by male supervisors and colleagues—burst onto the national consciousness during the televised hearings of law professor Anita Hill's charges against then–U.S. Supreme Court candidate Clarence Thomas. Though federal laws against sexual harassment have been on the books for more than 25 years, unwelcome sexual advances as a condition of employment or promotion are prevalent. Also illegal and just as prevalent are hostile working environments with obscene posters and sexist jokes that tell women: "You are an outsider. You don't belong here." These behaviors effectively keep women out of certain jobs and from advancing in the ones they have—the traditional aims of sexual harassment.

Studies show that from 45 percent to 85 percent of women have experienced sexual harassment during their working lives. Only 3 percent ever complain about it to their companies or file an official complaint with city, state or federal agencies. The U.S. Equal Employment Opportunity Commission reports that in 1990, only 5,572 charges of sexual harassment were filed; in 1985, there were 5,035. Aware that women will make up the majority of new hires in the 1990s and beyond—and understanding that successful lawsuits can cost employers bad publicity and thousands of dollars in damages—forward-looking corporate managers are formulating clear antiharassment policies to take immediate, corrective action in-house, before claims get to outside agencies or the courts.

Women have the right to feel comfortable at work and to do their jobs free of unwelcome sexual attention. They have the right to know they are equal with other workers and that their employers will not put up with illegal workplace activities. Sexual harassment can no longer be swept under the office rug, and employers are legally responsible for seeing it is not. Still, many women are understandably reluctant to make charges of sexual harassment. Many quit their jobs instead: They saw what happened to Anita Hill, when the accuser, not the accused, was put on trial. But employment lawyer Sheribel Rothenberg urges women to speak up when they are harassed, not to let the harasser get away with his destructive behavior. "If we don't speak up, what will we tell our daughters?" she asks.

LOOKING INSIDE AND OUTSIDE THE COMPANY

The realization that you have no place to go in your company, whether you're female or male, should trigger flashing lights in your mind's eyes: It's time to take action, whether you want to or not. If you're not advancing in your job, you are vulnerable to cutbacks and cost-saving demotions, but if you take charge of the situation right away and start analyzing where you are and what you can do about it, you will be able to choose where you want to go and when.

"The feeling of people in a dead-end job usually comes after three years of doing the same thing," says Marilyn Moats Kennedy, a nationally known career consultant. "The realization hits one day, and that's when it's time to make a change." Kennedy warns against doing anything impulsive. "Don't quit immediately," she advises. "Instead, try to restructure your job within the company so that you will be doing something challenging. Rewrite your job description and, in doing so, move yourself up one level in your company's job rankings. Present it to your boss and explain why this job change will be good for the company and for you. But never mention you are bored. If that doesn't work, and it's a large company with many departments and other holdings, ask for a transfer."

The career counselor tells of a client who started with a large company in customer service, got bored, applied for the job of supervisor, got it, got bored again and transferred to marketing. That led to her current job in sales at the same firm. "She loves selling and has doubled her income," Kennedy says. And she did it without leaving the company. If there's no hope of switching to something that's better for you within the company, look outside. If you want to tread water until you can find the job you really want, consider temporary work or a lateral move to a different company. (See Chapter 5.)

Never be obvious in your present job about the fact that you are job hunting. If you're planning to leave by choice, keep your job hunt secret. Get an answering machine for your home phone and, if you can afford it, a facsimile machine. Take vacation time or personal days to go out on interviews. If that's not enough time, make appointments to meet people during the workday away from the office. Arrange breakfast, lunch and after-work meetings. Changing jobs by choice gives you the power to determine your fate, but it must be done with utmost discretion. Never answer a blind ad that gives only a box number; it might turn out to be your present employers or someone who knows them. It's an additional pressure to job hunt in secret, but you have no choice.

When you do get job interviews and offers, calmly analyze which one will be best for you; after all, you already have a paying job. But some job switchers are so grateful to be offered employment they devalue their worth during the job interview. "Don't offer to work for less," warns Mort Hoffman, president of Corporate Careers, a White Plains, New York employment agency and search firm. "It raises a red flag." And if a company does make a job offer, he strongly advises getting it in writing before giving two weeks' notice. If your present employers say they don't want to lose you and make a counteroffer, Hoffman says: "Refuse it. They'll replace you soon anyway."

WHEN YOU'RE FORCED OUT

Not everyone, even the most skilled and experienced worker, has a choice in whether to stay on the job or go. John T. Thomas was executive vice president of Ero Industries, a $25 million manufacturing company. In a casual conversation with Thomas, the company's chief executive said he was thinking of deemphasizing its direct marketing business. Thomas, a highly credentialed marketing consultant, took no action. "I could smell something was about to happen, but I didn't think it would happen when it did," says Thomas, who had just relocated his family to Ero's headquarters. But six months later, the company sold off the division and the executive was out of a job. He then began the job hunting that, he says, "I should have done months before." Today, Thomas is a partner in Ward Howell International, a $30 million executive search firm specializing in middle and upper management positions. He's learned his lesson well: Thomas advises employees who suspect their company is ripe for a downsizing, merger, acquisition or takeover to look for clues. "The most obvious clue is a rumor, because where there's smoke, there's fire," he says. "And, if there's a sudden burst of activity on weekends by financial people, be suspicious. Executives don't work on weekends for fun." Former employees of Kraft, Time-Life, Exxon, IBM, General Foods, AT&T, Borg-Warner, General Motors, R. J. Reynolds Tobacco Company and Sears, Roebuck, to name a few, now know it's important to start job hunting the minute the rumors begin.

As bad as it is to lose your job through a merger or downsizing, nothing matches the humiliation of being fired. Janet Jones (not her real name) is a marketing researcher who recently was fired from her job with a Washington-based nonprofit agency. Her position was eliminated in a general staff cutback. Jones got another job with a small private business, and she thinks she was placed so quickly because she never mentioned she was fired. "I was canned for reasons that had nothing to do with my ability," says the researcher, who asks that her name not be used. "But what could I say in a job interview, that I had a crazy boss and was fired? That I did a good job but got fired anyway?"[6] Because she was sacked, Jones says, "if I admitted how I lost my job it would bring into question issues of competence and integrity. It would only raise eyebrows—and anyone who says otherwise is full of it."

But at least one veteran personnel executive is saying that being fired—whether it's called something as basic as being "laid off" or as esoteric as being "redirected"—is no longer fraught with negative emotional baggage in the world of job hunting. "With all the downsizing... even at companies that historically have never laid people off, being fired doesn't carry the same stigma," says Thomas J. Glynn, president of Fox-Morris Associates, a Philadelphia-based recruiting and outplacement firm. "If fired means being discharged without consent, then it's not a negative. However, if it means you've done something out of bounds, illegal or immoral, the stigma still applies in that connotation."

Often, "you're fired" can be the first step in a new and important professional direction. When Grace Mirabella of New York was fired as editor in chief of *Vogue*, she certainly had done nothing out of bounds. In fact, she had led the upscale women's magazine to a circulation of 1.2 million in 1988 from 400,000 in 1971.[7] The firing came as a shock, but within a year the veteran editor bounded back as publications director of a new and dynamic magazine bearing her name, *Mirabella*. The editor says she was eager to leave *Vogue* but never had the guts to do it, and that she sees her life after being fired as an adventure.

WHAT TO DO IF YOU'RE FIRED

Even if your former employer allows you to resign, it's important to face the fact that you were indeed fired, handle your exit with dignity, mourn your job loss briefly if you're inclined to do so—and then get on with the rest of your life. Remember, you live in a world where being fired is common, not only for people who deserve it, but also for many who do not. Consultant Glynn gives this advice about what to do if you're fired:

- Tell acquaintances, friends and anyone in a position to help that you are job hunting. Tell them the truth.

- Don't be afraid to follow up on leads from your network of contacts, even if they are people you don't personally know, for fear that too many people will know how you came to lose your job. They might be able to help you.
- Be aware that the number of opportunities will not increase the longer you are in the job market. When a good opportunity comes along, evaluate it for what it is rather than by how quickly it came.
- Look for a new job in a positive way. A future employer is not interested in your anger.

Whether or not you use the word fired, Glynn warns that "if you feel you were fired, it can work against you." Being fired may be the time for you to determine which values are most important to your happiness and to dream a little about what you would like to do in a perfect world.

THE GOOD NEWS

Whether you choose to leave your job or were fired, the psychological stress is severe, psychologists say. But there's light at the end of the tunnel: Reemployment is the quickest cure and brings fast emotional recovery, research by the University of Michigan shows.[8] A study of 400 blue-collar workers laid off or fired in widespread auto industry cutbacks shows that "distress from job loss dissipated relatively quickly for those workers landing a new job. Within a year, their emotional state was the same as or even slightly better than those working straight through the rough economic times. And despite the strain of finding new employment, many U.S. workers look forward with joyful anticipation to quitting their jobs. Switching jobs ranked eighth in a list of New Year's resolutions in a survey of 1,010 women and men by Summit Poll, a research organization.[9]

Brad Smith has changed jobs often and is upbeat about his work pattern. A partner in an accounting firm in Irvine, California, he has changed employers four times in recent years. Each change has been a good move for him, he says, because each time he has earned more money and gotten more autonomy. And Jane Pauley says she welcomed the change that moved her from the top-ranking job as coanchor of the early morning "Today" show to a new assignment at NBC-TV at prime time, a higher salary and better hours. Serious questions were raised in Pauley's behalf about why she allegedly was considered too old at age 39, a form of illegal age discrimination. But instead of grousing publicly about being forced out, Pauley is now making more money and has more time for her family.

Though you may feel negative about an unwelcomed job separation, try to be positive. Look for a position that has a potential for growth and advancement. "Negative motivation seldom pays off," says Joseph Carideo, partner in Thorndike Deland Associates, a New York executive search firm.[10] There often are unexpected benefits from acknowledging the reality and moving on to something different. A study by the consulting firm Right Associates shows that when executives who lose their job decide to do the same job in a new industry, they earn an average of 10 percent more than they did previously.[11] Executives who lose their jobs and stay in the same industry average a 4.3 percent pay cut.

CHANGING PROFESSIONS

When you hate to go to work in the morning and then hate what you do when you get there, it's time to explore other career possibilities. Changing professions is a trend expected to accelerate in the next century because of new technology; it will be as commonplace as buying a new car. But switching careers by choice is a challenge: Many people who have concentrated on preparing themselves for one profession fear taking such a big step. Part of the problem is that dissatisfaction with a career often comes in mid-life, when most people have family responsibilities and are less likely to want to take risks, even if they know they've gone as far as they can go in their current field. "If you stop to analyze it, your career is not a ladder—it's a progression," says Ken Dychtwald, president of Age Wave, a consulting firm that studies the impact of aging. "Every rung up the ladder that you move, there's room for fewer people. It's like the children's game of musical chairs, where every turn they take away a chair."

Whether you've been in your job only a few years or are a seasoned professional, deciding to make a change, which means acquiring the necessary skills and education, making connections in your new field and then starting to job hunt, can be both financially and emotionally rewarding. "I've seen a lawyer who changed to interior designing and a very successful accountant who became a camp director," says Sheila Pond, head of career planning at Career Vision, a nonprofit career guidance agency.[12] "And, I know of an air traffic controller who is in the process of becoming a physical therapist."

Over the years, the letters and phone calls I've received from people who want to or need to change careers sound far more desperate than those from people seeking new jobs in their current professions. A man in his late 30s wrote me that after 17 years of selling women's apparel to all types of retail operations, he wanted to make a career change. "How do I convince a company that I'm good at selling, that I can sell anything, even if it's a different product from the one I sell now?" he asked. "I have always been under the assumption that it's easier to learn about a product than to learn how to sell. I've answered hundreds of ads and I've been in direct contact with several manufacturers outside of women's apparel. But my efforts have produced little." Since he was making no headway in sales, I suggested he forget it and consider marketing, where his years of experience and college education will be valuable assets. Because he's currently employed, he can afford to take marketing courses and even to earn a master's degree.

A secretary, who has worked for the same company for 20 years and has never been considered for promotion, called me in desperation. "I'm at the end of my rope," she said. "I started out as a secretary because I believed I could work my way up into management if I hung in long enough. But they won't give me a chance. I've got to get out of here and try something different before it's too late." I advised the secretary to stay in her job for the time being simply to put food on the table, but to take positive action to prepare herself for a better job. In our conversation, she told me she spent weekends going to real estate open houses, even though she was not in the market for a home. She was fascinated by how homes are bought and sold. When I suggested switching to real estate sales and becoming a licensed broker, her eyes lit up, even though she realized she had many years of hard work ahead to qualify for the profession.

Both the salesperson and the secretary needed to take a step back and carefully examine their own strengths in order to prepare for a new profession. Switching professions does not have the urgency of finding a new job after you've been fired or laid off because you still have a job. Having a steady income gives you the luxury to be creative, to consider new ideas, to dream what may turn out to be the possible dream. You even have time to work with a reputable career consultant to find out what you are good at. Charles Handy, a researcher on issues concerning the workforce of the future, has a novel approach:

Go to 20 acquaintances, friends and co-workers and ask each to tell you one thing you do very well.[13] An advertising executive who did that, Handy says, got 20 helpful answers, but not one was advertising. Instead, the executive was seen as being a leader, knowledgeable in history, a wine connoisseur and a good organizer. He now conducts European tours of battlefields, historical sites and vineyards.

STARTING YOUR OWN BUSINESS

In your soul-searching about leaving your job or switching professions, there's another option: becoming an entrepreneur. You'll have a wonderful boss, someone you really like and trust, who has your best interests at heart. That person will be you. Of course, that's a simplistic approach to incurring the risks that surround starting your own business, but many people leave the corporate culture and decide to take the plunge on their own because they are tired of reporting to people they don't respect. They're tired of being described as "underqualified" by their current bosses and "overqualified" by prospective employers. Many female and minority entrepreneurs are former employees who became frustrated from beating their heads against the glass ceiling and from being unable to rise in their professions because of discrimination by their supervisors or the corporation itself.

"As a woman and minority, I finally got tired of wearing that navy blue corporate suit every day and always being ignored by my managers," says a former personnel administrator, an African American who now owns a temporary services agency. "It took me 12 years to leave, but when I finally opened my own business, despite the hard work and struggle it took to make it a success, I knew I had done the right thing." Carol Ross Barney agrees. She's president of her own architecture firm, which she opened after working for other firms for ten years. Now she has 12 employees and billings of more than $1 million. "I would not work for other people again," she says. "I make more money now and I am my own boss. Of course, I also have to work much harder." The temporary services owner and the architect are typical business owners because they "evolved" into being entrepreneurs after years of working in their fields. Though they are experts in their professions, they knew they needed additional skills and training in business administration.

A Washington, D.C., social worker, tired of the long hours and low pay at the nonprofit social service agency where he worked for eight years, wrote me about his plans to start his own consulting firm within two years. "I know social work, but my master's degree in it won't help me get a successful practice going," he wrote. "I don't have the foggiest notion of how to run a business." He's learning how to be a business owner by taking computer courses at night and studying for a degree in accounting. He is part of a trend projected to continue in 2000 and reflected by my three children: studies show that almost half of all women and men dream of owning their own businesses someday. That's why the most popular adult education courses are those on the do's and don'ts of starting your own enterprise. The National Federation of Independent Businesses reports that 64 percent of entrepreneurs start new businesses; the rest purchase existing ones. The proliferation of start-up firms is due in part to the fact that baby boomers like to do their own thing. The generation that is now middle-aged is made up of people with the experience, education and tax incentives to become entrepreneurs, say David Evans and Linda Leighton of National Economic Research Associates. The economists say that the new breed of business owners are more likely to be older than younger and have more education. Female entrepreneurs, they find, are apt to be women with advanced college degrees who have children under the age of three.

The location of new businesses is changing, too. Instead of being in traditional centers of industry and finance such as Chicago, Detroit, Los Angeles, and New York, industrial centers seem to be shifting rapidly. Small businesses "are reshuffling the country's economic deck," according to *U.S. News and World Report*, which has found the following patterns: High-technology firms are booming in Seattle; telemarketing companies in Omaha; financial services in Salt Lake City; insurance, Des Moines; supercomputers, Minneapolis; industrial exports, Peoria, Illinois; franchises, Wichita; sports equipment, Indianapolis; computer software, Columbus, Ohio; health care, Louisville, Kentucky; restaurants, Portland, Maine; credit cards, Wilmington, Delaware; small businesses, Manchester, New Hampshire; banking, Charlotte, North Carolina; tourism, Orlando, Florida.[14]

SWEET SMELL OF SUCCESS

People who want to start their own businesses are not deterred by warnings from the Small Business Administration that only 50 percent of new businesses that open each year will be around five years later. In fact, one of the characteristics of new business owners is their optimism. A three-year study of some 3,000 new businesses by American Express Small Business Services and the National Federation of Independent Businesses found that more than 90 percent of the entrepreneurs said they'd do it again, and 67 percent said their level of personal satisfaction was higher than they thought it would be before opening their own businesses.[15] The study also lists key reasons cited by the new entrepreneurs for their success:

- *Self-confidence.* Of those who believed from the beginning that their businesses had a 90 percent chance of making it, 82 percent were still in business.
- *Capital.* There was an 84 percent survival rate for businesses with an initial investment exceeding $50,000; it was 74 percent for those who started up with under $20,000.
- *Customer service.* 82 percent of entrepreneurs who worked between 60 and 69 hours a week were still in business—but they also reported "knowing when to stop."
- *Commitment.* Though many people start new businesses by moonlighting while holding a full-time job, 78 percent of the new owners who were successful said their business was their only job. Of those who held another job while testing entrepreneurial waters, 70 percent survived.
- *Product knowledge.* Eighty percent of business owners with prior work experience with the product or services they now offer remained in business; the survival rate for those whose previous jobs were very different was 72 percent.

OPENING NEW DOORS

When Gayle Sayers realized that his years as a Football Hall of Fame running back, a master's degree in education and administration, and experience as a college athletic director would not get him his dream job in the front office of a National Football League (NFL) team or allow him to buy an NFL franchise, he started his own business. Refusing to be stymied by what he attributes to the NFL's failure to hire black managers, he borrowed $300,000 on his home and opened his own business.[16] Today, the former football star owns Gale Sayers Crest Computer Supply Company, a successful mail order house. Sayers started a service business selling office and computer equipment because his market research showed high-tech supply firms are the wave of the future. In 1989, Crest had $16.5 million in revenue. He had done his homework.

Peter Greenhill, a former New York public relations consultant, lost his job at Rogers & Cowan when the company reorganized in 1984. His new business is baseball cards, a $7 million enterprise founded by his son David when he was 13 to help the family out. The former p.r. executive handles finances, advertising and administration for New York Card Company; his wife, a teacher, works the computers. And the family is well on its way to financial solvency.[17]

Joining the rising tide of entrepreneurs are dental hygienists, truck drivers, upholsterers, elder care providers, contractors, corporate child care consultants, facilities managers, meeting planners, travel agents, public relations specialists and independent video producers.

Women Business Owners

Of the nation's 19 million business owners, 4 million are women who own businesses with total annual receipts of $278.1 billion.[18] The Small Business Administration (SBA) says women will own 50 percent of the nation's businesses by 2000. "Women business owners are not a social cause," emphasizes Gillian Rudd, former president of the National Association of Women Business Owners. "We are a force for economic development, annually contributing over $250 billion to the economy, $37 billion to the federal government and $13 billion to state and local treasuries." In the United States, women are opening their own businesses at a rate that is six times that of men, according to the SBA, putting themselves in a risky position because of the high failure rate of new businesses.

"A peacock that sits on its tail feathers is just another turkey," says Sharon P. Cavanaugh, president and owner of Peacock Papers, a Boston-based manufacturer of paper party and gift products.[19] Cavanaugh is no turkey; she's a risk taker. Before she started her own business with less than $500,000 and one employee, she had worked for 13 years in real estate development. Cavanaugh was successful, but all along she "had a little idea for a business that mushroomed, like a bull running through a corral," she told me. By 1989, her business grossed about $10 million and had 65 employees. "If you want to do something and are willing to work hard and go after it, you're going to get it," she says.

Working from Home

One of the reasons so many women, especially those with children, start their own businesses is they want to work from home, a good place to launch a business because it saves so much time and money. Link Resources, a New York-based market research firm, predicts that by the year 2000, people who own home-based businesses will represent one-third of the work force, working out of kitchens, attics, dens, garages and basements.[20] Working from home clearly is economical and geographically convenient. "The home is viewed as the perfect place for entrepreneurship," say Kathleen Christensen, director of the National Project on Home-Based Work at the graduate school of the City University of New York. "There are tax advantages, minimal capital needs and low overhead. And it seems ideal for mothers of young children."

But working from home also has drawbacks. Christensen surveyed 7,000 female home-based workers, 5,530 of them self-employed, and found that the need for child care still is "absolutely critical; you cannot start a serious business without it." Her study shows that two-thirds of the women doing professional work and one-third of those doing clerical work hired child care. Women without children, on the other hand, often worked day and night because of the "tremendous amount of anxiety involved in trying to make it," Christensen says. "They are prime candidates for burnout."

Other problems she found:

- feelings of loneliness and isolation
- serious logistical problems, including how to separate the workplace from the house—and from the rest of the family
- lack of health insurance, pensions and other benefits

"But when it does work, home-based work is very satisfying," Christensen says. "Success is based on recognizing the problems that exist and dealing with them honestly. Those who want to succeed have to be clear with themselves that their work at home is serious work."

Plan Ahead

Whether you're going to a new job, switching careers or starting your own business, it's important to proceed in a professional manner. That means giving notice, training your replacement and leaving as pleasantly as possible. If your present employer has exit interviews for those leaving the firm, proceed with caution: This is not the time to make points or to get back at managers who have harmed your progress, even if they deserve it. If you want a strong, positive reference from your current employer, make no accusations about anyone or anything.

The next important step you must take before you leave is to make sure your financial house is in order. "Look carefully at your present employer's provisions for your retirement and profit-sharing plans to see if you want to take the cash or leave it in the plan," says Maryann Laketek, consultant with Hewitt Associates, an international employee benefits consulting firm. Laketek says if you have more than $3,500 in your plan, federal law requires the employer to let you leave the money in, if you want to. "But remember, if you don't take it when you leave, you may not be able to withdraw it until 59.5 years or at retirement," the consultant warns. If you take cash and are under 59.5 years, you must roll over the money into an individual retirement account (IRA) plan within 60 days of receiving it from the company; otherwise, you'll have to pay a 10 percent penalty plus income tax. If you're over 59.5 years and take cash, you're permitted to take a one-time special tax averaging, which puts you in a lower bracket.

"Don't throw away your retirement money," advises Jane Bryant Quinn, financial columnist.[21] "You may have received a lump-sum distribution from a pension plan, your tax-deductible 401(k)-contributions, matching contributions from your employer and tax-deferred earnings on the whole sum. None of this money has ever been taxed, and your goal should be to keep it that way. Do it by rolling the wad into an IRA." Health benefits are just as important as cash from pension and profit-sharing plans. Employers must allow you to continue health benefits at your expense for 18 months, and an existing life insurance policy may be converted into a personal policy. But consultant Laketek warns that if you or family members have a previously existing health problem, "it might lengthen the waiting period to one year to get enrolled in your new plan. Or, if you go to work for a small firm, you may endanger your being included at all."

MAKING THE RIGHT MOVES

What's exciting about working in the 1990s is that skilled job seekers will not be stuck in a dead-end job with no future or in a profession they hate. And if you are fired, laid off or caught in a downsizing or merger, you still will have viable options. In Chapter 7 you'll be able to analyze where you are now in your present job so that you can prepare for success in the future workplace.

7

SECURING YOUR FUTURE

Success is what this book is about. Success in the profession of your choice, one with a future and one you can advance in. Turning your career into a success story will take the same basic ingredients in the 21st century as it did in the 20th: motivation, enthusiasm, sacrifice and professional qualifications. In addition to the basics, jobs in the 1990s will require more teamwork, flexibility, communications and technological skills, managerial ability and continuous education. In the future, general knowledge will be more important than narrow expertise because everyone will be asked to do everything. There isn't a set list of skills or credentials needed to succeed in certain jobs, according to Raymond Brixley, director of human resources for Quaker Oats Company's U.S. Grocery Products Division, "... so we look for someone capable of doing lots of things well, and more importantly, someone who 'fits' into the organization's structure." That means, he says, getting along with colleagues and clients and mirroring the company's philosophy.[1]

In the future, companies are expected to be far less secretive about their activities and involvements, so it will be easier to ascertain how well you fit in. Without com-

119

promising your ideals of ethics, fitting in with the corporate culture—even actually believing in it—is an important factor in a successful career.

HOW TO BE SUCCESSFUL

What you are doing right now to prepare for a profession will determine how well you are positioned for the future. You cannot be passive about your career: You must take charge of it and make it move. Even if you are lucky enough to have a personal mentor, someone looking out for your best interests on the job, you are the one who must be aware of what's happening in the workplace and in your field. You are the only one who knows what makes you happy and, at the same time, self-sufficient. You have to identify your own problems and solve them, with a little help from friends and career experts. Here are some examples of creative problem solving based on letters and phone calls from readers of my nationally syndicated Jobs column. They illustrate how being aware that something is wrong and then doing something about it make the difference between success and frustration. All names and some of the details have been changed.

David E.—Advertising Sales

When David E. called me, he sounded desperate. He had been in advertising for eight years and for the past two had worked for a new local monthly magazine. "I made the magazine grow," he said. "I went out there and really hustled. I not only got people to advertise in a new magazine, sight unseen, I got repeat business by building trust and confidence. I was always available to help advertisers. I worked my tail off." But the day he called me, David had learned that the playing field was changed. His commission was reduced, and he would no longer get a draw on expenses. Three staff members, relatives of the publisher, had been hired at half his salary and commission and were being assigned to his clients. His job would be solely new advertising. "I'm supposed to take it quietly," he says. "But I won't."

David thought he had a secure job because he was productive, but it wasn't enough. Employers, especially owners of family-held businesses, can do whatever they want—but so can you, I told him. The handwriting was on the wall: The company wanted him out; it was simply a matter of time. David loved advertising and had an excellent reputation. Before his credibility was destroyed, I advised him to start job hunting while he still had a job. In our discussion of alternatives, David told me he had carefully studied the advertising and marketing plans of an older, established national magazine the new local magazine was competing with. He had done a report on the bigger publication's strengths and weaknesses and had used his insights to get the older magazine's advertisers to advertise in his publication, too. He knew the national magazine as well as his own. I suggested he set up an interview with the larger magazine at its headquarters to discuss his findings. I cautioned him not to knock his present employer but to emphasize that he could be productive for the more established one. David liked the idea but said he would have to move slowly and carefully. "Just be discreet," I warned him. "Don't let anyone know what you're doing."

Six months later, David called to say he was hanging in at his present job and had been granted an interview at the larger magazine. "I think they really were impressed with how much I knew about their operation," he said. As luck would have it—and it was partially luck—the magazine's advertising chief told David she was considering opening a branch office in his city and would keep him in mind. One year later—about the time the local magazine was going out of business—he was hired as manager of the new office. "I'm glad I didn't spend a lot of time agonizing about how I was being screwed," David said. "If I had, I would have missed this chance." And he wouldn't have gotten the excellent reference he did from the smaller magazine.

Today, David has a staff of five and does more than sell: He recruits, hires, trains and supervises. He does budget and payroll and is taking business courses at night, for which the magazine pays. "I couldn't be happier," he says.

Mary S.—Human Resources

Mary S. was an office manager at a large company, one that, despite its size, stresses employee loyalty and sees itself and its workers as one family. Mary, who has an undergraduate degree in psychology, had worked for the firm for 15 years when she wrote me. She started to apply for promotions after her second year but had not been able to move beyond her present title, although she received regular salary increases each year. "No one says it directly, but the general feeling is that I manage a staff of 20 people and have gone as far as I can go," Mary wrote. "But I like it here. I really care about this company and feel a part of it, and I want to go further."

In her letter, Mary wrote about her concerns: the glass ceiling that blocked her from moving ahead; the fact that a team of white men, who surely were not going to be shoved aside, ran the company; and that there was no clear corporate plan about how to get from one step on the career ladder to the next. What would happen, she worried, to women and minorities like her who had been highly recruited but had no room to advance? "I don't want the company to lose these valuable employees," Mary said. "And I don't want them to lose me. What will happen when the labor market has few qualified workers, which already is beginning to happen? How will our firm be able to attract them?"

In telephone conversations with Mary, I pointed out that she was talking about employee diversity. "I'll bet your company is talking about it, too," I told her. "Perhaps, since you care so much, your next move should be to personnel." Mary was enthusiastic about working in human resources, helping people and the company she was so closely identified with. She researched facts on the demographics of the labor force in 2000 and the projected shortages of skilled workers. She wrote a memo on her findings to the vice president of human resources detailing what she thought the firm should do to maintain its positive public image and to attract and retain the best workers. In a personal interview with the vice president, who told her he shared her concerns about all workers being able to achieve their full potential, Mary told him she herself felt stymied. It was true, he told her, that there was no room at the present time to move upward, but if she would take a lateral move at the same salary, he would be happy to have her in his department. He offered her a job as part of a newly formed human resources group working on issues of diversity that included recruitment, training, compensation, benefits and work-family issues—"all the things," says Mary, "that are close to my heart." She made the move, losing her managerial status. But eight months later she was named director of the company's new community outreach program.

John T.—Computer Sales

John T. works in a parking lot. "When you're black and from the ghetto, it's the only job you can get," he said when he called me. When I countered that what he said was scarcely true, John responded that it was 100 percent true for him. Bright and articulate, John works hard at his job. His courtesy and helpfulness to customers earn him good tips. "I make enough money to live on, but I'm only 22," he told me. "When I look down the line at when I get older, I get scared: The job is very hard on you physically, and so is the weather. I don't see many older parking lot attendants around."

John knew he had to prepare for something more stable, something with a future, and he was willing to do what it takes. He had a high school diploma and had thought about getting advanced technical training or even going to college, but his divorced mother needed his salary to help support his four younger brothers and sisters. John said he knew he was good with people—his tips showed that—but he didn't know what to do with his talent. He also wanted to become computer literate. "I've fooled around with computers a little and I have a feel for them," he said. We discussed that perhaps someday he would like to sell computers at the retail level. The idea excited him, and within two weeks he started taking courses in computer literacy at a community college at night. He soon was able to do word processing and some programming. He often stayed on after class working on the computers and talking to the instructor. The instructor, manager of a retail computer store, asked John to work part-time evenings during the pre-Christmas season, when school was not in session. John was so successful selling computers and programs and dealing with buyers' follow-up questions he was kept on after the holidays. He continues to work days at the parking lot, goes to school in the evenings and works at the store on the nights there are no classes.

John has long-term plans: When he completes his computer literacy course, he plans to continue at the community college and earn an associate degree. His next step is to get his bachelor's degree and then enroll in the university's one-year, intensive course in advanced computer applications. He estimates the entire process may take ten years. "I don't make enough money yet in sales to leave my parking job, but I've learned I'm very good at selling," he told me. "I'm gaining experience, building references and waiting for a full-time job to open up somewhere. Meanwhile, I'm saving my money and going to school. It's going to take me a long time to get to where I want to go—selling computers and other high-tech equipment—but I'm determined to do it."

FUTURE HIGHS AND LOWS OF TECHNOLOGY

David, Mary and John are in charge of their work lives—a powerful feeling. And they did it through their own efforts. Though David and Mary are better educated, far more established and higher ranking than John, he has an advantage over them: He's directly involved in computer technology, a profession at the cutting edge of change in the 1990s. Right now, John is at the low-tech level of selling the product, but after he finishes his intensive college training, he will be schooled in the high-tech of computer programming and analysis. He will be positioned for rapid advancement in the 1990s and beyond because he will understand the interplay of high-tech and low-tech in employment opportunities—the key today to planning a successful career. The new technology is the driving force behind the creation of new jobs, changing forever everything it touches.

To underline the fact that the crest of computer technology will affect almost every high-wage, high-skilled job by 2000, the U.S. Department of Labor has issued a special report stressing the need for all workers to have technological skills.[2] It cites as an example of what many workers will need to know the job responsibilities of a man identified only as Kareem. Kareem is an electronics specialist working as an electrician at an auto assembly plant. With the head of his plant's high-technology training program, he has been involved with the selection and installation of a robotics painting system. Kareem works with pneumatics, hydraulics, computer consoles and simulations of operations of the equipment he uses. At his plant, system downtime has been reduced by 22 percent.

"Just about everybody will work with computers in one form or another, but that doesn't mean they will be in the business of designing them," says P. Helmut Epp, head of the Department of Computer Science and Information at DePaul University in Chicago. "There's going to be a continuous struggle between those people who computerize and those who use the results. At any given point, there will always be jobs for people who look at existing systems and see how they can be improved upon, who can build systems upon systems. What we're seeing now is a form of infrastructure and information that builds upon itself." Dr. Epp, whose first job was as a computer programmer in 1967 when he was a teenager, says the future job market "will be so splintered that there will be low-tech jobs that will coexist with high-tech jobs, but there will not be so much room between the two as there is now—and they will continually shift." Whatever level of technology you will work at, says the professor, who heads DePaul's computer career program, what will be needed is "mental toughness that will get the job done, no matter what."

A DIFFERENT SKILLS MIX

At Motorola, a leading international supplier of mobile radios and semiconductors, preparing for jobs in the 1990s has been going on since the 1980s. "Every organization that's going to make it between now and 2000 will have to concentrate on bringing in employees who have a higher degree of math, reading and reasoning skills—or have in-house programs to bring them up to speed," said Rosalyn D. Wesley, manager of sourcing and development for Motorola's land mobile product center. "There will be no room for a person who can do only one thing. People will have to understand the technology, the product, the impact of competition and the global marketplace." A different mix of technological skills will be required in 2000. "We will need more software engineering designers as opposed to hardware," says Wesley. "They will also have to be able to work with clients." Wesley, who is responsible for training and ensuring workforce diversity, stresses that "more than half of all the jobs in 2000 will require education beyond high school. Liberal arts graduates not literate in technology will find themselves behind the eight ball."

But according to Michael S. Dunford, president of an executive search firm bearing his name, "high-tech and low-tech jobs still will be distinguishable in the near future. There will be no blur but perhaps a gradual blend." A professor of technology management at the School of Business at Illinois Institute of Technology has his own definition of what automation means in its impact on employment. "A high-tech job is one in which the rate of change in the underlying technology is very high," says Joel D. Goldhar, who has an undergraduate degree in chemical engineering, an MBA and a doctorate in business. "A low-tech job has a slow rate of change." In the future, the professor says, "there will be knowledge workers (high-tech), such as engineers, and touch laborers (low-tech), such as fast-food workers. The knowledge workers are the people who design the machines, but it only takes a few of them." To get ready for the jobs of the future, Goldhar urges people to "get as much education as you can to be able to deal with the information technology that will be pervasive in doing all jobs, whether high- or low-tech."

REALITY CHECK

Even if you're in the job you want—one that will not be obsolete in 2000—and even if you know what to do about it if it isn't right for you, it's important to take frequent readings of your employment health: Where are you going and why? How exactly are you doing? Here is a checklist of ten questions that will help you take the pulse of your present work condition:

	Yes	No
1. Do you look forward to going to work each day?	☐	☐
2. At the end of the day, do you have a sense of accomplishment?	☐	☐
3. Do you respect your employers, their goals, ethics and professional expertise?	☐	☐
4. Are you doing what you do best, using the skills and knowledge you have acquired for the profession of your choice?	☐	☐
5. Do you feel you are being paid fairly, including salary, benefits and other perks?	☐	☐
6. Are you positioned to move ahead in the next two or three years?	☐	☐
7. Does your company have a commitment to continuing education and training to keep you up to date in your field and in the new technology?	☐	☐
8. Does your employer know your professional goals and discuss with you on a regular basis the skills you need to move into the next job level?	☐	☐

	Yes	**No**
9. Is your present employer concerned about issues such as flexible hours, parental leave, job sharing, child and elder care and wellness programs?	☐	☐
10. Are you satisfied with the balance between your time commitment to your personal goals and responsibilities and your professional goals and responsibilities?	☐	☐

You should ask these self-examination questions once or twice a year to stay in touch with how you feel about work. If most of your answers are yes, that's good news. If most of your answers are no, it doesn't mean you should quit immediately; it does mean you should start evaluating how to remedy the situation. By taking action now, you will secure your future and will have a better shot at being successful.

Employment in the 1990s promises to be exciting and challenging. Your workplace—and it may be your home—will look different because of pervasive automation; your fellow workers will look different because of the new demographics. Instead of more leisure, you probably will have less; instead of reporting to a supervisor, you probably will be your own manager. And change, constant change, in the way you do your job, will be a given. Knowing these facts, having this information, you are well positioned to be successful in your job in the 1990s and beyond.

The future is coming, but only you can decide where it's going.

PART II

The 100 Best Jobs in the 1990s and Beyond

8

THE TOP JOBS

A student in my career planning class at Harold Washington College was thinking about going back to work in two years, after being out of the labor market for ten years raising her children. "I have a teaching degree, but I don't want to teach," she said. "What I really love is photography, and I think it's the kind of job that could give me the flexible hours I need. What's the future for photographers?" I told her photography is one of the top 100 jobs in the next century, but if she thought all she had to do to be a success was to snap pictures, she was mistaken. The impact of high-tech will radicalize the profession. She was lucky, I said, because she has time to become a broad-based professional. Unless she expanded her skills, she would not find enough work. I suggested she learn to develop and print her own photos. She should learn to transmit them over wire services and to call up work by other photographers on a computerized database such as the Associated Press's Electronic Darkroom. She would need to know how to crop and size photos, touch them up and send them to be printed through systems such as Scitex. "And it wouldn't hurt to learn desktop publishing, how to make videos, how to operate a TV camera, something

133

about biomedical photography and a lot about marketing, advertising, imaging, photography management and photo journalism," I told her. I didn't want to overwhelm her, but all those skills will make up the definition of "photographer" in 2000.

Another student with a bachelor's degree in finance wondered if he still would have a job in 2000. "I'm a corporate financial analyst, and I'm worried because of the current downsizing of accounting firms and a dwindling interest in mergers and acquisitions," he said. "I'm only 24, but I want to know how secure my job is." I assured him concern about security is a valid and realistic priority. Why invest so much time and energy in what might turn out to be a dead-end job? I explained that while financial services mirror the economy's cyclical ups and downs, long-term projections are good for those in his field: Corporate financial executive is one of the top 100 jobs in the 1990s, according to the U.S. Bureau of Labor Statistics. I urged him, since he was concerned, to make himself more marketable by becoming a certified public accountant and a certified financial planner, to think about earning an MBA and, down the road, to consider getting a law degree. Perhaps his present employer would pay for his studies. In this way, no matter what the economy did, he would be positioned for a variety of good jobs in the next century. Time was on his side.

Photographer and corporate financial executive are only two of the 100 best jobs mentioned in this section of the book. The jobs are not the futuristic ones that may evolve in 2000; you'll find those exciting job possibilities in Chapter 4. Instead, the jobs listed here are those that will be most plentiful, have specific requirements and a strong career track. They exist right now and will continue to expand in the coming decades, but they will be affected by the new technology and the new demographics.

The list of the 100 best jobs in the 1990s and beyond is divided into ten major industry categories, each covered in a separate chapter. The categories and the jobs in them are listed in alphabetical order. The categories are:

- Business and Financial Services
- Education, Government and Social Services
- Engineering and Computer Technology
- Health Care Professions
- Hospitality Industry
- Management and Office Personnel
- Manufacturing, Repair, Construction, Agriculture and Transportation
- Media and the Arts
- Sales and Personal Services
- Science

Some categories are much larger than others. Engineering's growth, for example, is due to the economy's shift to service and high-tech professionals. The growth in health care is due to the aging of the American population and to the thousands of Americans without health care coverage, which means they are much sicker and in need of critical care when they finally seek medical care.

SELECTION CRITERIA

Each of the 100 job listings begins with educational and employment requirements and current and projected salaries for the year 2000. You'll also find valuable inside tips on how to get on the fast track whether you're entering the labor market, switching jobs, changing careers or planning to open your own business.

Selecting the best jobs required more than two years of careful research and analysis. There is no similar list of these projected labor market winners. Jobs were chosen for this book based on information from the U.S. Department of Labor and its *Monthly Labor Review*,[1] from my own research and daily coverage of employment and from interviews with career counselors, leaders of professional associations, economists and human resources executives.

Not surprisingly, most opportunities are in the service sector. They range from aircraft technician, a medium-paying field that requires an associate degree and will have 20,000 openings by 2000, to the highly selective, highly competitive position of investment banker with its elite Ivy League requirements, advanced degrees and high salaries. The jobs have real employment opportunities, not only in percentage of increase, but in real numbers—among them, registered nurses, paralegals, retail salespeople, cooks/chefs, accountants and computer and health care professionals. I've omitted occupations that are just work, not careers with a future, such as janitors, waiters, waitresses, bartenders, taxi drivers, receptionists, parking lot attendants and refuse collectors— even though there will be many openings in these dead-end occupations. Despite the fact that many jobs in the 1990s and beyond will be driven by developments in computer-circuits and particle accelerators, I've also included a sprinkling of jobs that don't require college or graduate degrees but do have great potential as entry-level jobs or can lead to future entrepreneurship. Among them are truck driver, carpenter, secretary, appliance repairer, travel agent and correction officer or guard. Study the chart at the end of this chapter to see which jobs suit your abilities and interests. The information in the individual job listings in Chapters 9 to 18 will help you make an informed decision about where you want to go and how to get there.

JOB REQUIREMENTS

Each of the 100 best jobs has specific requirements, which I've listed as you might see them in a classified

want ad or job prospectus. Requirements include education, experience, certification, licensing and technical
skills needed to do the job. I've also included character
and personality traits that professionals in the field say
are a necessity to succeed and employers say they look
for. These traits often make the difference in getting a job
and then moving ahead in it. I compiled the information
for the requirements from the U.S. Labor Department's
Occupational Outlook Handbook, newspaper and magazine articles on the future job market and my own interviews with executives of professional associations and
human resources directors. Perhaps the most valuable
source was the people who actually do the job now. They
provide an accurate sense of what's expected of employees
in each of the 100 jobs. For instance, if lens grinding interests you—and optics is a fast-growing and changing field—
to become an ophthalmic laboratory technician you'll
need a high school diploma, a background in science and
mathematics, six to eight months of on-the-job training
and continuing education. On the other hand, to become
a management consultant you'll need at least a bachelor's
degree, at best an MBA, strong business and people skills
and the ability to create computer programs. Knowing
this information will help you evaluate if you can meet
the educational requirements for the job that interests
you and if you have the personality traits that will make
you successful in it.

SALARIES

American workers freely talk about their age, weight
and even their sex lives. But one thing they are reluctant
to discuss is their salaries—and employers like it that
way. Unless salaries are public knowledge, as they are for
union and government workers, they are one of the best
kept secrets in the U.S. labor market. Though workers

expect to make more money every year, the secrecy makes it difficult to know what a job should pay and what colleagues are earning for comparable work. Without accurate salary information, you have very little power in wage negotiations. Such information is essential to plan your career, keep it moving along and, above all, to make sure you are being paid fairly. Part II of this book breaks that silence and lists the 1991 salaries and projected 2000 salaries for the 100 best jobs.

All 1991 wages are average salaries or salary ranges, unless otherwise indicated. They come from sources such as professional organizations, magazine and newspaper articles, educational institutions, consulting firms, personnel directors and knowledgeable professionals in the field. Sources are listed in the notes at the end of the book. If there is no attribution, the 1991 figures are mine, based on the most recent data available from the U.S. Bureau of Labor Statistics and the *Occupational Outlook Handbook*, updated and derived by me.[2] Other sources I've used: the Current Population Survey; National Survey of Professional Administrative, Technical and Clerical Pay; Private Nonservice Industry Survey; Industry Wage Survey.

Salary projections for 2000 are educated guesses made by educators, economists, executives of professional associations, career counselors, personnel directors and professionals in the field. Unless otherwise indicated, the 21st century projections are mine. They are based on current salaries, the maintaining of an average 5 percent annual increase in this decade, the projected supply and demand for workers in a particular field, education required and the projected growth of the field itself. Most increases in these estimated average salaries range from 43 percent to 73 percent over 1991 figures. The estimates, subject to change if the economy fluctuates dramatically, will give you a sense of where a particular job is going in the year 2000 because the size of the paycheck reflects the importance of the job, at least in the eyes of employers. You will also be able to ascertain what kind of lifestyle a particular occupation might provide you. All salaries for 2000 are on the conservative side. Registered nurses, for instance, are expected to average $50,000 in the next two decades, but there will continue to be an extreme shortage of RNs and health care experts say nurses' salaries will increase astronomically. Some have told me they will average as high as $85,000. However, I list the figure I heard the most: $50,000.

Changing Salary Patterns

When studying the 1991 and 2000 salaries listed for each job, remember that real wages, adjusted for inflation, have been declining since the early 1980s. A study by United Way of America indicates that in 1983, U.S. workers who had turned 50 years old "found their real earnings actually had declined by 14 percent over the previous decade, reversing a long-standing trend."[3] Most workers view the years between 30 and 50 as their most lucrative earning period, but that expectation probably will not be realized in 2000.

Despite this bad news—especially for yuppies who want to live rich, die poor and make at least $1,000 more each year than their current age—the report also has some good salary news, not for individuals, but for couples. "The number of households headed by persons in the 35 to 50 age group with incomes of $50,000 or more is expected to triple by 2000—largely a result of two-income couples and the huge size of the baby boom generation," the report states. Because baby boomers will be mature adults, established in the work force, their salaries will reflect their seniority and bring up the average for all age groups.

Economists Bennett Harrison and Barry Bluestone predict that the shift to a service-producing society will result in lower wages except for the most highly skilled employees,[4] but the U.S. Department of Labor insists that low-wage jobs actually have been declining. In 1987, when the U.S. first became a service society instead of industrial, "over 40 percent of the 3.1 million new jobs created were in the very highest-paying occupational categories: managerial, professional and technical.... And 15.6 million people entered, for the first time, the ranks of workers earning $10 or more an hour—while those earning less than $5 an hour actually declined by 7 million."[5] However, everyone agrees that salaries for the top jobs will continue to rise. (See Chapter 5 for inside tips on where to find the best salaries and benefits.)

THE INSIDE TRACK

The section of each job listing titled "Inside Track" gives suggestions about how to begin your career, where to work, how to "pay your dues" and get a head start, the additional education you'll need, the personality and character traits that will serve you best and how high-tech will affect the job. You'll learn that lawyers are advised to consider the growing fields of bankruptcy and space law; carpenters must be willing to work long hours; dietitians who want to become private consultants must take business courses; restaurant and food service managers who are skilled *and* charming will move ahead rapidly; paralegals and other support staff with broad computer skills will be the first hired and best paid. From suggesting that accountants and auditors "use paraprofessionals to free you up to get more clients" to advising veterinarians to "have an equal commitment to animals and their owners," the advice of "Inside Track" will give you a chance to be one step ahead of your competition for the 100 best jobs in the 1990s and beyond.

The following chart cross-references the jobs, the industry categories and the appropriate chapters in this book so that you can easily find the ones you're interested in.

Chapter 9   Business and Financial Services

Jobs

Accountant/Auditor
Bank Loan Officer
Bank Marketer
Corporate Financial Analyst
Court Reporter
Economist
Financial Planner
Insurance Claim Examiner

Investment Banker
Lawyer
Management Consultant
Paralegal
Real Estate Agent/Broker
Real Estate Appraiser
Underwriter

Chapter 10   Education, Government and Social Services

Jobs

Corrections Officer/Guard/Jailer
Educational Administrator
Firefighter
Librarian
Mathematician/Statistician

Police Officer
Psychologist/Counselor
Social Worker
Teacher/Professor

Chapter 11   Engineering and Computer Technology

Jobs

Computer Operator
Computer Programmer
Computer Service Technician
Computer Systems Analyst
Database Manager
Drafter
Engineer

Information Systems Manager
Manufacturing Specialist
   (CAD/CAM and CAI)
Operations Systems Research Analyst
Peripheral Electronic Data Processing
   Equipment Operator

Chapter 12   Health Care Professions

Jobs

Dental Hygienist
Dentist
Dietitian
Health Services Administrator
Home Health Aide
Licensed Practical Nurse
Medical Records Administrator
Occupational Therapist
Ophthalmic Laboratory Technician
Optician

Paramedic
Pharmacist
Physical Therapist
Physician
Physician Assistant
Podiatrist
Radiologic Technologist
Registered Nurse
Speech Pathologist/Audiologist
Veterinarian

Chapter 13   Hospitality Industry

Jobs

Cook/Chef
Flight Attendant
Flight Engineer
Hotel Manager/Assistant

Pilot
Restaurant/Food Service Manager
Travel Agent

Chapter 14   Management and Office Personnel

Jobs

Clerical Supervisor/Office Manager
Corporate Personnel Trainer
Employment Interviewer

Human Resources Manager/Executive
Labor Relations Specialist
Secretary/Office Administrator

Chapter 15   Manufacturing, Repair, Construction, Agriculture and
                  Transportation

Jobs

Aircraft Technician
Appliance/Power Tool Repairer
Architect
Automotive Mechanic
Carpenter
Farm Manager

Industrial Designer
Landscape Architect
Office/Business Machine Repairer
Operations Manager/Manufacturing
Radio/TV Service Technician
Truck Driver

Chapter 16   Media and the Arts

Jobs

Actor/Director/Producer
Advertising and Marketing Account
   Supervisor
Arts Administrator
Commerical and Graphic Artists
Editor/Writer

Interior Designer
Photographer/Camera Operator
Public Relations Specialist
Radio/TV News Reporter
Reporter/Correspondent

Chapter 17   Sales and Personal Services

Jobs

Cosmetologist
Insurance Salesperson

Retail Salesperson
Wholesale Sales Representative

Chapter 18   Science

Jobs

Agricultural Scientist
Biological Scientist
Chemist

Environmental Scientist
Food Scientist
Physicist/Astronomer

9

BUSINESS AND FINANCIAL SERVICES

Accountant/Auditor
Bank Loan Officer
Bank Marketer
Corporate Financial Analyst
Court Reporter
Economist
Financial Planner
Insurance Claim Examiner
Investment Banker
Lawyer
Management Consultant
Paralegal
Real Estate Agent/Broker
Real Estate Appraiser
Underwriter

Business and financial services are among the fastest-growing segments of the service-producing sector, according to *Projections 2000*, published by the U.S. Department of Labor. Some 3.3 million jobs in this category are projected to open up by 2000, all of them requiring computer knowledge. The category includes the most sought-after semiprofessional, the paralegal, and one of the highest-paid professionals, the lawyer. Business and financial services will be a dynamic field in the 1990s and beyond.

ACCOUNTANT/AUDITOR

Job Requirements: Bachelor's degree in accounting with continuous updating to keep current and to retain state license as certified public accountant. Also helpful: accreditation as certified management accountant by the Institute of Certified Management Accountants. MBA and master's degree in taxation are important. Must know how to use sophisticated computer systems.

◆ **Salary:**

1991	*2000*
$28,400[1]	**$43,000**[2]
(starting)	(starting)

Inside Track: Despite the downsizing of accounting and consulting firms in the early 1990s, some 211,000 entry-level jobs for accountants and auditors will be added to the labor market by 2000. Employment prospects are good for those specializing in bankruptcy, debt restructuring, benefits consulting, corporate reorganization and fraud investigations. Starting in 2000, new members of the American Institute of Certified Public Accountants will have to have a total of 150 credit hours of education, which means the traditional 120 hours of undergraduate study plus 30 more hours of graduate work. "The upper 10 percent of successful accountants and auditors work in large firms that have sophisticated training programs," says David Birkenstein, president of the CPA firm of Hochfelder, Birkenstein, Lipinski & Weber, Ltd. To move ahead, Birkenstein, a CPA and attorney who stresses the importance of having the highest ethical standards, get your CPA license within three years. Knowing how to use microcomputers is essential. Experienced accountants and auditors will find a law degree helpful, especially if you want to start your own business. Use paraprofessionals to free yourself up to get clients.

BANK LOAN OFFICER

Job Requirements: Bachelor's degree in accounting or finance. Experience, such as in credit analysis, is necessary. MBA needed for advancement. Computer and communications skills, judgment and tact are essential. Must have knowledge of computers and data processing equipment. Banks give intense training programs for this critical position.

◆ Salary:

1991	*2000*
$26,250 to $44,000[3]	**$40,000 to $65,000**
(starting)	(starting)

Inside Track: Banks of the future will be supermarkets of financial services, but the loan department will still be the number one money maker. The savings and loan scandal of the early 1990s that cost American taxpayers some $1 billion makes this job a critical one. "It's the top job in a bank—some 70 percent of bank presidents are former loan officers who came up the ranks," says C. Paul Johnson, chairman and CEO of the fast-growing First Colonial Bankshares. "The job is more an art than a science," the successful banker says. "You have to be a good judge of character because once you check out all the facts on a loan applicant you have to sense whether the person requesting the loan plans to pay you back."

BANK MARKETER

Job Requirements: Bachelor's degree in marketing or journalism required. Experience in banking necessary. Especially helpful: certification from special bank marketing courses given by Colorado, West Florida and Cornell universities. Must be able to do planning, research, development, advertising, direct marketing, telemarketing, sales, communications and community events. Will have to work long hours, often under pressure of deadlines. Success dependent on creativity in introducing new products and attracting customers.

✦ **Salary:**

1991	*2000*
$36,382 to $220,000[4]	**$50,000 to $300,000**

Inside Track: Marketing and journalism are different routes leading to this important job, so you can choose the area that interests you more. Once you have your undergraduate degree, get a job, any job, in a bank, and start working toward your goal. It would be ideal to start in marketing, but that will be impossible without banking experience.

Banking will change radically in the 1990s as banks become one-stop supermarkets for a variety of financial services. Bank marketers will be promoting loans, insurance, income tax preparation, stock brokerage services, financial counseling, consumer discount and travel agency services, bank-managed mutual funds, checking and savings, safety deposit boxes and credit cards. The more you know about each of these areas, the more valuable you will be. Bank marketers attract new customers and keep old ones by innovative plans.

Despite the downsizing of bank personnel, "you can go to any city and there's going to be a commercial bank that needs you badly," says J. Douglas Adamson of the Bank Marketing Association, a professional organization for public relations and marketing executives for commercial and savings banks. "To get ahead, you really need to have good instincts and appreciate the customer's perspective. You have to be able to focus on that customer and be proficient in advertising research and product development."

CORPORATE FINANCIAL ANALYST

Job Requirements: Bachelor's degree in accounting, finance or business administration. Credentials such as certified public accountant, certified financial planner, an MBA and a law degree give an extra edge in getting ahead. Job involves giving sound financial advice and preparing financial reports for company records and to meet government and regulatory agency requirements. Need knowledge of business management to help direct and project firm's financial future. Opportunities best for those familiar with computer systems, data processing systems and the entire spectrum of financial services. Must be a team player.

◆ **Salary:**

_1991_	_2000_
$73,867[5]	**$101,400**

Inside Track: Between 1988 and 2000, an additional 130,000 financial managers will be needed because of the increasing variety and complexity of financial services, competition, changing laws and growing emphasis on ethics and accuracy of financial data. In-house financial planners work directly for corporations. As these firms become part of the global economy, financial analysts will also have to know international law and be up to date on events in the global marketplace. Analysts with global knowledge will be in great demand at manufacturing firms. If you position yourself right in the profession, attend seminars and read the literature on international finance and events, you can use the job as your route to a top spot in the company. Job openings will be good in health services, which will be struggling to cut costs and to operate more efficiently. Most jobs will be with firms with 50 or fewer employees, but the career track is faster and company-paid educational and training opportunities better in larger firms.

For advancement, it's critical to keep up to date on the new technology in your field. Companies coming out of recessionary times look for financial executives with strong skills. "Recruiting firms are often asked to find financial strategists . . . who can lead the corporation out of a nongrowth environment," said Miles McKie, a managing director of Russell Reynolds Associates, an international executive recruitment firm.

COURT REPORTER

Job Requirements: This important business service requires certification in court reporting from a two-year vocational or community college program. State certification also is required to record court proceedings, depositions and business meetings. Must have specific training in computer programs for this automated profession, especially computer-aided transcription. Need to be able to concentrate for long periods of time and get along well with people. Must be mature and not react emotionally to the proceedings. Promptness, ability to meet deadlines and to function under extreme pressure also required.

◆ **Salary:**

1991	*2000*
$26,460[6]	**$37,000**

Inside Track: As the legal profession expands in the 1990s, so will jobs for court reporters. The secret to a good job in this field is passing state certification. Court reporting—which goes beyond the courtroom into lawyers' offices for depositions, into board meetings and into important business meetings—provides the opportunity to make good money if you're willing to work hard and long. It can be very lucrative not only to do the basic work required, but also to provide additional transcripts of the material to clients. Court reporters work directly for the various court systems, for court reporting firms and as independent contractors.

"You have to be able to absorb a lot of knowledge and retain it, have an extensive vocabulary and a curiosity about words," says Cathy Mrozek, co-owner of Rubin, Mrozek Associates, a successful court reporting firm. Mrozek, who also is a court reporter, says the people who do best in the field are those who are flexible and enjoy diverse atmospheres. "You never know where you will be or where you may be going," she says. Court reporters sometimes are invited to "go with the case," which means following it to another city or even another country. This is one of the few fields that requires only two years of training, can pay well and might lead to owning your own business. Knowing the location and spelling of cities and countries worldwide will be important in legal matters involving international trade and the global marketplace.

ECONOMIST

Job Requirements: Master's degree and doctorate in economics needed for advanced jobs, especially for teaching at colleges or universities. Those with bachelor's degree find entry-level jobs in business or government, working on reports, research and analysis. Must be able to communicate findings in simplistic terms to colleagues, clients, the public and the media. Must know in depth and on a global basis: economic theory, mathematics, statistics and computer applications. Must have at fingertips latest information on prime rate, U.S. dollar versus currency of other countries, consumer price index, gross national product, U.S. civilian unemployment rate and U.S. corporate profits after tax. Individual research projects on economic issues are expected. Those skilled in quantitative techniques have best prospects.

◆ **Salary:**

1991	*2000*
$27,600[7]	**$40,512**
(starting, bachelor's degree)	(starting, bachelor's degree)

Inside Track: Jobs for economists are projected to expand by 27 percent by 2000, reflecting industry's growing reliance on quantitative methods of analyzing business trends, forecasting sales and planning purchasing and production. There's an old saying that if you ask ten economists to forecast the economy you'll get ten different answers. Despite this truism, economists offer vital input. Most jobs are in academia and government, but business and industry are increasingly relying on staff or private economic consultants for information. Labor economists will be in demand at banks, corporations, universities and federal and regional governments.

Government jobs usually do not pay as well as other areas, but economists who work in this sector say they have a strong sense of public service. Government work, however, can lead to lucrative private consulting contracts. Among the best-paid economists are PhDs who are professors of finance at top business schools. Their salaries currently range from $120,000 to $250,000. Some top economists make even more than that as private consultants to Fortune 500 companies.

FINANCIAL PLANNER

Job Requirements: Bachelor's degree in finance to set up spending, savings and investment programs for individuals and corporations. For credibility, need certification in financial planning from American College in Bryn Mawr, Pennsylvania, or University of Denver. State registration required. Must be up to date in latest computer programs and the various money instruments and markets available. Knowledge of federal, state and local tax law essential. Background in international finance increasingly important for global investments. Certified public accountant training, MBA or law degree important to career advancement. Able to work well with people, inspire trust—and study hard.

✦ **Salary:**

_1991_	_2000_
$18,900 to $31,500[8]	**$30,000 to $50,000**
(starting)	(starting)

Inside Track: Financial planning is a growth field because of the profusion of investment opportunities and the complexity of financial services. By 2000, both the profusion and complexity are projected to increase. Financial planners work for themselves or for insurance and financial services firms. This is a relatively new business services field, and one of the problems it has that pushes at the limits of ethical behavior is that some financial planners represent the products they suggest customers buy. That means the planner has a vested interest in recommending the product and gets paid both a fee by the client and a commission by the company offering the product. Many planners, especially those who work for insurance companies, banks or other financial institutions, tell their clients up front what the situation is. Other planners, usually private consultants, refuse to represent any of the products they suggest clients buy. You will have to decide which way you want to go in this field.

"Financial planners must understand people and their motivations, have good technical skills and be trustworthy," says Charles M. Finn, president of the International Association for Financial Planning. Finn suggests new entrants to the field "start out with a clearly successful financial planning firm. Spend five years learning from them how the business functions, and then decide whether to stay as a full partner or to go out on your own." He says top planners today make more than

$250,000 a year and expects the six-figure salaries to continue to increase to the year 2000.

INSURANCE CLAIM EXAMINER

Job Requirements: Prefer college graduates but will hire those without degrees who have specialized experience, such as knowledge of automobile body shop work for auto claims or extensive clerical background for office work. Some courses in insurance, economics and business administration needed to investigate claims, negotiate settlements and authorize payments to claimants. College background in engineering needed to adjust industrial claims, such as fires and other accidents. Legal background helpful to handle workers' compensation and product liability cases. Some medical knowledge for life and health insurance claims. Most firms have intensive on-the-job training and home-study courses through the Insurance Institute of America. Certification important from the Institute and other insurance associations. Computer literacy will be the backbone of this job in the 1990s, as all information on clients and data on policies will be stored in desktop computers. Laptop computers used outside office. Also needed: good math and communications skills. Customer service stressed: a sense of fairness, efficiency and ability to smooth relations with customers.

✦ Salary:

1991	*2000*
$22,176	**$32,260**

Inside Track: Some 172,000 additional insurance claim examiners and investigators will be needed by 2000, mostly because of the new demographics of an aging society. Mature people with both careers and families have the greatest need for life and health insurance and protection for homes, autos and other possessions. Insurance claim examiners—they're not called "adjusters" anymore—are considered administrative support staff by the industry and average salaries are low. But it's a job that is plentiful and getting in at an entry level such as this can lead to important positions in the insurance industry. Career mobility often is rapid because hard workers who perform well are noticed and appreciated.

Specialties of the 1990s will be international business insurance, marine cargo, workers' compensation and product and pollution liability. Your employer will sponsor you in courses in these areas. Take the ones that interest you most and build in-depth knowledge. You can expect to spend three to five years at this level, learning the business. Your next step up should be a big one, probably into sales or management.

INVESTMENT BANKER

Job Requirements: An MBA is needed just to get a foot in the door of this high-powered, lucrative profession of investing money for corporations, governments or yourself. Skill in corporate finance, global markets and cutting-edge computer technology essential in this high-risk world of stocks, bonds, restructuring, mergers, acquisitions, divestitures, buyouts and takeovers. Intense competition for few jobs at the top, but opportunities continue to grow for entry-level trainee jobs. Specialists needed in small and midsize entrepreneurial growth companies. In the 1990s and beyond, must be willing to stay with investments and "grow" businesses rather than take them over and sell off pieces to make a quick buck. In demand: Those who want to make a lot of money but not at the expense of customers or the public. Profession has been in boom and bust cycle but will be on the rise again by the end of the decade as mergers and takeovers rebound.

◆ Salary:

1991	*2000*
$45,000 to $50,000[9]	**$77,000 to $86,000**
(starting)	(starting)

Inside Track: The very companies that have been laying off top investment bankers are hiring: Firms such as PaineWebber Group, Smith Barney, Prudential Securities and Dean Witter actually have increased the size of their staffs. "When you lose someone higher up, with heavy-duty salary, someone has to take over the work," says Joyce M. Short, president of the Wall Street Registry, a New York employment service that refers college graduates seeking work in investment banking.[10] "Housecleaning creates movement into firms, and you can position yourself for the time the industry goes into a growth cycle." Don't expect the fast career rise of the 1980s—those days are gone. "Investment banking no longer is the way to a quick fortune," says Dennis Devere of Thorndike Deland Associates, an executive search firm. "The glory days are over, to a large extent." But rewards still are great for those who make it in this high-risk field, where top performers make millions of dollars.

William Jordan of the Securities Industry Association makes no bones about what it takes to be successful. "Get an MBA from a super-elite or Ivy League school, preferably Harvard, Columbia, University of Pennsylvania, Stanford, Northwestern or the University of Chicago," he advises. "Then go to work for an elite New York investment banking firm." He also adds that in addition to starting salaries, investment bankers can earn a bonus of from $15,000 to $25,000 in their first year.

LAWYER

Job Requirements: Bachelor's degree, usually in political science, followed by law degree from three-year accredited law school. Must pass state bar examination and be admitted to state bar. Must be able to work long, hard hours, bring in clients and be current on the law and legal decisions. Computer literacy needed. Must be good negotiator, have a strong business background, inspire confidence and be able to work well with people. Also will need scientific knowledge for new technology involving biotechnology and space litigation.

✦ **Salary:**

<u>1991</u>	<u>2000</u>
$57,170[11]	**$88,000**

Inside Track: There was a surplus of lawyers in major urban areas in the late 1980s and early 1990s, but jobs for lawyers will have a 71 percent growth by the end of the century. An estimated 176,000 additional lawyers will be needed as a result of population growth and international economic expansion. The United States is a litigious society, and lawyers will continue to be in demand, particularly in the specialties of bankruptcy, litigation, personal injury, environmental, biotechnology and space law.

Space law is the closest Lt. Col. F. Kenneth Schwetje, space lawyer with the Joint Chiefs of Staff at the Pentagon, can get to aviation. "I can't find a plane without my glasses," he says, "but being a space attorney is like being part of a new era."[12] He says you must know the law, physics and technology to work on cases of space salvage, liability for space debris, patent rights for inventions and personal injury suits. To have a qualified staff of legal specialists in biotechnology, particularly in patent disputes, law firms are recruiting scientists with doctorates in biology and sending them to law school. These lawyers must be familiar with genetically engineered substances produced through recombinant DNA techniques known as gene splicing.[13] The need for environmental lawyers also will be critical. "It's not unusual for the cost of cleaning up one contaminated site to be anywhere from several hundreds of thousands of dollars to several million," says Lynda J. Oswald, assistant professor of business law at the University of Michigan.

Despite lower average salaries for attorneys in general, star law school graduates are starting in top firms at salaries that range from $77,000 to $80,000. Public interest firms start lawyers at $26,000. Many lawyers make well into six figures, some in the millions. Big firms provide the best pay and experience, but smaller firms—and they are the ones that will be doing the most hiring—provide a faster career track and a variety of experience.

MANAGEMENT CONSULTANT

Job Requirements: Bachelor's degree in business administration. Master's degree preferred. Must know organizational behavior, finance, sociology and demographic patterns to advise management on personnel and business strategy. An MBA is preferred but can be acquired during career. Must be computer literate and know production, the labor market, family and work problems, marketing. Ability to work and communicate with both top executives and employees is essential. Biggest responsibilities: training a diverse workforce and helping firms meet employees' work and family needs.

◆ **Salary:**

1991	*2000*
$40,021 to $45,510	**$60,000 to $72,000**

Inside Track: Some 46,000 additional management consultants will be needed by 2000 because of competitive pressures on organizations to produce more efficiently and to attract and retain qualified employees. Educational training and personnel skills will be as important as financial and production expertise as large corporations turn to management consultants for help in meeting the challenges of the new workforce of the 21st century. Opportunities will be best for those with advanced degrees and experience. Jobs will expand at the entry level in public accounting and benefits consulting firms, despite downsizing at upper echelons in the early 1990s.

Big firms pay the most money and have the best benefits, but smaller management firms, usually with only two or three people, will proliferate and will be doing most of the hiring. Join associations and professional groups. Take continuing education courses in management, business and marketing to keep up to date in this fast-changing field. If your goal is to open your own firm—and that's generally the way to make the most money—give yourself at least five years working for someone else, updating your skills all the while.

PARALEGAL

Job Requirements: Formal training in programs at community colleges, vocational schools, colleges and universities leading to certification as certified legal assistant. Biggest law firms insist on four-year college degree followed by certification. Must be interested in the law and able to work under a lawyer's supervision interviewing clients and witnesses; doing legal research; drafting wills, contracts and other legal documents. Must pay attention to detail and have patience with clients and attorneys. Important to know litigation, real estate, mortgages, corporate law, employee benefits and general legal processes. Must be on cutting edge of computer technology to do job.

♦ **Salary:**

1991	*2000*
$30,171[14]	**$39,840**

Inside Track: This is the fastest-growing semiprofessional job, expected to grow by 104 percent and to add 62,000 jobs by 2000. The growth is directly related to the increase in numbers of new lawyers needed in this decade and to the new technology that has freed up attorneys to assign more responsibility to legal technicians. Most paralegals work for law firms, and that's where most jobs will be, but opportunities will also open up in corporations, government, insurance firms, financial institutions—and in working by yourself. Registered nurses with paralegal degrees are being recruited by medical malpractice firms. Five years ago, there was no career path for paralegals, but now those employed by corporations will have the chance to move up into management. There are few career paths at law firms except for those that have large staffs of paralegals and need paralegal supervisors. Paralegals with bachelor's degrees will advance most quickly, and salaries are expected to catch up with the growing responsibilities of the job. "The more you prove yourself, the more you get to do," says Janet Cohen, paralegal with a New York law firm and graduate of New York University's Institute of Paralegal Studies.

One new career path leads to opening your own business. Barbara M. Spain, a certified legal assistant who has a bachelor's and master's degree and who has done doctoral studies in history, says owning her own paralegal business after six years working for a law firm "changes the balance of power between paralegals and attorneys." It allows her to earn more money and her clients to save money by using an outside consultant who does not charge as much as a law firm would for her time.[15] Declarations of independence such as Spain's will become more prevalent in the 1990s because the shortage of paralegals will continue into the next century.

REAL ESTATE AGENT/BROKER

Job Requirements: High school diploma. Must pass written exam for state license. Bachelor's degree in real estate preferred. Agents, who sell property owned by others, must have 30 hours of classroom experience. Brokers, who sell real estate and rent, manage and develop new properties, must have 90 hours. Real estate firms offer courses to potential agents. Must be able to sell, have thorough knowledge of the housing market, an outgoing personality, concern for people and good communications skills. Latest knowledge of computer technology. Must be ambitious and committed to hard work.

✦ Salary:

1991	*2000*
$30,870	**$46,200 +**

Inside Track: Despite the sluggishness of the real estate market in the early 1990s, some 72,000 more real estate agents and brokers will be needed by 2000. The growing "bulge" of the population between the ages of 25 and 54 will cause sales of residential and commercial properties to soar—creating more jobs in real estate, especially in home purchases and rental units. New construction and worker relocation also will fuel the need for agents and brokers. The basic ingredient of success is the ability to sell; then comes working long and hard hours, including nights and weekends.

Agents and brokers frequently become developers of new property, and the ones on a fast track are establishing themselves across the Atlantic as well as at home, setting up offices and forming partnerships with European firms to capitalize on the growing global market.[16] "Most real estate companies already have relationships with corporations that are asking questions about real estate in Europe," says Tom Driscoll, president of the Office Network, which represents 28 companies with 108 offices around the world. "You want to be able to answer them." The aging of the U.S. population is precipitating interest in the building of "granny flats," similar to the Australian portable, factory-built, four-room cottages that fit in the back yard. But more firms are interested in managing or renovating buildings than in building them. The demand for physical access to buildings and offices for disabled persons will drive renovations in the next decade and provide job opportunities.

Start your real estate career in your own community, where you know the neighborhood, schools and tax and zoning laws. Then, get top-notch training, either through a real estate firm or private or community college. "The secret to success," says Diana M. Beliard, partner in the successful firm of Beliard Gordon & Partners, Ltd., "is to be flexible in every way and roll with the punches."

REAL ESTATE APPRAISER

Job Requirements: College degree increasingly important in evaluation of property. State certification or licensing. Must be 18 and pass written exam. Experience as real estate agent or broker helpful. Qualifications determined by professional organizations include 60 hours of education in the field for residential appraisers; 150

hours for commercial appraisers. Both require 15 additional hours of professional training, two years' experience and passing grade in exams. Background needed in finance, mathematics, real estate, international affairs and economics. Must know how to measure buildings, evaluate construction and location, search public records and prepare formal reports. Must be computer literate and able to work with real estate and legal databases. Must be unbiased.

✦ **Salary:**

1991	*2000*
$33,075	**$50,000**

Inside Track: Appraisers are the linchpins in real estate transactions: They are the experts who give an objective opinion as to the worth of the property, usually in deals involving substantial amounts of money. Riding the tide of the projected increase of agents and brokers, job opportunities for appraisers will be on the rise in the 1990s. Most are employees of banks, savings and loans, mortgage companies and multiservice real estate companies. Job growth will be in smaller, independent companies that do appraisals for a fee. Today, analyses of property and future construction are being fed into computers that come up with answers as to whether or not the proposed transaction is worth pursuing. It's a highly competitive field, and not everyone is successful in it. Traditionally, the only route to appraising, which can be very profitable for top producers, was from real estate sales, management or finance. But those with the best chance of making it in the 1990s and beyond are college graduates who have studied real estate, finance, business administration and English. On-the-job training is intense, pending licensing. Continuing education is the secret to success in this field. Programs are offered by the Appraisal Institute and the American Society of Appraisers.

UNDERWRITER

Job Requirements: Large insurance companies want college graduates with degrees in business administration or accounting. Liberal arts degree in any field plus courses in business law and accounting also acceptable. Job requires selecting billions of dollars in risks of policy holders that insurance companies will insure. Must be able to analyze insurance applications, medical and loss control reports and actuarial studies. Must be computer literate to process information and applications. Best credential sought by employers: certification as a fellow of the Academy of Life Underwriters. Another prestigious designation: chartered property-casualty underwriter, by the American Institute for Property and Liability Underwriters. Must like working with details, evaluating information, making prompt decisions and communicating information accurately and effectively.

✦ **Salary:**

1991	*2000*
$31,303	**$45,427**

Inside Track: The projected rise in volume and complexity of insurance products will result in an additional 30,000 jobs for underwriters by 2000. The aging of the U.S. population will mean a growth in the number of people who have the greatest need for life and health insurance. New businesses will need coverage on an international basis. Underwriters begin as trainees, supervised by experienced risk appraisers. Good judgment is the secret to success in this field. Openings are in the so-called F.I.R.E.

industries—finance, insurance and real estate—which are projected to have good growth in the 1990s and beyond. Continuing education in tax law, health insurance changes and life and property insurance is necessary to make sound decisions about what risks your company should take and about your own career advancement. Earning an MBA while on the job, with the employer paying for it, is ideal. Experienced underwriters often are promoted into management jobs, where salaries are high. Hot areas in the coming decade: life, health and property liability insurance.

10

EDUCATION, GOVERNMENT AND SOCIAL SERVICES

Corrections Officer/Guard/Jailer
Educational Administrator
Firefighter
Librarian
Mathematician/Statistician
Police Officer
Psychologist/Counselor
Social Worker
Teacher/Professor

After a decade of cutbacks in federal, state and municipal services, the government will once again become an important employer, replacing workers who leave or retire and increasing job opportunities nationwide by 10 percent. There will be more job openings in government in the next 20 years than there now are qualified people to fill them. Jobs in the social services will grow, propelled by the aging of America. The high-tech, information society of 2000 means people will need more education to get jobs and move ahead, so teachers and professors will be in great demand. There already is a shortage of PhDs in the United States. Opportunities will abound for job seekers interested in this category, which is made up of the "caring" professions.

CORRECTIONS
OFFICER/GUARD/JAILER

Job Requirements: Must be 18 years old and have at least a high school diploma, but for jobs with a future must have associate or bachelor's degree in psychology, criminology or counseling. Federal, state and muncipal governments have individual recruitment standards and special training programs. Most states require certification. Usually a civil service job. Administrative and people skills extremely important to do job right. Must be computer literate. By 2000, security will be an automated, high-tech profession in apprehension, supervision and handling of inmates. Strong sense of public service and problem-solving skills important. High ethical standards and honesty are basic.

✦ **Salary:**

<u>1991</u>	<u>2000</u>
$17,000 to $20,000	**$21,000 to $35,000**

Inside Track: Jobs in this field are projected to grow by 32.2 percent in the 1990s. Corrections will add 76,000 officers; guards, 256,000. As the crime rate rises and public concern grows about crime, vandalism and terrorism, correctional facilities will expand and additional officers will be hired to supervise and counsel incarcerated inmates. Best jobs for guards are in private industry and contract security firms, protecting facilities and personnel. Corporate security jobs have higher salaries, more benefits, better job security and more opportunities for advancement. The field will gain higher status and be made more professional in this decade. A bachelor's degree is necessary to move ahead. Many professionals add courses or degrees in social work or the law. To open your own firm, you'll need business and management courses. Inside tip: The growing retail industry will need store detectives and other security personnel. Jobs in retail have a career path that can lead to management positions within a store.

EDUCATIONAL ADMINISTRATOR

Job Requirements: Must have teaching and administrative experience to run an educational institution as its principal, curriculum supervisor or administrative support person. Must be an accredited teacher with advanced degrees in education and administration. Must have classroom experience, good communications and business skills and ability to get along with people. A commitment to learning is basic. Creativity needed in developing innovative programs for quality education that will attract and instruct students. Computer literacy needed to create new programs and instructional videos and to access latest information on education.

◆ **Salary:**

1991	*2000*
$55,125[1]	**$70,000**

Inside Track: Some 62,000 more educational administrators will be needed in this decade as school enrollments increase. Nationwide emphasis will be focused on improving the quality of education to prepare students for the new workplace demands of the 21st century. Jobs will be across the board, in elementary, secondary and high schools; community, vocational and technical schools; colleges and universities. Growth areas will be in child care and job training centers and with corporations, either as private consultants or staff members. Education is a national priority, and salaries are expected to rise. "Administrators must have a good understanding of both pupils and teachers and be active in family and community issues," says Terry Astuto of the National Policy Board for Educational Administration. Astuto says administrators are "a graying profession and will have turnover at all levels." She warns that currently, qualifying for administrative jobs "is haphazard because there are no national standards for education, training or skills you should have." Her group is working to develop specific standards, a goal that is critical in view of the growth and importance of the profession.

FIREFIGHTER

Job Requirements: Must be 18 years old and a high school graduate. As skills required become more technical, college degree increasingly necessary. Must pass medical and physical tests of strength and score high on municipal tests. Usually a civil service job and unionized in many cities. Must have mechanical ability, be able to work as part of a team and live congenially with other firefighters when on duty. Must be mentally alert and fully aware that this is one of the most hazardous occupations. Automated equipment and recordkeeping require high-tech and computer skills.

✦ **Salary:**

1991	*2000*
$30,870	**$42,000**

Inside Track: An estimated 29,000 more firefighters will be needed by 2000 because of the expected increase in the number of homeowners and their need for fire protection. There will be intense competition and long waiting lists for jobs in urban areas, but smaller communities with growing populations and rural areas will be paying top dollar to attract full-time, qualified personnel. Get experience as a volunteer and supplement your training with community college courses in fire science. A bachelor's degree puts you on a faster career path. Advancement is based on ability, experience, examination and seniority. If you qualify and pass tests, you can progress up the ranks to lieutenant captain, battalion chief, assistant chief, deputy chief and, finally, chief. Continuing education in safety procedures, fire-fighting techniques and computer literacy to access information will position you for success in this vital community service profession. A lucrative aspect of the field is in becoming a consultant to private industry, including business, manufacturing and insurance institutions.

LIBRARIAN

Job Requirements: Master's degree in library science. Accreditation by American Library Association. Must be computer literate and able to communicate electronically with databases and other libraries in the United States and throughout the world. Doctorate needed for college teaching or job in large library system. State certification needed for public school libraries. Must have advanced degree, business experience and strong research skills for jobs with corporations and law firms. Constant upgrading of high-tech skills necessary.

◆ **Salary:**

1991	*2000*
$28,665 to $88,200	**$40,300 to $124,000**

Inside Track: Because of turnover and retirements, there will be an additional 14,000 jobs by 2000 for school and public librarians, but pay will be at the low end of the scale. Well-paying jobs are growing rapidly in libraries of corporations or law firms, where computer literate librarians will be needed to acquire, organize, store and communicate the latest information to managerial and professional people. Upward progress is slow in school and community libraries, but corporate librarians have a career path to management. Specialties in demand: banking, insurance, law and government. Library technicians with associate degrees will be a fast-growing technical occupation as support staff to accredited librarians. Librarian consultants who can transfer information on paper to laser discs and who can bring the world of information to individuals' desks through personal computers will be on the cutting edge of change and on their way to professional and financial success. "This [laser discs] is an effort to finally do what people have been talking about for so many years," says Mickie Voges, law librarian.[2]

MATHEMATICIAN/STATISTICIAN

Job Requirements: Degree in mathematics from four-year college for entry-level jobs, followed by graduate degree and constant updating of skills and information. Strong background needed in computer science. Must be good researcher, goal-oriented and willing to work long hours. Mathematicians must be skilled at collecting, analyzing and presenting numerical data. Statisticians must be able to design, carry out and interpret numerical results of surveys and experiments, creating computer studies and programs.

✦ **Salary:**

1991	*2000*
$29,900[3]	**$45,000**
(starting, bachelor's degree)	(starting, bachelor's degree)

Inside Track: Some 3,000 additional mathematicians and 3,300 more statisticians will be needed by 2000. The growing shortage of PhDs in applied math will make mathematicians with doctorates in demand at colleges, in research and in industry. Statisticians—mathematicians who create research tudies—will be needed to prepare projections for business and government agencies. Best opportunities in both fields are for those with strong backgrounds in computer skills. The American Mathematical Society says "knowing how to apply and develop various theories to work-related issues is an important skill in our technologically advanced society." Business statisticians need an additional skill: to be able to sell the value of their services to their colleagues. "Right now, statistics is a booming field to go into," says Barbara Bailar, executive director of the American Statistical Association. "Statisticians are actively involved in new applications in every field, designing clinical trials for new drugs and new products. They're being hired by industrial firms, especially automobile, food and chemical manufacturers. There's new emphasis on quality assurance, which is based on conclusions derived from statistical techniques."[4] Statistician Frank J. Rossi, who sells statistical software products to manufacturers, says, "Industry is the place for statisticians to go. Businesses are getting clobbered by all the data available. . . . Statisticians know how to use the new tools automation provides because we're the ones who invented them."

POLICE OFFICER

Job Requirements: Requirements vary by community and agency, but best background is a degree from a four-year college or university. Associate degree from community college acceptable. Courses in law enforcement, police science, criminal justice and public administration are important. Must know how to use computers to gather and communicate information and to keep records. To qualify for entry-level job, must be 21 and pass rigorous physical, intelligence and psychological tests. Intense on-the-job training. Dedication to serving the public, a humanitarian concern about people, community involvement and high ethical standards are essential. Job is usually under civil service.

◆ **Salary:**

1991	*2000*
$30,870	**$42,750**

Inside Track: Jobs for police officers, detectives and special agents will increase by 68,000 in the 1990s because of the need for greater protection. Crime, terrorism and drug use are expected to rise in this decade, making the police officer's job a more highly skilled position nationwide. Better-educated police will be more productive, more effective and better paid. There will be competition for higher-paying jobs in metropolitan police departments and at federal law enforcement agencies such as the Federal Bureau of Investigation and the Secret Service. Police officers on the fast track move up to detective. The expanding industry of private security firms that work on a contract basis for corporations will actively recruit police officers for management jobs. Police officers with experience and management skills will open their own private security or consulting firms, which is the way to make money in this field.

PSYCHOLOGIST/COUNSELOR

Job Requirements: Must have bachelor's degree followed by master's degree in psychology for entry-level jobs in administration or testing. Doctorate in psychology necessary for teaching, counseling and consulting. State certification or license needed for private practice. Must be emotionally stable, mature, caring and able to deal with people. Patience, perseverance and commitment to helping others essential. Experience in working with the elderly and understanding of people with diverse backgrounds, from all parts of the world, a plus. Background in research and computer literacy important.

◆ **Salary:**

1991	*2000*
$36,225 to $55,125	**$45,000 to $75,000**

Inside Track: The projected increase of 28,000 jobs for psychologists is based on the needs of aging Americans, continued public concern about mental health and the expected proliferation of testing and counseling of job seekers, workers and students. Jobs will be in hospitals, private practice, not-for-profit agencies and as consultants to industry. Corporations will hire staff psychologists to counsel and manage employee assistance programs dealing with substance abuse, wellness, family and marital problems, stress and addictive behavior. Psychologists with extensive training in quantitative research methods and computer science will have a competitive edge in the business world. Opportunities are best for those with doctorates in clinical and counseling psychology and in research; with master's degrees, in child psychology. Those with only an undergraduate degree have few career prospects. Though a drug-free workplace will be a popular theme in the 1990s and beyond, the major problem employees have involves their marriages, and psychologists skilled in dealing with family problems will do best in corporate America. "We have a federal drug czar but no czar of marital and family problems, which are much more prevalent," says Dr. Bruce E. Bennett, a psychologist. "Employees tend to bring domestic problems to the workplace with them. They don't leave them at home."[5] Job growth for psychologists and counselors will be fueled by inclusion of their professional services in health insurance policies.

SOCIAL WORKER

Job Requirements: Must have master's degree in social work for entry-level job. State licensing or registration required. Must want to help others, have empathy for clients and be resourceful. Maturity, emotional stability and confidence essential in this demanding profession.

Must have sense of satisfaction from work. Experience in working with the elderly, understanding of people with diverse backgrounds and ability to speak languages in addition to English are pluses. Must be computer literate to file reports and access information.

◆ **Salary:**

1991	*2000*
$32,793	**$45,000**

Inside Track: An additional 110,000 jobs for social workers will open up in this decade to serve the elderly, children, mentally impaired and developmentally disabled. This is one of the fastest-growing occupations, but the pay is low in contrast to its educational requirements. Jobs will be in government agencies, hospitals and private social agencies. Additional courses and advanced studies in social work lead to better-paying administrative and managerial jobs. Clinical social workers are opening their own consulting firms, as more and more states allow insurance companies to reimburse private social workers. Opportunities for social workers are expanding in drug counseling, protection services and counseling for sexually abused and battered children.

Social workers feel a great sense of satisfaction in their profession. "The appeal is in tangible human rewards you can't get in other jobs, especially if you want to make a difference in the world," says Lucy Sanchez of the National Association of Social Workers.[6] Though salaries will be better in 2000 than they were in the early 1990s, social workers do not become rich. "Earning money never entered my mind," says David J. Pate, a social worker who works with an agency that educates teenagers about the problems of early pregnancy. "I want to help others, and this is the way to do it."

TEACHER/PROFESSOR

Job Requirements: Must have bachelor's degree in teaching from four-year accredited college, student teaching experience and state certification to teach kindergarten through grade 12. Additional training necessary for renewal of state license. Must have PhD to teach at college level. Must know one's field and be able to communicate clearly with diverse student body. Must be well organized and highly motivated. Teachers must be involved in the community and be able to relate to both students and parents. Professors also must be able to do meaningful research. Computer literacy required to access data, do research, create teaching programs and transmit information in the classroom, within the institution and throughout the world.

◆ Salary:

1991	*2000*
$32,202 (teacher)[7]	**$46,733 (teacher)**
$43,720 (professor)[8]	**$71,211 (professor)**

Inside Track: A projected 208,000 more kindergarten and elementary school teachers and 224,000 more secondary school teachers will be needed by 2000, due to the emphasis on educational excellence, increased enrollment, smaller classes and the large number of teachers who will reach retirement age by the end of the decade. In addition to public and private schools, there will be good job openings in vocational schools, technical schools and community colleges. Teachers most sought after will be those who are free to relocate and who are bilingual in Spanish and English. Best employment opportunities will be for teachers who specialize in arithmetic, science, computer skills and special education. The path to administrative positions in schools lies in advanced degrees in educational administration and high visibility in the community. Job openings for college and university faculty will expand by 23,000, with the best opportunities for professors of business, engineering and science. PhDs with strong human relations skills who want to teach and do significant research will have their choice of jobs.

There will be a shortage of 7,500 natural scientists and engineers with doctorates by 2000; shortages in the humanities and social sciences are occurring now; and the dearth of accountants with doctorates is so severe that some universities are offering new PhD graduates $70,000 a year and full professors, $100,000. "There now are three jobs for every new graduate in management," says Dr. Robert A. Ulbrick, dean of the Graduate School of Management at Clark University.[9] And Allen R. Sanderson, associate professor at the University of Chicago, says: "Everyone is going after the same talent pool of PhDs; the job market is tightening, and salaries are being bid up significantly."

11

ENGINEERING AND COMPUTER TECHNOLOGY

Computer Operator
Computer Programmer
Computer Service Technician
Computer Systems Analyst
Database Manager
Drafter
Engineer
Information Systems Manager
Manufacturing Specialist (CAD/CAM and CAI)
Operations/Systems Research Analyst
Peripheral Electronic Data Processing
    Equipment Operator

Computer-related technical jobs are the fastest-growing occupations in the economy and are projected to grow by more than 70 percent by the year 2000. Because of the emergence of a high-tech society and the increasing automation of almost every occupation, the engineer will be the number one professional in demand in this decade. Some 351,000 new engineers will be needed; of that number, 192,000 jobs will open up for electrical and electronics engineers. It's estimated that one job is created in engineering and computer technology for every $100,000 spent on research by the federal government. The demand for technicians and support workers will also grow rapidly in data processing and systems, hardware and software analysis. This category of jobs is on the cutting edge of change, and workers in it will help determine how successful the United States will be in a highly competitive, technological international workplace.

COMPUTER OPERATOR

Job Requirements: High school diploma; business school training or associate degree in data processing from community college or technical school acceptable. On-the-job training provided by employer. Bachelor's degree preferred by largest firms and necessary for advancement. Must be able to oversee the operation of expensive computer hardware systems, especially large mainframe systems. Able to anticipate problems and make needed changes and adjustments. Hands-on experience on equipment and related operating systems needed. Ability to work from operating instructions prepared by programmers or operations managers, set controls, monitor computer consoles and respond to user complaints. Must be able to work independently without supervisor, be adaptable to constant equipment and program changes, willing to learn and have good communications skills.

◆ Salary:

1991	*2000*
$20,466 to $27,707[1]	**$33,000 to $42,000**

Inside Track: Estimates are that 92,000 additional computer operators will be needed by 2000 due to the increased use of computers throughout the economy to store important information. Previous work experience is the key to landing an operator job in large establishments; in smaller organizations, you may be able to start at entry level. Continuous formal education in analytical and technical subjects is needed to move up to higher-level responsibilities in computer and information networks. Because you work closely with programmers and systems analysts, you will be the first to know when those jobs are open. You will be able to move from employer to employer to position yourself for the best career advancement, including management jobs.

COMPUTER PROGRAMMER

Job Requirements: Many programmers are high school, vocational school, community college or college graduates who have taken computer courses, but increasing demand is for bachelor's degree in computer programming, data processing, science, engineering or physical science. Graduate degree needed for advanced applications. Business courses in accounting and inventory control helpful. Certification in computer programming from Institute for Certification of Computer Professionals often required. Must have experience in writing detailed instructional or software programs that access information in a logical way computer must follow. Strong technical and communication skills necessary. Ability to think logically and do exacting analytical work. Patience, persistence and ability to work with extreme accuracy under pressure. Ingenuity and imagination required. Diligence and determination needed to devise and apply programs to business, government and educational uses. Must be able to write users' manuals for software packages.

◆ **Salary:**

_1991_	_2000_
$31,900[2]	**$52,632**

Inside Track: An estimated 250,000 additional computer programmers will be needed by 2000. To move up to systems programmer or management, you must have a bachelor's degree in computer science and training in accounting, management, engineering or science. Training in computer science is one of the strongest job credentials in this technological age. You will need to know programming languages, such as COBOL for business applications, FORTRAN for science and one of the more advanced artificial intelligence languages. A good way to enter the field is to combine work experience with formal training while in school: Get a summer or part-time job in data processing; apply for an internship; participate in a college work-study program. Once you get a job, keep up with rapidly changing technology by continuing your technical training. Take courses offered by your employer or software vendors.

Job openings are everywhere, but the best chances for advancement will be in the Northeast and West, where high-tech firms proliferate and will rebound after the economic slowdown of the early 1990s. The U.S. Department of Labor says utilities companies will pay the highest salaries in the coming decade. The cutting edge of change for programmers is creating material for "smart" machines. Artificial intelligence programming requires a doctorate and promises the highest salary. Neural network programming is modeled after the nervous system of life forms. It can be learned by experience and is a futuristic business opportunity for these professionals.[3]

COMPUTER SERVICE TECHNICIAN

Job Requirements: Also called field engineers, customer service engineers or service technicians. Need one to two years' training past high school in electronics or electrical disciplines to keep increasingly sophisticated machines working. Courses in physics, computer theory, computer math and circuitry theory needed. Degree from vocational, technical or community college important. Ability to work closely with electricians, test equipment and do preventive maintenance. Strong diagnostic skills and mechanical ability. Firms often hire high school or college graduates and then train them to maintain their computers and peripheral office equipment. If working for private repair firm or representing manufacturing, public relations skills needed to represent employer to clients and to promote customer satisfaction and good will. Maturity needed to go from one work site to another on a daily basis to make repairs—and to fit in at each place.

♦ **Salary:**

1991	*2000*
$34,177	**$52,000**

Inside Track: An additional 44,000 repairers—a 35 percent increase—will be needed as more computers and office machines are used in homes and offices. The Bureau of Labor Statistics names the computer service technician as one of the 20 fastest-growing occupations in the 1990s. Three-fourths of all technicians work for equipment manufacturers, retail establishments and firms with enough equipment and funding to have an in-house repair staff. Repairers who can service several models and brands of equipment or who know how to take care of the most complex equipment will be in greatest demand. Knowing the basic equipment and what makes it tick often leads to high-paying jobs in sales and management. Take courses to keep up with changing technology. The most successful technicians take business courses and often open their own repair shops, become independent dealers or buy a sales franchise.

COMPUTER SYSTEMS ANALYST

Job Requirements: College degree in four-year computer science information systems, business or related majors such as engineering, mathematics or science. Must have previous experience as computer programmer to plan and develop new computer systems or devise ways to apply existing ones more efficiently. Familiarity with programming languages and broad knowledge of computer systems. Master's degree usually required; a doctorate is even better. Titles of certified data processor and certified systems professional from Institute for Certification of Computer Professionals are important credentials, indicating five years' experience and specialty training. Ability to work as a team with managers and other professionals to harness computer's potential and to communicate with technical and nontechnical personnel. Must have patience and perseverance.

◆ **Salary:**

1991	*2000*
$31,200 to $42,997[4]	**$48,000 to $67,000**

Inside Track: Reduced enrollment in computer science courses at colleges and universities will lead to a major shortfall in computer systems analysts in this decade. Some 214,000 will be needed as computer capabilities and applications increase. Job prospects will be best for college graduates who combine courses in programming and systems analysis with training and experience in applied fields. In this high-tech age, professionals who can plan and develop computers to help businesses, industries and educational institutions get work done faster and more efficiently will be in great demand.

In the 1990s, systems analysts will be needed to upgrade expensive computer systems already in use. This is a field that has low turnover, so pick your place of employment carefully, making sure you have a chance to get additional training and to move into management and administration. A lucrative field for systems analysts is working as independent consultants to the many companies that cannot afford in-house analysts. Hottest area is networking, which allows users of microcomputers (PCs) to enter and retrieve data from one mainframe computer and to "talk" to one another. Systems analysts who are current in their profession and show leadership skills can be on track for high-paying jobs of manager of information systems and chief information officer.

DATABASE MANAGER

Job Requirements: Bachelor's degree in four-year computer science information systems needed. Job entails making sure the company's data is accurate, safely stored and available as needed. Large corporations prefer master's degree in management or computer science. Must be security conscious and know database languages such as COBOL for business applications; FORTRAN for science and one of the more advanced artificial intelligence languages. Must have at least two to five years' experience to qualify for position that is central to the daily operation of business, government and educational institutions. Must be reliable, methodical, able to work with other managers and to schedule a 24-hour staff. Ability to inspire confidence and trust among colleagues and withstand stress.

◆ **Salary:**

1991	*2000*
$38,587[5]	**$50,000**

Inside Track: Database managers hold in their hands the success or failure of newspapers, insurance companies, hospitals, government agencies and other businesses and academic institutions. If a computer system "crashes," data is lost and time is wasted. It's the responsibility of the database manager to make sure the system isn't overloaded and workers are able to do their jobs without delays or problems. Professionals in this job are watched carefully for possibility of advancement to higher managerial levels. "You get ahead by constantly upgrading your skills and keeping up with computer technology," says Karin Kushino, director of career counseling and placement at DeVry Institute of Technology. As more and more manufacturing plants are automated, job opportunities will grow for database managers. Other good job areas for the 1990s and beyond: financial data processing, insurance, utilities and government agencies. "This is a growing profession," says Kushino.

DRAFTER

Job Requirements: High school diploma plus two-year associate degree in drafting from technical institute, junior and community college or extension division of university. Background in mathematics, physical sciences, mechanical drawing and drafting. Knowledge of computer-aided systems to prepare detailed drawings showing exact dimensions and all parts of buildings, products and equipment necessary, but still must be able to work by hand and be adept with compasses, dividers, protractors, triangles and other drafting devices. Must be able to specify exact dimensions and materials to be used. Skilled in drawing freehand three-dimensional objects. Artistic ability a plus. Able to work with engineers, surveyors, engineers and architects on team projects.

◆ **Salary:**

_1991_	_2000_
$16,537 to $40,000[6]	**$20,000 to $60,000**

Inside Track: The expected large increase in the demand for drafting services is projected to add 39,000 more jobs. A good career track is to start out as a generalist and then to pick a specialty such as architectural, aeronautical, electrical, electronic, civil or mechanical drafting. By 2000, it's expected that most drafters will do their work by computer, but the systems are expensive and some firms will still need drafters with hands-on abilities. Best jobs are with engineering and architectural firms. Entry-level drafters work under close supervision. With experience, you may advance to senior drafter or supervisor. Good training and a bachelor's degree lead to higher-paying jobs. Some drafters go back to school to become architects or engineers, which are more prestigious and better-paying professions. "Experience in large professional firms is best because they have the most advanced equipment," says John T. Dygden, professor of engineering graphics at Illinois Institute of Technology. "When you use a computer, it looks as if all you have to do is push buttons, but you still have to understand the principles."

ENGINEER

Job Requirements: Bachelor's degree in engineering from four- or five-year accredited engineering program. Degree in science and mathematics sometimes acceptable. Generalist training important to move into specialties such as chemical, electrical, electronic, mechanical and civil engineering. Undergraduate preparation in practical design and production work to apply principles of science and mathematics to economic solution of technical problems. Master's and doctorate needed for theoretical mathematical and scientific projects such as artificial intelligence and particle accelerators. State licensing required in some areas of engineering: Consulting engineer in independent practice must be licensed. Good mechanical ability, reasoning powers, creativity, attention to detail, ability to work with a team and good communications skills are necessities. Able to use computer-aided design systems to produce and analyze designs for everything from constructing new highways to probing outer space. Must be available for international assignments.

◆ **Salary:**

_1991_	_2000_
$34,300[7]	**$68,000**
(bachelor's degree)	(bachelor's degree)

Inside Track: Engineers are on the cutting edge of change in a high-tech society and will be the most valued professionals of the 21st century. Though cutbacks in the defense industry in the early 1990s temporarily affected jobs for engineers, the chronic shortage of these professionals will lead to the creation of 351,000 new jobs by 2000; of that number, 192,000 jobs will be for electrical and electronic engineers skilled in data processing and system, hardware and software analysis. Consumer electronics is one of the fastest-growing fields. Much of the growth in the profession will come from the building of new industrial plants to meet global demand for more goods and services and to increase productivity. Other industries in need of engineers: aerospace, chemical, civil, industrial, metallurgic/ceramic and petroleum. Robotics or artificial intelligence is the "hot" area because the shortage of skilled workers will accelerate the need to create machines to do the work once performed by humans. Ceramic engineers of the future will work with charged particles to build ceramic diesel engines; electronic engineers literally will make worldwide connections; chemical engineers will work at pharmaceutical companies designing biotechnological products.

"The first thing to do is to get that master's degree," says Richard Saeks, dean of the College of Engineering at Illinois Institute of Technology. "Many engineers with bachelor's degrees get jobs and earn their master's degree part-time while working. After five to eight years at a large company, engineers move up to management." It is essential to continue your technical education because this is such a rapidly changing profession. Engineers will be in so much demand that private engineering consulting firms will boom.

INFORMATION SYSTEMS MANAGER

Job Requirements: A high-ranking, top-level job. Experience as computer systems analyst essential. Bachelor's degree in engineering, finance or mathematics.

Master's degree required in most cases, preferably an MBA. Must have experience running computer systems and managing teams of people in order to keep corporation's expensive and intricate information systems running smoothly. Advanced skills in networking—wiring diverse computer stations for workers to share information in a variety of locations. Need to understand computer networks, satellites, databases, workstations, factory automation, supercomputing and peripheral equipment including telephones, electronic mail, fax machines and copiers. Must be able to make instant strategic decisions about voice and data systems and, at the same time, plan for the future. Ability to work with corporate strategy and planning executives. Able to handle constant pressure to utilize new technology for competitive ends, upgrade software and develop new systems. Business management skills and ability to work as team member are important. Must be mobile for international assignments.

◆ **Salary:**

1991	*2000*
$146,081	**$225,250**

Inside Track: As the average salary indicates, this is a job of enormous importance with many responsibilities. The challenge is to create ways to link the company's many computers and other high-tech devices through networking, the accessing and sending of information to mainframes and to personal computers. You will have to stay abreast of the latest technologies and variables for your particular business's networking needs. Professionals who are up to date in microelectronics, fiber optics and digital technology are prime candidates for this job. Demand will be greatest in financial services industries.

"Companies are looking for people who are business executives first and technologists second," says Herbert Z. Halbrecht, president of an executive search firm that specializes in information managers. "Those with ability to manage people and who have an interest in strategic planning will move ahead quickly."

Though most present information systems managers work for Fortune 500 companies, the lack of in-house computer professionals in the next century will be a serious constraint to business success and productivity of small and medium-sized corporations that want to compete in a global, high-tech marketplace. "The rapid obsolescence of computer technology, combined with the accelerating convergence of computer and telecommunications technologies, has also aggravated shortages of qualified technical managers," says Robert Atkins, a Department of Commerce analyst.[8]

MANUFACTURING SPECIALIST (CAD/CAM AND CAI)

Job Requirements: Minimum of bachelor's degree in electrical and mechanical engineering with specialized courses in using the computer to create designs (CAD), to plan and produce the product (CAM) and to give objects three-dimensional form (CAI). Business experience important to plan and design manufacturers' production systems and new products for everything from industrial design to fashion. Good sense of spatial relations needed and ability to make scientific measurements. Must be familiar with variety of software systems for manufacturing designs such as AutoCAD, CADAM, CADDS, Scicards, Prep 7 and Unigraphics. Technician assistants with high school diploma and courses in basic computer and drafting skills also needed. Must be team player.

♦ **Salary:**

1991	*2000*
$34,177[9]	**$45,000**

Inside Track: These technical specialists will be in great demand in manufacturing plants whose owners want to increase productivity in the face of global competition. If you combine creativity with routine hard work, you will quickly become an invaluable staff member on a career track to sales and management. "The best thing to do is to get experience working in a big corporation," says Daniel Waldstein, director of career development programs, Illinois Institute of Technology. "Manufacturing design specialists are on the cutting edge of technological change." Waldstein says advanced degrees are necessary to do senior research or to go into management. Selling the software needed for CAD/CAM and CAI systems is also a growing field, one to be considered after you have professional on-the-job experience. Being a private consultant to manufacturers is the most lucrative end of the business. "Entrepreneurship should be considered down the road," says Waldstein, "but you'll need marketing expertise to open your own business."

OPERATIONS/SYSTEMS RESEARCH ANALYST

Job Requirements: Employers look for college graduates who have strong backgrounds in quantitative methods and computer programming. Graduate degree preferred in operations research, management science, mathematics, statistics, business administration or computer science. Must be computer literate. Intensive on-the-job training to learn how individual employer prefers solving problems related to business strategy, forecasting, resource allocation, facilities layout, inventory control, personnel schedules and distribution systems. Must be able to work closely with managers and adapt work to corporate requirements. Must be able to collect information from those directly facing a procedural problem, define the problem, break it into component parts, collect information and then select analytical technique to solve it. Must be a problem solver and troubleshooter and have background in quality control, inventory, personnel, business forecasting, products and distribution. Ability to explain complicated problems and solutions in simple terms and to communicate well in writing and verbally.

◆ **Salary:**

1991	*2000*
$40,633	**$62,500**

Inside Track: To remain competitive in a global marketplace, business and industry will need an additional 30,000 operations research analysts by 2000 to help make smart business decisions. That's a 55 percent increase in job opportunities. To move ahead, take training programs, keep up with new developments in operations research techniques and stay abreast of advances in computer science. Skills you will acquire and overall knowledge of the business you will learn will position you for important management slots. The job is a fast track to leadership positions, especially if you are successful in coming up with methods of doing business that are more productive and save money. Demand will be strong in the retail industry to research store locations and layouts; in motels, to determine size and location of new chains; in manufacturing, which for the first time is beginning to use mathematical models, to distribute finished products and to position sales offices. This is an important mid-level job in the 1990s and beyond.

PERIPHERAL ELECTRONIC DATA PROCESSING EQUIPMENT OPERATOR

Job Requirements: To operate related computer devices such as printers, disc drives, tape readers and fax and duplicating machines, must have previous work experience and a bachelor's degree in computer science or data processing. Intensive on-the-job training in large firms, where most jobs are available. Must understand computer hardware systems and anticipate problems before they happen. Able to keep peripheral equipment running by loading it with tapes, discs and paper as needed, set and monitor controls and locate and solve problems. Prepare printouts and other material for distribution to computer users and maintain daily records of machine problems. Help analyze, test and debug new programs. Ability to work efficiently with programmers and other colleagues. Must be able to deal with workers frustrated by nonworking equipment.

◆ **Salary:**

_1991_	_2000_
$22,050	**$30,000**

Inside Track: As more organizations use less expensive midsize computers rather than mainframes, a growing number of peripheral equipment operators will be needed to oversee smaller high-tech machines. This is an entry-level job that gets you in on the ground floor of high-technology systems and can lead to the next step up, a job as systems analyst. It can put you on track for well-paying jobs in information management and networking. Jobs for these technicians will be in wholesale trade, manufacturing, data processing, banks, government, accounting, auditing and bookkeeping. Sharon Katterman, director of job placement for Moraine Valley Community College, advises peripheral equipment operators who want to move ahead to keep up to date and continue your education in the field. "More experience and more training will give you more salary," she says.

12

HEALTH CARE PROFESSIONS

Dental Hygienist
Dentist
Dietitian
Health Services Administrator
Home Health Aide
Licensed Practical Nurse
Medical Records Administrator
Occupational Therapist
Ophthalmic Laboratory Technician
Optician
Paramedic
Pharmacist
Physical Therapist
Physician
Physician Assistant
Podiatrist
Radiologic Technologist
Registered Nurse
Speech Pathologist/Audiologist
Veterinarian

Health care includes more of the best-paying and fastest-growing jobs for the 1990s than any other occupational category. The number of health care workers grew by 50 percent in the 1980s, according to the U.S. Department of Labor, and the insatiable demand for health care professionals is expected to continue unabated. Health services will add a staggering 3.2 million jobs for an estimated total of 12 million by the 21st century. The increase will be driven by the aging of America, new technology that keeps people alive longer, the AIDS epidemic and the growing public awareness of the importance of health care. Among the ten fastest-growing of all occupations in the United States, six are in health care: licensed practical nurse, occupational therapist, physical therapist, physician assistant, radiologic technologist and registered nurse. This category of jobs needs technically trained, caring people willing to work long, hard hours and is wide open for advancement.

DENTAL HYGIENIST

Job Requirements: To provide preventive dental care such as scaling and cleaning teeth and to encourage patients in private dentist offices to have good oral hygiene habits, must have degree from accredited dental hygiene program, usually two to three years leading to associate degree. Usually need at least one year of college for admission to program. State licensing includes written and clinical exams. National board certification given by the American Dental Association Joint Commission on National Dental Examinations. Background in biology, health, chemistry, psychology, speech and math. Bachelor's degree a plus. Must enjoy working with patients, able to take direct supervision by dentist and able to put patients at ease. Manual dexterity important. Current in fast-changing dental technology.

◆ **Salary:**

1991	*2000*
$27,397	**$39,800**

Inside Track: There will be a need for 16,000 additional dental hygienists by 2000 because of the population growth, the aging of America, public awareness of the importance of oral hygiene, rising real income and proliferation of dental insurance. New technology allows the hygienist to free up the dentist to service more patients. Expanding trend of group practice and dental offices in large retail stores also will increase job opportunities. The U.S. Department of Labor predicts that "qualified hygienists will be in strong demand and should have little trouble finding or keeping jobs." Dental hygienists who want to be autonomous should first get experience, take business courses and then set up their own private practices under the supervision of a dentist. If you want to teach in public schools or private clinics or do research in your profession, you will need a master's degree in science. Two attractions of the profession are its flexible hours and fairly good pay. "To get ahead, you have to enjoy working with individuals and groups and keeping people well—and really want to be in the field," says Sammie Sumlin of the American Dental Hygienists Association.

DENTIST

Job Requirements: Bachelor's degree with broad background in humanities, especially psychology and communications, and in science, especially biology, chemistry, health and mathematics. Followed by degree from four- or five-year accredited dental school. Must have state license and pass written and practical exam given by the National Board of Dental Examiners to become doctor of dental surgery (DDS) or doctor of dental medicine (DDM). Experience in dental clinics. Need manual skills, diagnostic ability, good sense of spatial relations, good visual memory. Administrative skills needed to schedule patients and keep records. Up to date on latest dental technology. Good doctor-patient communications.

✦ Salary:

_1991_	_2000_
$79,065	**$125,000**[1]

Inside Track: After an oversupply of dentists in the 1980s and the consequent decline of enrollment in dental schools, there will be a need for 22,000 more professionals by 2000. Nine out of ten dentists will be in private practice, so business skills—especially aggressive marketing techniques—are as important as technical ones. Aging Americans will need more dental care; so will a growing population in general. A good route is to start out working for an established dentist, then to share space with other dentists until you have enough money, to take business courses and then to establish your own practice—the last estimated to cost $100,000.

The practice of dentistry is becoming more specialized because general practices are diminishing: Cleaning teeth and filling cavities are no longer time-consuming, arduous tasks because of high-tech equipment and mild anesthetics, and because fluoridation of water has improved the dental health of Americans. The best opportunities for specialists, who will need additional training and licensing, will be for orthodontists, who straighten teeth; oral and maxillofacial surgeons, who operate on the mouth and jaws; periodontists, who treat gums; prosthodontists, artificial teeth, and endodontists, root canal work. Be aware of the dangers of catching patients' diseases, from colds to AIDS, and take the necessary precautions.

Despite high-tech changes in delivery of dental care, some old-fashioned basic attributes will still matter. "Motivation and devotion to patients are the key factors in success," says long-time dentist Bertram Weisenberg.

DIETITIAN

Job Requirements: Bachelor's degree with major in foods, nutrition, institutional management or home economics needed to help people develop healthy eating habits. Must have approved work experience, serve an internship and be registered by Commission on Dietetic Registration of The American Dietetic Association. To counsel individuals, food manufacturers and corporations on nutritional needs, need managerial, organizational and administrative training; courses in chemistry, microbiology, physiology, mathematics, statistics, sociology and economics. Computer literacy essential to set up databases with information and to plan and record specific diets. Good communications and collaborative skills important.

◆ **Salary:**

1991	*2000*
$27,562 to $71,662	**$40,000 to $80,000**

Inside Track: Employment is expected to increase by 11,000 jobs to meet the growing demand by Americans for healthy foods and fat-free diets. Dietitians' credentials are carefully defined, but anyone can be a "nutritionist." The best opportunities for qualified dietitians will be in hospitals, clinics, physician groups, nursing homes, hotels, restaurants, health clubs, food manufacturing companies and social service programs. Some dietitians are specialists in diabetes, cancer, heart problems and pediatric or geriatric nutrition. Most work with patients in hospitals or other medical settings, but earning a master's degree will position you for two growing fields:

1. Management dietitians do large-scale meal planning for catering firms, restaurant chains and health clubs and for major institutions such as schools, colleges, prisons and company cafeterias.
2. Research dietitians work for educational or community health organizations and usually are part of a team of scientists, physicians, nurses and biomedical engineers studying a particular food subject.

Experienced dietitians with advanced training or degrees can move into administration and management.

Nutritional diets are now a way of life, and individual weight reduction food plans are an expanding area of opportunity for dietitians as meal planners and consultants. In the 1990s, dietitians who make the most money will be sales representatives for equipment or food manufacturers and for weight loss plans. Keep your computer skills up to date and be informed on the latest research on cholesterol, effects of drugs on the body and behavior modification. Kay Manger-Hague of The American Dietetic Association says there will be good opportunities for private consultants with master's degrees or doctorates in nutrition. "You will have to be entrepreneurial, promote and market yourself aggressively and develop your own business plan," she says.

HEALTH SERVICES ADMINISTRATOR

Job Requirements: Master's degree in health administration followed by one- to two-year internship to plan, organize, coordinate and supervise the way health care is delivered. Must be knowledgeable in hospital administration, public and business administration and personnel. Need strong financial and organizational management skills and hands-on experience in running a specific department. Must be computer literate and able to create your own computer programs. Ability to oversee entire facility or day-to-day management of specific services such as surgical care, geriatrics, rehabilitation or long-range planning. Jobs also include community outreach, planning, policy making, negotiating with employees and dealing with government agencies. Graduate degree in health services administration, nursing or business an asset. Clinical experience as nurse or therapist also helpful. Must be a self-starter, good public speaker and have strong leadership and interpersonal skills.

◆ **Salary:**

1991	*2000*
$38,587 to $66,150[2]	**$71,250**

Inside Track: Some 75,000 more jobs will open up by the end of the century because of the continuing growth of the health care industry. Employment in hospitals, offices of physicians and other medical practitioners, outpatient facilities, health maintenance organizations and long-term care facilities will grow the fastest. Best opportunities will be in major medical centers and ambulatory surgery, alcohol and drug abuse, rehabilitation, hospices, nursing homes and home health care. There will be few jobs in rural communities. Administrators on a fast track with a bachelor's degree will begin as assistants in large hospitals or department heads in small hospitals or nursing homes. It's not easy to transfer from one type of institution to another because employers want experience in their area—so make sure the place you choose to work is in the aspect of the industry in which you want to be. With master's degrees, administrators are positioned to handle millions of dollars in facilities and equipment and hundreds of employees. The best route to take is to gain experience in a large hospital to find out where your skills can be used. Then become a specialist in that area rather than a generalist. By 2000, the medical facilities with the best administrators will be the ones that are still in business.

HOME HEALTH AIDE

Job Requirements: The minimum requirement to help elderly, disabled and ill people live in their own homes rather than institutions is to be able to read and write. But as hospital costs rise and more patients are sent home to recover, health and homemaking assistance will become more professionalized. For a patient to qualify for Medicare reimbursement, the aide must have a high school diploma and training in a certified program at an adult education institution or community college. Most institutions and private agencies give in-house training. Must be mature, stable individual, ready to step into new situations. Care is given in people's homes, away from medical centers and direct supervision, so must be competent and self-sufficient. Must be strong and in good health, dependable and good observer of patient's progress. Low stress level to avoid burnout.

◆ **Salary:**

1991	*2000*
$15,435	**$20,000**

Inside Track: The number of "frail elderly," women and men in their 80s, is expected to rise dramatically in the 1990s and will fuel the addition of 207,000—63 percent—more home health aides. The trend to care for the chronically ill at home and new technology to facilitate home health care will spur the fast growth of this profession. Most aides work for public or private agencies such as home health agencies, visiting nurse associations, hospitals, public health and welfare departments and temporary help firms. This is an entry-level job into the booming health care services industry, and you can work part-time or full-time. Aides with previous experience or training as health or nursing aides will be in most demand. Next step up is to become a licensed practical nurse, and many employers will pay for your additional education.

Salaries of U.S. home health care workers are low; few receive benefits. But some employees are forming their own agencies. Annette K. Dance, who works for Cooperative Home Care Associates in the South Bronx, cares for an elderly woman with a pacemaker and diabetes. Dance is clinically trained and certified and licensed by the state of New York. She also has a good salary, benefits, a profit-sharing plan—and is one of 90 worker-owners of the company. "Would you believe I have power to say if the president of the company stays on?" asks Dance, who previously worked as a nurse's aide. "I'm also excited about this company because it offers training, education and a chance for advancement."[3]

LICENSED PRACTICAL NURSE

Job Requirements: High school diploma preferred to be accepted for training to care for the sick under direction of physicians and registered nurses. Must be licensed by state following 1 to 1½ years' training in state-approved practical nursing program and pass the national written exam. Supervised clinical experience. Computer literacy to keep records. Need background in nursing, pharmacology, computation and technical skills. Must be adaptable, energetic, able to get along with people and communicate well. Must take and execute orders to give basic bedside care and evaluate patients' needs. In offices of doctors, health maintenance organizations and clinics, will need clerical and recordkeeping skills. Deep regard for people and emotional stability important in stressful job.

◆ **Salary:**

1991	*2000*
$23,152	**$42,000**

Inside Track: In response to the health care needs of a growing and aging population and the shortage of registered nurses (RNs), 229,000 additional licensed practical nurses (LPNs) will be needed by 2000. Hospitals and nursing homes will offer the most job opportunities. Employment will grow rapidly in physicians' offices, walk-in clinics and health maintenance organizations. There will be job growth in home health care, but pay is low. This is a good entry-level job into the health care field and one that should lead to becoming an RN, which pays much better. Most hospitals will pay tuition and arrange hours for you to attend school. LPNs who want to become RNs will be encouraged to do so in the 1990s. As educational and training requirements are upgraded for LPNs, it will be easier to advance on the career ladder.

MEDICAL RECORDS ADMINISTRATOR

Job Requirements: Two-year associate degree or bachelor's degree in medical records administration from accredited program to set up permanent files for every patient doctors and hospitals treat. Voluntary accreditation for graduates as accredited record technician by passing written exam given by American Medical Records Association. Medical records are the database for hospital decisions and provide background and documentation for insurance reimbursement and legal and personnel matters, so skilled understanding of recordkeeping function and how it fits in with medical, hospital, state and legal requirements is basic. Must be knowledgeable in "diagnostic related groups" (DRGs) to determine Medicare reimbursements. Must be able to pull everything together, refine information and make it accessible. Must be up to date in financial information and computer technology. Able to use computer recordkeeping and billing programs and tabulate statistics. Accuracy in coding and abstracting data.

✦ **Salary:**

1991	*2000*
$43,549	**$64,000**

Inside Track: If health institutions want to get paid or defend themselves in litigation, they must have good records. The need for skilled financial management and quality control will produce 28,000 additional jobs for medical records administrators by 2000. The key is to be a graduate of an approved program. Records administrators increasingly will have to document the quality of medical care in view of the surge of medical malpractice suits. Continuing training in computer use is necessary to move ahead because the work is expected to be paperless by the end of the century. Most jobs are at hospitals, but opportunities also will be good at nursing homes, home health agencies, health maintenance organizations and large medical groups. You can advance by specializing, managing or teaching. Teaching will require a master's degree in education or health administration. The focus on people who do this job and its importance to the survival of the institution will in itself position you for advancement into management. Keeping up with advanced information systems and recordkeeping techniques will put you on a fast track.

OCCUPATIONAL THERAPIST

Job Requirements: Graduate of accredited program with bachelor's degree in occupational therapy. Must be licensed by state to help disabled people develop, recover or maintain daily lives and work skills. National certification as registered occupational therapist awarded by American Occupational Therapy Certification Board. Background in biology, anatomy, psychology, health, physiology, art and social sciences. Computer programming skills necessary to help patient regain manual dexterity and thought processes on computer. Ability to work independently and good people skills needed to help patients relearn skills. Essential to be creative in planning therapies and activities, able to motivate patients and to use games, crafts and other therapeutic tools. Must be strong physically and emotionally for demanding job. Skilled in making patients feel confident and good about themselves.

◆ **Salary:**

1991	*2000*
$29,767	**$51,000**

Inside Track: Some 16,000 jobs will open up for occupational therapists by 2000 because of the aging of the population. The anticipated growth in rehabilitation services is a reflection of the increase of middle-aged Americans, who statistically are more vulnerable to heart disease and strokes. Most jobs will be in hospitals that are adding rehabilitation centers, and in hospital subsidiaries such as home health care, rehabilitation programs and outpatient clinics. Schools will be the second largest employer. As direct insurance reimbursement is allowed by states, occupational therapists will open independent practices to provide follow-up services to long-term patients recently released from hospitals. To have a private practice, you must have business skills and be part of a network of physicians and other referral parties. Jobs for occupational therapists will grow as consultants to businesses with disabled workers and in university research labs. An area with great future potential in opportunity and salary is consulting with rehabilitation professionals and design engineers on computer-aided equipment, such as microprocessing devices that permit paralyzed patients to communicate, operate equipment or wheelchairs, and to eat, walk and dress. Home health care will also expand for occupational therapists.

The profession is demanding, but one in which you can see the results of your work. "It was exciting to discover a career where I can work with people of all ages and where my contributions are so greatly needed," says Barbara Georges, certified occupational therapist who works in the home care program of St. Joseph's Hospital in Kirkwood, Missouri.[4]

OPHTHALMIC LABORATORY TECHNICIAN

Job Requirements: High school diploma necessary for these technicians, who are also known as manufacturing opticians, optical mechanics or optical goods workers. To make prescription eyeglasses, grind and polish glass and plastic, need courses in science and mathematics. Skills such as lens grinding, cutting, edging, beveling and assembly generally are learned on the job in training sessions of from six to eight months. Certificate from six-month or one-year vocational program desirable. Manual dexterity and skills in precision work are essential. High-tech machines constantly changing the way work is done, so must be up to date in use of latest equipment. Able to follow prescription specifications accurately.

◆ **Salary:**

1991	*2000*
$12,763 to $19,143	**$16,785 to $26,000**

Inside Track: Job opportunities for these technicians will grow by 7,300 because of the projected growth of marketing of glasses as a fashion item. Another factor is the aging of America with the consequent increased demand for corrective lenses. About half the jobs will be in retail optical stores and chains that manufacture prescription glasses and sell them directly to the public. Jobs also will expand in optical laboratories. Salaries are low in this entry-level job, but so are educational and training requirements. Jobs will be plentiful, so you can use yours to position yourself to become—with a college degree and additional credentials in optical technology, business, management and marketing—a dispensing optician, supervisor or manager. Technicians in retail stores and labs can move up to better-paying administrative jobs. You can learn how the business is run while you are there, on the inside. With hard work and carefully honed skills, you may eventually be able to open your own store. Stores that will be expanding most rapidly are those that make prescription glasses on the premises and give fast and convenient service.

OPTICIAN

Job Requirements: Most firms prefer high school graduates with courses in science, math and physics to train in filling prescriptions and helping customers select eyeglasses and contact lenses. Best chances for those with associate degree in opticianry from community college. Knowledge of algebra, geometry and mechanical drawing desirable. Substantial on-the-job training, often from two to four years. Licensing required by 22 states following apprenticeship of from two to five years. Certification from American Board of Opticianry and National Contact Lens Examiners. Continuing education to maintain certification. Background as ophthalmic laboratory technician helpful. Must have strong marketing and people skills. Fashion sense to help customer select corrective frames. Good sense of spatial relations and careful work habits important. Computer and high-tech skills important to use rapidly changing measurement devices.

◆ **Salary:**

1991	*2000*
$28,665	**$40,000**

Inside Track: Employment for opticians is projected to increase much faster than the average for all other occupations through this decade because of the need for corrective lenses by an aging population. This job is one step above that of ophthalmic laboratory technician and is a good route into the thriving field of opticianry. Technical ability is essential but not enough to succeed in this field. You also have to be able to put clients at ease, assess their total personality in suggesting frames and boost their confidence when fitting them with contact lenses and helping them adjust to wearing lenses. Courses in psychology, computer science and optics, especially in the use of new types of laser equipment for measuring, will move your career along more quickly.

More than half the jobs will be working for ophthalmologists or optometrists who sell glasses directly to patients, but an expanding area is independent or chain optical shops, department stores and drugstores. The "hot" spot to work will be at "superoptical stores," the fastest-growing segment of the business, where eyes are examined and glasses made on the spot. Pay is relatively low, but experience in a retail setting can lead to owning your own business. "If I wanted to get rich, I would have stayed as a pilot for the U.S. Air Force," says Jeffrey C. Snodgrass, owner of three optical shops. "But being an optician is good, steady work. It's satisfying to help people see."

PARAMEDIC

Job Requirements: Must be at least 18 years old, have high school diploma and valid driver's license. Instruction in 110-hour emergency medical care in basic life support systems is mandatory. Must be registered by the National Registry of Emergency Medical Technicians. Must be technically trained in assessing patient's medical condition and providing correct treatment. Must perform under strict guidelines consistent with level of training. Computer technology important in assessing patient's condition, administering equipment and applying other life support skills. Must remain cool and assuring under pressure. Must be able to communicate patient's problems clearly to hospital and follow doctor's orders accurately. Courage and physical strength essential in freeing patients trapped in a car accident or building collapse. Must have good memory, keep good records, maintain ambulance, know fastest traffic routes and cope with physical and emotional demands of job. Ability to work as member of a team. Continuing education to maintain certification.

✦ **Salary:**

_1991_	_2000_
$26,460	**$36,000**

Inside Track: Some 10,000 jobs will be open for paramedics by the end of the century because of increasing health needs of an aging population and because of high turnover in the job. As the work becomes even more technical, salaries will increase. With additional training, emergency medical technicians can move up to higher levels of emergency work as specified by state law. With experience and additional education, you can advance through ranks of management starting as a field supervisor and moving up to operations manager and ultimately executive director. To become a teacher, you will need a bachelor's degree in education. Newest area of training is in electrical defibrillation, which qualifies paramedics to administer electrodes to revive certain types of heart attack victims.

Opportunities are best in municipal governments and in private ambulance services. The latter is growing rapidly as many communities are contracting with private services to handle emergencies. Hospitals will not be a good area of employment because many no longer provide emergency paramedic services and more will cut back in this area. To open your own company, you will need at least five years of field experience, management and operations responsibilities and courses in business administration. Technical and medical knowledge alone are not sufficient for success in this field: You also must be able to handle constant stress without burning out. One of the rewards of this challenging job is the satisfaction of knowing you are saving lives.

PHARMACIST

Job Requirements: License to practice required in all states. Must be graduate of accredited five-year college of pharmacy, pass state board, be over 21 and have good standing in the community. Need experience or internship supervised by registered pharmacist. Continuing education for license renewal. Need one to two years of prepharmacy at junior college or college to be admitted to pharmacy school. Emphasis on math, chemistry, biology, physics, humanities, social sciences and business administration. Must be computer literate to access new information and to create programs to store data on patients, prescriptions, inventory control and billing. Must be accurate, orderly and sympathetic; willing to work nontraditional hours; and able to communicate with the public.

◆ **Salary:**

1991	*2000*
$44,000	**$60,605**

Inside Track: Because the population will be larger and older in 2000, some 44,000 jobs will open for pharmacists. Studies show that people over 65 use twice as many prescription drugs as those younger. Scientific advances and new technology will bring more medicines onto the market, and job prospects will be excellent. Expanding health insurance coverage of medications will also spur the growth of pharmacists, as more people will be able to afford prescriptions. In fact, the demand for pharmacists is expected to outstrip supply. Jobs in hospitals, community pharmacies and large retail drugstore chains will be plentiful. Pharmacists with a strong background in cost control will be most in demand. Those with one- to two-year residencies or doctorates in pharmacy will be on a fast career track at hospitals and health maintenance organizations; these credentials, coupled with courses in business administration, are also the best route to starting your own business. One of the fastest-growing and best-paying areas is sales. A sure prescription for success selling products for a major pharmaceutical company: a bachelor's degree in pharmacy, several years of experience and an MBA. Pharmacy is a fast-changing profession, becoming more automated and complex, so continuing education in the field will be necessary for success.

PHYSICAL THERAPIST

Job Requirements: Bachelor's degree or certificate from accredited four-year college program. State licensing to work hands-on with patients to improve mobility, relieve pain and restore strength to limbs, neck and trunk. Master's degree preferred. Need clinical experience or internship. Must be able to assess and test patient's physical and emotional needs, make an evaluation, develop a treatment, observe and document progress. Must know basic sciences such as anatomy, biomechanics, biology, physics and physiology. Also need background in sociology, communications, psychology. Must be patient, tactful, resourceful. Need manual dexterity and physical stamina. Must be able to use computer to program treatments, keep records and create assistive devices. Continuing education required for state licensing.

◆ **Salary:**

1991	*2000*
$31,421 to $66,150	**$45,000 to $96,000**

Inside Track: This is third fastest-growing ocupation in the United States. It is expected to expand by 57 percent, adding 39,000 more therapists. In addition to the general need for long-term care and rehabilitation for an aging population, the fastest-growing area will be in health maintenance. The prevalence of repetitive motion illnesses such as carpal tunnel syndrome also drives demand for therapists. Another somewhat ironic reason for the expansion of the profession is the nation's continuing emphasis on sports, fitness and physical activity. As a result, sports medicine will be the most lucrative specialty. Hospitals are the main employers, but an increasing percentage of physical therapists will be working in ambulatory services, home health care agencies, corporate clinics and fitness centers. The best opportunities will be in private clinics, either working with a physicians group or in private practice. A growing number of physical therapists will open their own independent offices to treat patients referred by medical doctors. The growth will be spurred by rising hospital costs, which result in patients being released quickly, requiring continued care outside of the hospital. Another factor is the increasing number of states that allow therapists to be reimbursed directly through private health insurance and Medicare benefits.

"The demand for physical therapists outside of hospitals will continue to increase—the demand is incredible," says Kenneth D. Davis, a physical therapist and director of the American Physical Therapy Association.[5] In the future, it's expected that entry-level physical therapists will have to have master's degrees. It will be a necessity if you're planning to go into business for yourself. Physical therapists will be so scarce that most hospitals and clinics will pay for additional education and advanced degrees. Kathleen M. Gombas, a physical therapist who works for a clinic specializing in sports medicine, went to college at night to earn her MBA. "The most rewarding part of my job is seeing someone who comes hobbling in and then returns in a few months, free of pain and back to normal activities," said Gombas, who plans to go into administration, either in marketing or management. She says there are so many employment opportunities for physical therapists that "you could quit this morning and get a job this afternoon."

PHYSICIAN

Job Requirements: Bachelor's degree followed by graduation from accredited medical school program of four years or from accredited institution that combines college and medical school in six years rather than eight. One year internship. Two to five years' residency for specialization. Must be licensed by state to give medical examinations, diagnose illnesses and treat people with injuries or disease. Need technical skills and empathy for patients. Continuing education and board certification in specialty. Continual improving of skills. Must be up to date in cutting edge of computer technology in such areas as imaging systems, genetic engineering and other biotechnology research and innovations. Strong marketing and business skills essential for private practice. Good communications skills and concern for patients. Able to work long, irregular hours and handle stress. Emotional stability and decisiveness. Business administration skills to run private practice and good management techniques important.

◆ **Salary:**

1991	*2000*
$157,500	**$233,906**

Inside Track: A growing and aging population and medical technology inventions will expand the health industry so dramatically that 149,000 additional physicians will be needed by 2000. Enrollment dropped in the 1980s at U.S. medical schools because of the perceived oversupply of doctors and the high expense and tremendous demands of a medical school education. But demand for doctors in certain specialties is driving the large number of openings: Doctors will be needed in geriatrics, family medicine, primary care, surgery, cardiovascular work, organ transplant, psychiatry, ophthalmology, pathology, radiation, physical medicine and rehabilitation. The U.S. military and rural areas of the country have serious shortages of doctors. Doctors of the future will have radically different choices from their predecessors regarding where and how to practice: Instead of establishing expensive individual practices, many will take salaried jobs in group medicine, clinics and health maintenance organizations. A good way to get experience for setting up your own practice is to join a group practice or to affiliate with a major hospital in a large urban area or adjoining suburb.

It takes many years of hard work to prepare for the medical profession. A physician's training is costly, too, and many are graduated with large debts in private and government loans. On the other hand, salaries for physicians are among the highest in the labor force. Physicians point to their long years of preparation and hard work, the dreaded possibility of malpractice suits and the burdensome paperwork they must do to be reimbursed as justification for making so much money. However, doctors will have to deal with the public perception that they are greedy. "When you consider that we work a 60-some hour week, that we put 12 years of training in and we owe 50 grand when we start on average, I don't think anybody is robbing the bank," said Dr. Philip R. Alper, an internist in Burlingame, California.[6] In addition to hefty incomes, physicians also get enormous gratification from the work they do. Dr. W. French Anderson, chief of molecular hematology at the National Heart, Lung and Blood Institute, is one of the world's first genetic surgeons and hopes to counteract vulnerability to deadly infections by infusing patients with genetically engineered cells. "This is what I do," Dr. Anderson says. "I eat, sleep and breathe gene therapy 24 hours a day."

PHYSICIAN ASSISTANT

Job Requirements: High school diploma, two years of college and work experience to enroll in two-year accredited program to perform under doctor's supervision many essential but time-consuming tasks involved in patient care. Training must include classroom instruction and clinical experience. Licensed by all states except Mississippi and New Jersey. Must be certified by National Commission on Certification of Physician Assistants and licensed by state. Knowledgeable in basic primary care and high-tech surgical procedures. Able to relieve physician of tasks such as taking medical histories, performing examinations, making preliminary diagnoses, ordering tests, studying results, prescribing treatment, performing minor surgery and assisting in major surgery—under supervision of doctor. Need background in anatomy, biochemistry, physiology, clinical medicine, home health care, geriatrics, obstetrics and internal medicine. Must have leadership abilities, self-confidence and emotional stability. Must keep up to date in latest medical and technological advances. Ability to work with medical staff as team member and follow orders accurately.

◆ **Salary:**

1991	*2000*
$35,000 to $60,000[7]	**$47,250**

Inside Track: The aging of America, an expanding health services industry and a growing reliance on paraprofessionals to provide primary care will open up 14,000 jobs for physician assistants. Not enough people are studying to be physician assistants, so there will be a shortage of these professionals in the near future. Physician assistants can do about 80 percent of what physicians can do—but that 20 percent is a critical difference. You must remember you are not a medical doctor and work cooperatively and constantly under supervision. With only two years' training, you can qualify for this well-paying, responsible job because of the intense and continual on-the-job training you get.

Opportunities will be best in doctors' offices, but growth areas also will be in veterans hospitals, rural and suburban clinics, community hospitals, family practices and health maintenance organizations. Medicare allows physicians to bill for services provided by physician assistants, which also will enhance employment. For a fast track, you must continue your education and go on for advanced degrees. But there's only so far you can go: Your usefulness is in the fact that you are not a physician and that your services are relatively inexpensive compared to those of a medical doctor. "It's a field that's absolutely going to grow, especially in geriatric care," says Nancy Tilson of the American Academy of Physician Assistants. "There are seven jobs for every physician assistant available." Mark Helgeson, a physician assistant at the Eagle Bend Clinic in Eagle Bend, Minneapolis, who is in practice with the tiny town's family practitioner, says he looks on himself as the extension or "tool" of the physician, who visits the clinic twice a week. "The doctor takes on the legal risk and responsibility [of a physician assistant] in exchange for the chance to make a profit," says Helgeson.[8]

PODIATRIST

Job Requirements: Four-year undergraduate degree in premed. Must pass Medical College Admission Test for admission to one of the nation's seven accredited podiatry schools. Podiatric medical training is four-year program in diagnosing and treating disorders of foot, ankle and lower leg. Must be state licensed. Board certification by the American Board of Podiatric Surgery, the American Board of Podiatric Orthopedics and the American Board of Podiatric Public Health. Must be skilled in reading radiologic films, magnetic resonance imaging and computer printouts. Must be qualified to perform surgery. Scientific aptitude, manual dexterity and good communications skills necessary. Ability to handle business, administrative and managerial responsibilities required for private practice. Enjoyment in helping others.

✦ Salary:

1991	*2000*
$44,100	**$68,412**
(starting)	(starting)

Inside Track: There will be a need for 5,700 additional podiatrists by 2000 because of the increase in numbers of older Americans and the continuing American participation in sports. Eighty percent of podiatric patients are 50 years and older, and there will be 50 million Americans over the age of 60 in 2000. Other factors: Podiatrists now are accepted as members of hospital staffs and can be reimbursed by health insurance for podiatric services. Most podiatrists are in private practice, and the best route to your own business is to start out working for someone else, either in a hospital, clinic or health maintenance organization. The American Podiatric Medical Association says podiatrists in private practice can earn up to $200,000 annually. Continuing education in the field and in business are important to start your own practice. One growth area of specialization is in working with diabetics who have foot problems. Hospital affiliation is important and highly competitive; it gives podiatrists the credibility the profession seeks. Dr. Robert I. Steinberg, podiatrist, is optimistic about the future of his profession: "There are more feet than people in this world," he says.

RADIOLOGIC TECHNOLOGIST

Job Requirements: Qualifications vary, but basic requirement is two-year associate degree in radiologic science or two-year hospital-based certification to use sophisticated, high-tech computer-enhanced radiation equipment—imaging, ultrasound and x-rays—to produce images and to treat disease. Background in mathematics, physics, chemistry, biology and anatomy helpful. State certification and licensing required. Must have training in radiography, radiation therapy technology and medical sonography. Skills in CT scanning, ultrasound, angiography and magnetic resonance imaging (MRI). Training in MRI provided by hospitals and equipment manufacturers. Registration by the American Registry of Radiologic Technologists and the American Registry of Diagnostic Medical Sonographers. Must be dependable, mature and caring. Able to work under doctor's orders. Physical strength and gentleness required for positioning patient for procedure. Accurate recordkeeping skills essential.

◆ Salary:

1991	2000
$25,358	**$41,000**
(starting)	(starting)

Inside Track: Technological advances, dependence on radiologic diagnosis and treatment, expansion of facilities that provide radiologic services, and the growth and aging of the American population will mean that 87,000 more technicians who are graduates of accredited programs will be needed. Job opportunities will be exceptional. The field has a built-in career track because of the intense on-site training given by hospitals on the use of state-of-the-art diagnostic equipment. Radiologic technicians are in such short supply that many hospitals are paying a hiring bonus to new employees and then training them. In addition to hospitals, there also are jobs at doctors' offices, health maintenance organizations, mobile units, clinics, industrial plants, research centers, government agencies and off-site emergency health care centers. Specialties are constantly emerging in the use of sonography, positron emission scanners and fluoroscopy. A new area is lithotripsy, which uses sound waves to pulverize kidney stones. Technologists also can move into administration and commercial sales and marketing.

Salaries are expected to accelerate in the next century. Because of the nationwide shortage, this is a profession that will take you to whatever part of the country you want to live in. "The crisis in employment is not coming, it's already here," says Don Hixson, chief technologist in nuclear medicine at Georgetown University Hospital.[9]

REGISTERED NURSE

Job Requirements: Must hold two-year associate degree from community college, three-year hospital diploma or bachelor's degree from four- or five-year nursing program or college. Bachelor's degree preferred to care for the sick and help the well stay healthy. Must pass state boards and be licensed to practice. Periodic renewal of license. Supervised clinical experience in hospital. Background in the sciences, humanities and computer literacy important. Professional skills, good judgment, caring attitude. Ability to handle stress. Must take responsibility and be decisive. Demanding profession. Stamina, flexibility and courage necessary. Must keep up to date in complex medical technology and computer-driven equipment. Administrative skills needed. Strong desire to help others and sensitivity to their needs.

✦ **Salary:**

_1991_	_2000_
$27,000[10]	**$50,000**
(starting)	(starting)

Inside Track: Registered nurses (RNs) are in great demand: 613,000 new jobs will open up by the end of the century. Sophisticated technology and an aging population are spurring the growth. Another factor generating a severe shortage of RNs is that patients admitted to the hospital nowadays need far more care, so hospitals need a higher ratio of nurses to each patient. The shortages in hospitals are of staff, surgical, critical care, emergency room and geriatric nurses. Midwives, nurse anesthetists and nurse practitioners require advanced degrees and also are in demand. The shortfall of nurses, which is only now beginning, is so severe that hospitals are taking positive steps to recruit, train and retain RNs. Nurses with associate degrees or diplomas will be able to study for their bachelor's degree while working full-time or part-time, and their employers will pick up the tab. Other perks to attract nurses include extra pay for night and weekend work, flexible schedules, child care, input into administrative decisions and freedom from unnecessary administrative work.

Some health care authorities expect salaries of RNs to rise astronomically in the 1990s, especially for emergency room nurses. Hospitals are the major employers of nurses, but also experiencing critical shortages are nursing homes, home health care agencies, clinics, doctors' offices, health maintenance organizations and community and public health centers. RNs also will be in demand in such fields as medical supply sales, with insurance and law firms, benefits management, research and product development. After decades of being viewed as handmaidens of doctors, RNs are getting the respect—and salary—they deserve both from hospital administrators and physicians.

Hospitals will offer RNs formal on-the-job management training, moving them up to assistant head nurse or head nurse. Graduate programs for RNs who want to get master's degrees in hospital administration will be necessary to advance your career. Areas of growth for nurse managers will be in ambulatory, acute and chronic care services and as administrators or owners of home health agencies.

People have long been attracted to nursing because they want to help others. Jan Stover, a registered nurse, enjoys the fast pace of the hospital emergency room she works in. "I like the idea that you have new patients all the time to help," she says.[11] But what will be different in the 21st century is that for the first time nurses will also have the power to control their work lives. "I'm doing the same work I did at a previous hospital, but now I am doing it with dignity and pleasure," says Annette Evans-Sheppard, an RN in neurosurgery. "I choose my own hours and I have input on decisions that affect me. I love my job, I love being a nurse. I love having hands-on contact with patients and helping them in every way. I used to be burned out in my other jobs, but not now!"[12]

SPEECH PATHOLOGIST/AUDIOLOGIST

Job Requirements: Pathologists work with people with speech and language disorders; audiologists treat the hearing impaired. For state licensing, must have bachelor's degree followed by master's degree in speech language pathology or audiology and 300 hours of clinical experience. To work in public schools, must have state practice certificate for classification as special education teacher. Must have background in acoustics, psychology and the anatomy, physiology and mechanics of speech and hearing. Can be certified by the American Speech-Language-Hearing Association by having a master's degree, completing a nine-month internship and passing a national written exam. Must be computer literate to access and create learning programs. In addition to being a skilled technician, must be compassionate, patient and able to communicate clearly with clients. Determination and commitment essential.

◆ **Salary:**

1991	*2000*
$31,421	**$46,000**

Inside Track: In response to the growing number of people 75 years and over—when hearing loss usually becomes a problem—15,000 more speech pathologists and audiologists will be needed by 2000. The baby boomers also will be in the age group when strokes that cause hearing and speech loss may occur.

Almost half of these professionals work in elementary and secondary schools, colleges and universities. The rest work in hearing centers, hospitals, nursing homes, offices of physicians and outpatient care facilities. A fast-growing area will be private practice, which means additional training in business administration. Private consultants do examinations, testing and rehabilitation for patients referred by hospitals, HMOs and private physicians. Businesses will also call on these professionals to help solve problems of industrial and environmental noise in manufacturing plants. Consultants will increasingly be asked by medical manufacturers for input about hearing aids. Hospitals are another fast-growing area for jobs: Many of these institutions, looking for ways to add income without bringing patients into the hospital for expensive overnight stays, will establish their own outpatient clinics staffed by speech therapists. One of the rewards of the career is seeing firsthand the rehabilitation of children and adults with hearing and speech problems.

VETERINARIAN

Job Requirements: At least three years of undergraduate work, preferably a four-year bachelor's degree followed by four years of accredited veterinary school and additional three to four years of study. To diagnose medical problems of animals, perform surgery and give medication, must have doctor of veterinary medicine (DVM) degree and pass state board proficiency examination. Must be licensed by state. For specialties, must complete internship and residency of from two to three years in animal hospitals or clinics and meet state board requirements. Strong background in physical and biological sciences, especially anatomy and biochemistry. Experience in diagnosing and treating animal diseases. Must have strong technical and business skills and love and compassion for animals. Ability to work long hours and under stress. Skilled in latest high-technology medical equipment and computer. Good communications skills to discuss problems with animal owners.

◆ **Salary:**

1991	*2000*
$25,000	**$34,000**[13]
(starting)	(starting)

Inside Track: Americans love their pets, and the expected growth in the U.S. animal population, emphasis on scientific animal husbandry and public demand for health and disease control programs for animals will create 12,000 new jobs for veterinarians by 2000. Admission to schools of veterinary medicine will continue to be highly competitive, but since the demand will be so strong it will be somewhat easier to get into accredited veterinary schools. Many vets work for zoos and aquariums, where they can do research and enjoy the rewards of public service and species conservation, but most work for private clinics treating small pets. In rural areas, vets treat livestock. Strong business administration and managerial skills are needed to open your own private practice. A good route is to get experience first working for clinics or in public health, take business courses and then open your own practice.

Fastest-growing specialties will be pathology, preventive medicine, toxicology, laboratory animal medicine and work in a particular species. Another area expected to grow will be the care and breeding of thoroughbred or pleasure horses. Few opportunities are expected to open up for food animals specialists—where veterinary medicine was focused earlier in the 20th century—because of the decline of the U.S. agricultural industry. Jobs will continue to move from rural to metropolitan areas. Teaching jobs, which require doctorates, will be plentiful.

The goal of most veterinarians is to open their own practice, according to Dr. Lester E. Fisher, veterinarian and director of the Lincoln Park Zoo in Chicago. "But unlike physicians who have hospital facilities provided, you have to provide your own," he says. "For that reason, many professionals are starting group practices." Dr. Fisher emphasizes the caring qualities of successful veterinarians. "Vets need a true commitment to animals and an equal commitment to owners," he says.

13

HOSPITALITY INDUSTRY

Cook/Chef
Flight Attendant
Flight Engineer
Hotel Manager/Assistant
Pilot
Restaurant/Food Service Manager
Travel Agent

The hospitality industry—travel, hotels and restaurants—is one of the fastest-growing segments of the economy. Many employment experts expect this industry to be the number one U.S. employer by the end of the century. Americans love to travel, see new sights and eat good food. By the year 2000, the combination of the continued influx of women into the workforce and the graying of America will mean there will be more people with money and vacation time to travel and more people eating out. Projections indicate that 586,000 chefs, cooks and other kitchen workers and 146,000 restaurant and food service managers will be needed by 2000. The hospitality industry is globalizing faster than most others, and workers will be able to use their skills to work wherever they want throughout the world. Because of its critical labor shortage, the hospitality industry will be extremely receptive to hiring beginners, older workers, students and young mothers. Opportunities in this category range from the relatively unskilled job of cook to highly skilled managers and pilots.

CHEF/COOK

Job Requirements: A cook is an entry-level job; a chef is a well-paid professional. Both are responsible for preparing food. Fast-food or short-order cooking experience needed for entry-level jobs for cooks. For chefs, on-the-job training and courses in culinary arts at trade, vocational and community colleges. For upscale chef jobs, must have training by prestigious culinary schools in United States and abroad. Must have health certificate from state and knowledge of hygiene and sanitation. Need basic skills of handling, preparing and presenting food. Certification and three-year apprenticeship program offered by the American Culinary Federation important for high-level cooks and chefs. Background in mathematics and business administration. Experience is the best teacher in this field, and actual practice is what employers look for. Summer workshops and on-the-job training offered by school districts, junior colleges, state departments of education and school associations. Must be able to work with a team, have good personal cleanliness and acute sense of taste and smell. For cooks, patience, good work habits and attendance are important. For chefs, a flair for the unusual, a strong aesthetic sense and engaging personality. Computer literacy necessary for ordering and inventory.

◆ **Salary:**

1991	*2000*
$13,230 (cook)	**$26,000 (cook)**
$40,000 (chef)	**$60,000 (chef)**
(starting)	(starting)

Inside Track: Chefs, cooks and other kitchen workers will add 586,000 jobs by the end of the century. That projection is based on the increasing size of the population and economy, higher disposable incomes and more leisure time for older Americans. Entry-level food preparation jobs usually are filled by workers under age 25, and the decline of people in this age group will make jobs plentiful. Many of the jobs in this field are dead-end and without benefits. But in the 1990s and beyond, cooks will be able to advance up through the ranks to become qualified chefs, to work where they want, make good salaries and to take their skills with them anywhere in the world. Jobs will be in institutions such as schools, employee cafeterias, hospitals and nursing homes and in restaurants and fast-food chains. Specialists in demand will be pastry chefs and specialty cooks for fine dining. For the most talented chefs and best communicators, jobs will also open up in teaching cooking at resort hotels, spas, wineries and on cruise ships. The dream of most cooks and chefs is to own their own restaurant. Those who do are among the stars of the profession and often make six-figure salaries. To do so, you will need excellent technical skills, innovative ideas, a following and people who will invest in your business. Some successful cooks and chefs open their own catering businesses. Courses in business administration and management are important if you want to be an entrepreneur. To move rapidly upward in your career, you must be willing to work long hours and be able to get along with those around you. Training is the key to success in this field.

Jan Leider, a graduate of the University of Kansas, worked as a waitress and then became an apprentice chef at Chicago's Westin Hotel. "I worked 800 hours in sauces, 700 in pastry, 300 in meat and 700 in cold foods and fancy art work," says Leider, who is now a certified chef. "I took courses at the hotel and was certified in sanitation. The apprenticeship program wasn't only theoretical; it's the real thing. And I'm much better prepared."[1]

FLIGHT ATTENDANT

Job Requirements: Must be high school graduate, but college degree preferred. Intensive training by airline to be responsible for safety and comfort of passengers on planes. Good communications skills, excellent health and vision and height proportional to weight. Ability to deal with public. Must be flexible for constantly changing schedule. Fluency in several languages important in global marketplace. Must know emergency procedures and first aid. Trained in serving food and drinks. Must be able to deal with stress and be decisive in handling on-board problems. Yearly training in emergency procedures and passenger relations. Must enjoy meeting people and traveling. Cheerful personality important.

◆ **Salary:**

1991	*2000*
$24,888 to $43,989	**$34,000 to $53,422**

Inside Track: By the year 2000, 34,000 additional flight attendants will be needed as international business and pleasure travel increase. Larger planes also will mean more flight attendants will be needed. In the 1990s, flight attendants may be trained to supervise passengers on their first vacation trips throughout the universe on spaceships. Salaries are based on seniority but are expected to rise along with demand for workers. Many people go into this field in order to travel and to take advantage of its flexible hours, but those who are committed to a full-time career as a flight attendant will be able to advance by taking business administration courses and moving into management. The first step up is flight service instructor, followed by customer service director and recruiting representative.

Unions of flight attendants deserve credit for upgrading the profession, which is predominantly female. Over the years, the unions have filed lawsuits making it illegal to fire members who are over age 25, or those who get married and have children. A recent victory by the Association of Professional Flight Attendants was a more reasonable weight standard for its members, all of whom work for American Airlines. Easing of these sexist restrictions will make jobs more competitive as more people will be able to qualify for them. As the various forms of discrimination are challenged, the image of flight attendants will continue to improve. Speaking of the previous weight tables, Cheryle Leon, president of the union and an active flight attendant based in Euless, Texas, says: "They played on the old image of 'stewardesses' and the 'fly me, sky-girl' stereotype. But those days are gone forever."[2]

FLIGHT ENGINEER

Job Requirements: Same qualifications as for pilot to assist pilots in monitoring and operating aircraft instruments and systems, making minor in-flight repairs and watching by computer and visually for other aircraft. Must have commercial pilot's license with instrument and multiengine rating to meet standards set by the Federal Aviation Administration (FAA). For airlines, must be at least 23 years old and have at least 1,500 hours of flying experience. College graduates are preferred. Military training a plus. Good vision corrected to perfect. Good hearing, no physical handicaps. Must pass drug screening test and written exam. Background in principles of safe flight, navigation techniques and FAA regulations. Must know latest computer technology, be able to handle stress and to work as a team. Good decision-making ability. Continuous upgrading of skills.

◆ **Salary:**

1991	*2000*
$46,305	**$65,000**[3]

Inside Track: Because of the projected shortage of pilots in general and the boom in air transportation, the job outlook for flight engineers will be favorable in the next century. "Many pilots are hired as flight engineers while in training," says Kit Darby of Future Aviation Professionals. "On older airplanes, they're used as a third pilot. This is where pilots start out." A flight engineer is in the least senior position on the aircraft, ranking below pilot, copilot and captain. Though the training for this profession is extensive and demanding, it's an entry-level job in aviation. That's why salaries are about half of what pilots make. However, the job leads to the well-paying, prestigious position of pilot.

Many existing aircraft need a flight engineer, but virtually all new aircraft, which will have computerized controls and video displays, will need only two officers in the cockpit. Airlines that can afford to will have two pilots, but many believe the introduction of computerized controls and information systems will make the lower-paid flight engineer in demand as the second pilot. The projected shortage of pilots will also affect the demand for flight engineers. In the future, flight engineers will have to be skilled in reading computerized data from a national Traffic Alert and Collision Avoidance System. The complex data is now in 50 percent of all planes and will be in all aircraft by the end of the decade. Expertise in reading windshear detection instruments will also be required. Those who prove themselves as flight engineers will be the first to be promoted to the highly desirable pilot status.

HOTEL MANAGER/ASSISTANT

Job Requirements: College degree in hotel or restaurant management to ensure guests are comfortable and the hotel is profitable. Also acceptable: liberal arts degree plus experience and additional training in hotel administration at a vocational, trade or community college. High school diploma plus vocational training and experience in hotel management also are acceptable, but promotions will take much longer than for those with bachelor's degree. Restaurant management an important entry-level credential for hotel management. Need background in hotel administration, accounting, finance, economics, marketing, housekeeping, food service and hotel maintenance. Computer science a must to supervise reservations, accounting, housekeeping and food supplies. Sales ability and good communications skills important. In international marketplace, fluency in several languages a plus. Must be able to handle stress, be a self-starter, solve problems, motivate staff and be willing to work around the clock. Must have pleasant personality and commitment to the guests.

◆ **Salary:**

_1991_	_2000_
$55,252	**$80,000 +**

Inside Track: The projected growth of the travel industry and of international business will create 27,000 more jobs in hotels, motels and resorts. The hotel industry is exploding due to widespread new construction, and new managers will be needed to supervise thousands of entry-level employees. The hours are long and hard, but the payoff is there for those who are determined. Among the top administrative slots are resident manager, executive housekeeper, front office manager, food and beverage manager and meeting planner. The fastest-moving career track in the booming hotel business is in the food and beverage department, which is where the hotel makes its money. In this department, good performance and seniority lead to fairly fast promotions into the higher echelons of hotel administration.

"Dedication to the hotel guest is the secret of success," says Evelyn Echols, president of Echols International Travel and Hotel Schools. "If you are good at what you do, you'll be noticed by hotel executives and moved ahead." The major international hotel chains offer the best opportunity for advancement. You have to be able to absorb all you can from intensive in-house training, be willing to relocate every two years and prepared to work anywhere in the world. In the hotel business, managers often are selected from within the ranks and trained for the next slot up, so pick the hotel you want to be with and stick with it if possible. Salaries increase as your responsibilities increase, and managers of well-known hotels make six-figure incomes. Remember, Ivana Trump was paid $350,000 a year to run the Plaza Hotel.

PILOT

Job Requirements: Must have commercial pilot's license, instrument and multiengine ratings and required flight time to meet standards set by the Federal Aviation Administration (FAA). For airlines, must be at least 23 years old and have at least 1,500 hours of flying experience. College graduates are preferred. Military training a plus. Good vision corrected to perfect. Good hearing, no physical handicaps. Must pass drug screening test and written exam. Background in principles of safe flight, navigation techniques and FAA regulations. Must be able to handle stress, work as a team. Good decision-making ability. Must be able to pass periodic tests of flying skills and physical health. Good communications skills, pleasant personality and fluency in foreign languages important. Must be up to date in latest aircraft computer technology.

◆ **Salary:**

_1991_	_2000_
$92,610	**$125,000**[4]

Inside Track: Some 26,000 more jobs will open up for aircraft pilots by the end of the century. Employment opportunities will increase because 25 percent of pilots currently flying for major airlines are expected to retire by 1997, and because the travel industry is projected to expand. The best job opportunities will be in flying jumbo jets for major international airlines; they look for college graduates with a commercial pilot's or flight engineer's license and with experience flying jets. For helicopter flying, pilots must be 18 years old, have 250 hours or more of flight experience and be licensed. The FAA has certified 600 civilian flying schools, including colleges and universities.

The Armed Forces are a major and preferred source of pilots, but it's not the fastest route ahead: Promotions are based solely on seniority, and military pilots usually move to the civilian sector after years of service. The best route, outside of military training flying jumbo jets, is to start as a corporate pilot, move to a regional airline and then go to a major one as a flight engineer. The next promotions are to pilot and then captain. The average new airline pilot has 4,000 hours of flying experience. Most of them have a college degree, perfect vision, an excellent health profile and are nonsmokers with low cholesterol. This is a prestigious job with good salary and benefits and a certain amount of glamour. Captain Bill Neuens, a chief pilot for United Airlines, flies 727s and 747s. "Pilots are always going to school," says Neuens, who is nearing the mandatory retirement age of 60. "I've always loved to fly, and I still do."[5]

RESTAURANT/FOOD SERVICE MANAGER

Job Requirements: High school diploma plus specialized training from vocational school, community college or four-year college or university. Graduates of programs or colleges specializing in restaurant and food service management preferred. Background in accounting, business law and management, food planning and preparation, and nutrition. Intensive on-the-job training by food service management companies and national and regional restaurant chains. Must have food and beverage experience. Internships helpful. Personal qualities stressed: good health, stamina, self-discipline, initiative and leadership skills. Able to solve problems quickly. Good communications skills. Must be willing to relocate and able to handle long hours of work. Ability to supervise employees, do payroll and scheduling. Computer literacy essential.

✦ **Salary:**

1991	*2000*
$40,792	**$65,000**[6]

Inside Track: Growth in the eating and drinking places at hotels, restaurants and resorts—and high employee turnover—will create 146,000 jobs for restaurant and food service managers. Though in the past it has been possible for those with only a high school education to be promoted to an administrative position within a company after many years of service, the best and fastest career opportunities are for those with degrees in restaurant or institutional food service management. Major corporations will help employees get a college degree or do advanced studies to move up in the ranks. Those with advanced courses in business administration or an MBA can skyrocket quickly in food service management at hotels and restaurant chains. Another sure route to success is to get to know the kitchen, good food from bad and the economics of the industry. Those who get to work early and stay the latest are noticed and moved ahead.

This is an industry in which it is important to accept a move to another city or country or a lateral move to learn about another department. Those who are skilled and charming, who have great patience and tact, will move ahead the fastest. At the large chains and at the most successful restaurants, top professionals in this field earn six-figure salaries. Many restaurant and food service managers hope to open their own eating places one day. To do this, make sure you have the necessary technical and business skills, well-heeled investors and a faithful clientele.

TRAVEL AGENT

Job Requirements: High school diploma plus specialized training at vocational school, community college or four-year college or university. College education increasingly important. In some states, must be licensed. Experience in some phase of the hospitality industry. Comprehensive in-house training by employers, but background needed in geography, foreign languages, history, accounting and business management. Computer skills are a basic requirement for employment. Must know how to access reservations systems worldwide. Being well-traveled is helpful. Must be good salesperson, have pleasant personality, good communications skills, a great deal of patience. Accuracy and up-to-date information are essential. An additional attribute: love of travel.

◆ **Salary:**

_1991_	_2000_
$21,110	**$27,000**

Inside Track: As business and pleasure travel continues to boom, so will jobs for travel agents. The U.S. Department of Labor projects 77,000 additional jobs will be created by 2000. This is an entry-level job and pay is low to start, but travel is free. With the expansion of travel, especially international travel, those who are the best trained, have the best sales skills and work hardest will be able to move ahead rapidly. Advanced courses can speed up the progress of your career. The Institute of Certified Travel Agents offers the title of certified travel counselor to those who complete its 18-month, part-time course. The American Society of Travel Agents gives a certificate of proficiency to agents who pass its three-hour test. Travel agents work on commission, so the ability to market your skills will be the difference between success and failure. The area of travel expected to grow the fastest will be international business travel as the global marketplace expands. The ideal place for a travel agent to start out is with a travel agency that specializes in business travel because that's where the most opportunities will be.

Travel agencies also are downsizing and merging, and smaller agencies are falling by the wayside. Major corporations are consolidating all travel management with "mega-agencies" such as American Express, Carlson Travel Network and Thomas Cook Travel.[7] The big companies can get better discounts on airfares and hotels, offer better analysis of travel costs and put together complex itineraries. Ursula Pedzimaz plans business meetings for Himmel & Associates, a travel agency known for its meeting planning. It's her first job after earning her high school diploma and taking a 12-week travel training course. "I've always wanted to be in the travel business because I'm excited by detail work, pressure and deadlines," says the travel agent. "Salary's not important to me at this point because I have a job with a future. I hope to move up and become a supervisor in three years."[8] The ultimate goal of many travel representatives is to own their own business. To do so, you will need courses in business administration, at least $50,000 in capital and a loyal following.

14

MANAGEMENT AND OFFICE PERSONNEL

Clerical Supervisor/Office Manager
Corporate Personnel Trainer
Employment Interviewer
Human Resources Manager/Executive
Labor Relations Specialist
Secretary/Office Administrator

The business of running a business—executive, managerial and administrative jobs—is a major occupation that will show faster than average growth. Though jobs in this field were once expected to decline because of automation, they are being expanded instead because of the increasing complexity of organizations and the need to recruit, train, manage and retain a diversified workforce. Though middle managers' ranks were severely depleted in the 1980s, the need for skilled managers in personnel and human resources, especially in retail and business services, will grow rapidly because of the coming labor shortage, the government predicts. High-tech inventions and the continuing automation of the workplace will radicalize the way work is done, but human hands and brains still will be needed to do it. One major change: 571,000 additional secretaries will be needed by the year 2000, and the job will be transformed into a secretary/office administrator who manages a group of executives. At the same time, there will be a loss of 36,000 jobs for stenographers by the end of the century. The challenges of the shortage of skilled employees and of managing a diverse labor force will accelerate the growth of jobs for those who hire, train, monitor illegal labor practices such as discrimination and supervise human resources departments.

CLERICAL SUPERVISOR/OFFICE MANAGER

Job Requirements: Associate degree acceptable, but bachelor's degree preferred to supervise the flow of work. Not an entry-level job. Must have a broad base of office skills, be able to set priorities, be well organized and have the ability to build support staff into a team. Flexibility in daily schedule and willingness to move from department to department are necessary. Skilled in recruiting, interviewing and training new employees. Ability to use computerized information systems to run department and assign and monitor work of staff. Because of complexity of office technology, specialized training or advanced degree important. To be promoted from within, must prove yourself first as an office worker who can handle stress and is competent, conscientious and loyal. Seniority also a factor.

◆ **Salary:**

1991	*2000*
$19,845 to $44,000	**$25,000 to $60,000**

Inside Track: Though the future workplace is projected to be paperless, clerical work is expected to expand, creating the need for 136,000 supervisors and managers. Opportunities will be good in retail trade, which includes food and clothing, and in business services such as temporary firms. These positions often are filled from within the company and often are a rare opportunity for clerical workers to advance into management. If you're a clerk, "let your supervisor know you're interested in additional responsibility and in moving ahead," says Anne Ladky, executive director of Women Employed, a national advocacy and career training organization for women. "Take extra courses in basic management skills, such as supervision of people." Once in the job, Ladky suggests you "coordinate important projects, introduce new systems and volunteer for office events that will give you visibility."

The secret to moving up from this position is to master new or updated software packages and to make sure the staff understands how to use them. Being a computer expert is the fastest track into other managerial positions because you will be invaluable to the firm. Continuing education courses in administration will be necessary for advancement. While planning your own upward career moves, you also must be aware of work problems and aspirations of those you supervise and be supportive of your staff. Your ability to retain skilled workers in a tight labor market will upgrade the quality of work and productivity of your department, save the company money in recruitment and training, and enhance your value and future.

CORPORATE PERSONNEL TRAINER

Job Requirements: Undergraduate degree in liberal arts or business with background in personnel, human resources or labor relations to help develop skills of new and current employees. College courses in personnel administration, human resources management, training and development most desirable. Combination of courses in social sciences, business and behavioral science useful. Background in psychology, sociology, education and at least one foreign language preferred. Must be able to assess employees' needs at both support staff and managerial levels, and to plan and run training programs to meet those needs. Also must be able to plan and present sessions to sensitize managers to a diverse work force. Advanced degrees often necessary in industrial relations, educational administration or management. Computer technology and video presentation techniques needed. Good communications skills and ability to motivate people.

◆ **Salary:**

_1991_	_2000_
$30,870	**$50,000**

Inside Track: Employee training will be one of the fastest-growing areas of human resources. "Concerns of the business community for a skilled workforce have never been greater," according to a report by the U.S. Departments of Education and Labor. Large corporations will need in-house professionals because of the growing shortage of trained personnel and emphasis on in-house job training. The high illiteracy rate in the United States and the projected shrinking labor pool will drive job growth in this field. Employers will be forced to hire illiterates and teach them basic skills such as reading, writing and mathematics. Managers, still predominantly white men, will have to learn how to supervise an entry-level labor force that will be overwhelmingly female, minority, immigrant and older. In addition to large corporations, other important employers are unions, management and consulting firms, hospitals, schools, banks, department stores and personnel agencies.

A growing area of employment for these professionals is retraining of older workers, necessitated by the shortage of younger, skilled personnel. "Between now and the year 2000, employers will have no choice but to encourage older workers," says Ronald C. Pilenza, former president of the Society for Human Resource Management.[1] And Raymond W. Zukowski, a training manager for Aerospace Electronic Systems of General Electric Company in Utica, New York, who runs an in-house technical renewal program, says: "The tendency to give only newer employees more challenging work means you're building in your own obsolescence."

Many corporate trainers are opening their own businesses. The best way to do so is to get the educational background you need, work for a large corporation for at least five years, prove your ability, take courses in business administration and then open your own consulting firm—with your present employer as your first account.

EMPLOYMENT INTERVIEWER

Job Requirements: A minimum of two years of college or an associate degree, but bachelor's degree preferred to help job seekers find work and employers find qualified staff. For placing or hiring secretaries, word processing operators and other support staff, outgoing personality, determination and selling skills more important than educational background. For doing executive search or headhunting—finding, placing or hiring professionals such as accountants, doctors, lawyers, managers, sales executives and engineers—prefer training or background in the field or a master's degree in business. Must have technical knowledge of field in which you place applicants. Good communications skills, desire to help people, understanding of office procedures and a warm, outgoing personality needed to deal with job seekers and with management or clients. Must be articulate, inspire confidence and able to handle a fast-paced work environment. Computer skills essential: up to date in latest programs to facilitate hiring process and to keep informed of employment laws and regulations. Must be aware of federal, state and local antidiscrimination laws governing hiring.

◆ **Salary:**

_1991_	_2000_
$17,640 to $30,000	**$25,000 to $48,000**[2]
(starting)	(starting)

Inside Track: More than 33,000 additional employment interviewers will be needed because of the rapid expansion of employment agencies and temporary firms and the corporate emphasis on hiring of qualified workers who will fit into the corporate culture. At entry level, interviewers work for private or state employment agencies and in training positions at corporations. The best opportunities for interviewers will be as full-time employees of temporary agencies, which will expand rapidly in this decade. With experience and advanced degrees, employment interviewers go to work for private executive search firms, where pay is the best. To succeed in the highly competitive headhunting profession, you will have to be able to sign up large corporations, small businesses and nonprofit organizations as clients and then locate, interview, screen and recommend applicants for jobs. Advancement to supervisory positions will be competitive, but that is not where the action will be. The most successful interviewers and headhunters are more highly valued than managerial personnel in this field, except in personnel offices of business and industry. The most successful interviewers form their own businesses, usually in a specialty they know best. To do so, you must have some background in business administration and a wide network of contacts.

Employment interviewers and executive search firms must be careful not to ask applicants discriminatory questions about race, religion, national origin or private matters. The workforce of the 21st century will be diverse, and you are legally obligated to be fair with a variety of job applicants. What employers fear most are lawsuits, and a study by the American Bar Foundation shows that in the two decades between 1969 and 1989, the volume of employment discrimination suits rose by an "astonishing 2,200 percent, nearly ten times faster than all other federal civil laws suits."[3]

Working on the staff of a corporate personnel department, for private employment agencies or in your own business, the secret to success in this highly competitive, demanding field is determination. "Top employment interviewers are those who stay in the field, work hard and move ahead," says Bob Allison of the National Association of Personnel Consultants. His professional organization certifies qualified personnel consultants.

HUMAN RESOURCES MANAGER/EXECUTIVE

Job Requirements: Must have bachelor's degree followed by advanced degree in human resources management, business or personnel administration to run personnel department or a division of it such as hiring and separation, employee benefits, training, compliance, safety programs or industrial relations. Must have personnel experience and familiarity with finance, especially benefits and compensation. Strong managerial skills and ability to advise and guide staff and employees. Ability to evaluate and establish administrative systems, procedures and training programs. Strong communications and people skills. Must be up to date in latest computer technology and software for human resources programs. Expertise in human relations, analysis and problem solving. Must be able to work with company employees, executives and unions and be current in executive compensation and bonuses, health and retirement benefits. Sensitivity to discrimination and harassment charges and to a diverse need for day care, maternity leave and flexible hours. Able to handle disciplinary problems such as alcoholism and drug abuse. Demanding, responsible job for mature, experienced person.

✦ **Salary:**

_1991_	_2000_
$81,585	**$122,160**

Inside Track: The projected shortage of skilled employees and the demands of managing a diverse workforce will make human resources managers, formerly called personnel directors, essential for business and industry. "By the 21st century, nearly all human resources executives will report directly to the chief executive officer," says Jeffrey Christian, president, Christian & Timbers, an international executive search firm based in Cleveland. The fastest-growing areas are for compensation and benefits managers, both of which require finely honed financial expertise. Computer skills will be an important part of the job to provide human resources information and to run the department. In the next decade, the personal computer will be used to run entire human resources information services—and you will have to know how to use this artificial intelligence. In the 1990s, human resource managers will be on the cutting edge of change, the innovators in solving work and family problems and compensation strategies.

Human resources is a growth field that is attractive to college graduates from both liberal arts and business schools. "Graduates with degrees in areas where jobs are in short supply are coming to us for advanced study in human resources," says Lawrence K. Williams, administrator of graduate studies at Cornell University's School of Industrial and Labor Relations. Top human resources directors make very good salaries: Compensation of more than $150,000 annually is not unusual at top corporations.

LABOR RELATIONS SPECIALIST

Job Requirements: Also known as equal employment officer (EEO). Must have bachelor's degree in personnel administration, industrial relations, psychology, sociology, counseling or education to assure employer's compliance with local, state and federal antidiscrimination laws and regulations. Graduate study increasingly important, especially a master's in labor relations or human resources. Law degree extremely helpful. Must have experience in human resources, particularly in recruitment and severance of workers, and understanding of the organizational structure of business. Up-to-date knowledge of laws regarding equal employment, especially affirmative action, and discrimination, especially sexual harassment. Sensitivity to needs of a diverse workforce and to employee complaints of discrimination. Must investigate and resolve grievances, monitor corporate policies and compile and submit EEO statistical reports. Computer literacy an important tool to perform job well. Skill in organizing sensitivity workshops for management and staff. Ability to work with unions, individuals and managers. Must be sincere about fairness to all employees and able to communicate that feeling. Able to inspire trust and confidence and to challenge wrongdoing of employers and managers in a positive way. Demanding, responsible job for mature person.

✦ **Salary:**

1991	*2000*
$40,091	**$61,818**

Inside Track: Job opportunities for labor relations specialists will grow faster than the average by the end of the century to meet the needs of managing a new workforce that will be increasingly female, minority, older and foreign. Midsize and large businesses, eager to reduce turnover, retain qualified employees and avoid costly lawsuits, will hire EEO officers to handle these responsibilities. Cultural diversity is the watchword of the 21st century, and you will be dealing with it hands on. There has been a shift from lawsuits alleging discrimination in hiring, which are difficult to prove, to discrimination in firing, and EEO officers in the future will have to focus on that procedure to make sure it is fair. "In 1964, when Title 7 of the U.S. Civil Rights Act was passed," says Eleanor Holmes Norton, head of the Equal Employment Opportunity Commission from 1977 to 1991, "the country was openly racist and few women and minorities could get entry-level positions. Companies that excluded them altogether had few complaints. Now the law is being pressed to new levels in the workplace, where it is sorely needed."[4]

The route to success in this field is to have a real understanding of and compassion for people—and at the same time to be a successful troubleshooter for the company. Experience in personnel—working with and counseling workers and management—is an important part of paying your dues in this field. To move upward from EEO to labor negotiations and high-level corporate jobs, you will need an MBA or law degree. Just as important will be a reputation for fairness and honesty. If you want to go into teaching or become a private consultant on these increasingly important matters, you will need a master's degree in industrial relations or human resources. This job is on the cutting edge of the many dramatic changes in the workforce that are projected for the next century, and if you can do it well, representing both employer and employees fairly, you will quickly move up the career ladder. It is an excellent takeoff point for important and high-level human resources positions.

SECRETARY/OFFICE ADMINISTRATOR

Job Requirements: High school diploma a basic requirement, but associate degree or diploma from secretarial or vocational school preferred. Those with college degrees and with certification as certified professional secretary from the Institute for Certifying Secretaries are highly sought after. Must have good command of grammar and be able to type letters, memos and reports quickly and accurately. Good communications skills essential both in person and on telephone. Must have word processing skills and up-to-date knowledge of various computerized business programs as well as technical skills necessary to use and oversee a variety of automated office equipment. Management and administrative skills necessary to organize workday schedules and assignments for yourself and the executives you work for. Must be able to handle stress and constant interruptions. Professional demeanor important. Must be adaptable, versatile.

◆ **Salary:**

1991	*2000*
$19,361	**$24,000**[5]

Inside Track: Employment opportunities will be good for secretaries, as 571,000 new jobs will be created by the end of the century. But the job will be changed because of automation: Secretaries will assume far more managerial and professional responsibilities and will handle support work for several executives rather than just one. To attract and retain secretaries, management will have to make sure they have upward mobility in the corporation. Smart secretaries will insist on being put on career tracks leading to positions of administrative assistant, administrative secretary, executive secretary and, ultimately, office manager, all of whom will be in demand. They will have demonstrated their ability in these areas by managing the detail work of a group of executives and planning their own work schedules.

"College-educated secretaries have a better chance to advance," says Anne Ladky, executive director of Women Employed, a national advocacy and training organization. "To enhance your job progress, it's important to take courses that build your expertise, such as office organization, business writing and computer science." Courses in finance, marketing and personnel also will be needed to advance out of the secretarial ranks, and your company should pay for these studies because they will benefit both you and the organization.

Secretaries/office administrators will be paramanagers in charge of work flow, purchasing and personnel administration. They will be "office translaters" who resolve top management's "technophobia," according to Professional Secretaries International. Reggio & Associates, a human resources consulting firm, predicts a complete change from clerical support to administrative support in the coming decade—the latter being part of the professional staff. Despite the severe shortage of qualified secretaries, their salaries on average are painfully low. Those who work for government agencies and belong to unions make an additional $50 to $60 a week, according to the American Federation of State, County and Municipal Workers. Most secretaries are not unionized, so to be paid fairly you must insist on a title that accurately describes what you're doing. "What difference does a title make?" asks Cecilia B. Walker, president of the professional secretaries group. "Roughly, $2,650 a year."[6]

15

MANUFACTURING, REPAIR, CONSTRUCTION, AGRICULTURE AND TRANSPORTATION

Aircraft Technician
Appliance/Power Tool Repairer
Architect
Automotive Mechanic
Carpenter
Farm Manager
Industrial Designer
Landscape Architect
Office/Business Machine Repairer
Operations Manager/Manufacturing
Radio/TV Service Technician
Truck Driver

The five industries in this chapter have been grouped together because they all represent occupations that are highly specialized, requiring mechanical and technical skills and often physical strength and endurance. Some of the industries, such as construction, repair and transportation, are among the few blue-collar fields that will grow in the 1990s. In fact, truck drivers are one of the top four workers most in demand in this decade because of projected increases in the amount of freight transported by trucks. Other industries, such as manufacturing and agriculture, are declining, but they are not going to disappear. U.S. manufacturers are serious about expanding their shrunken industry by increasing exports, so this sector will continue to be an important though smaller part of the U.S. economy.

Today's automated, high-tech factories, equipment and structures are the birthplace of new jobs with new responsibilities for those who can learn and adapt. The specific occupations in this section are projected to provide good-paying jobs with a future. Though the emphasis in the 1990s and beyond will be on brains not brawn, these jobs still require mechanical ability and physical endurance.

AIRCRAFT TECHNICIAN

Job Requirements: Must be certified by Federal Aviation Administration (FAA) as airframe mechanic, power plant mechanic or repairer. Must have at least 18 months of work experience, pass written and oral tests and demonstrate ability to do the job. Graduate of FAA-certified trade school preferred. Must have strong background in mathematics, physics, chemistry, electronics, computer science, mechanical drawing and knowledge of materials used to build planes. New degree in field is bachelor's of technology. Ability to submit concise and accurate reports is essential. Must be up to date in technological advances in aircraft, especially engine, navigation and communications equipment. Must be highly motivated, able to diagnose and solve complex problems. Have to work fast, often under pressure.

◆ **Salary:**

1991	*2000*
$23,152 to $31,972	**$30,000 to $45,000**[1]

Inside Track: The increase in air traffic, both domestic and international and for business and pleasure, will create 20,000 additional jobs for aircraft technicians and engine specialists by 2000. The need for more aviation technicians is so critical that American Airlines has become the first U.S. airline to sponsor an aviation maintenance training program, located at Midway Airport in Chicago. It has invested $5 million to provide post–high school training for aircraft technicians. "The academy will provide modern training in a field that has many high-paying job opportunities," says Luther G. Brewster, a director of aircraft maintenance for American. "We recognized the growing need for aviation technicians and took the initiative to fill the void."[2]

The best-paying jobs will be with major airlines, but smaller airlines, private plane owners, airports and government will have the most openings. "Specialists in large turbo or jet planes, which will be aging by the 21st century, will be highly sought after," says Kit Darby of Future Aviation Professionals. The key to advancement for aircraft technicians is to earn an inspector's authorization. To be eligible, you must hold an airframe and power plant certificate for at least three years, pass written and oral tests and demonstrate you can do the work. The inspector's certification leads to positions such as crew chief, inspector, lead inspector and shop supervisor. These positions are necessary to move into executive positions. Many successful technicians become FAA inspectors, where pay is usually lower but gratification higher because of performing a public service. If you want to open your own aircraft maintenance shop, make sure you have at least ten years of experience and have taken courses or advanced degrees in business administration and management.

APPLIANCE/POWER TOOL REPAIRER

Job Requirements: High school, vocational or community college courses in repairing kitchen appliances, ovens, washers and dryers, vacuum cleaners, lawn mowers and power tools. Must have strong background in electronics and electricity. At least three years of on-the-job training in repairing appliances and power tools given by employer, manufacturer or retailer of products. Must also know solid-state circuits, microprocessors and sensing devices. Some states require licensing to work on gas appliances. Ability to keep good billing records, concentrate, solve problems and please the customer. Mechanical aptitude and good communications skills also important. Must be flexible about working long hours, evenings and weekends. Tact and patience with customers needed.

◆ **Salary:**

_1991_	_2000_
$27,562	**$40,000**

Inside Track: The switch to electronically controlled appliances means a decrease in the need for power appliance repairers, but neither the power tools nor the need for repairers will disappear completely. Instead, the best repairers will be in great demand and their skills will be even more highly sought after. It is also important to be expert in repairing electronic equipment, as the two jobs eventually will overlap. One route to success in this field is to spend at least ten years repairing appliances and tools. At the same time, earn a college degree and take advanced courses in business and management. The next step up will be supervisor, assistant service manager or service manager.

Service management, which pays well, will be increasingly important by 2000, when the focus will be on customer service. "As technology increases and the global economy intensifies, most of the big companies are looking toward the service function to get revenues," says Andrew Kuczmar, senior national service manager for Echo Inc., manufacturers of outdoor power equipment. Echo is a Japanese-owned company. "Where you truly make profit is over the life of the product: Service brings in a lot of revenues."[3] The secret to being a successful service manager, Kuczmar says, is "to have a background in repair and to spend a lot of time in the field with distributors answering questions about the product. Service managers should not be in an ivory tower."

Another route to success is opening your own business, which can be done if you have at least ten years' experience as a repairer and have taken advanced courses in business administration and management. "To start your own repair shop, you need good repair skills, a business plan and the ability to deal well with people," says Sharon Katterman, job placement director of Moraine Valley Community College. She also advises getting all the information, counseling and training you can from regional offices of the federal Small Business Administration before opening your business.

ARCHITECT

Job Requirements: Must be licensed by state to provide architectural services. To get licensing, must have a professional degree in architecture from accredited architecture school, complete an internship of three years and pass the architect registration examination. Fastest route is to enroll in a five-year bachelor of architecture degree program. Graduate degree, especially master's of architecture, preferred and is essential for teaching or research. To design buildings must be skilled in design, mechanics, engineering, management and supervision. Must be able to prepare and present drawings for projected building, understand its structural system, specify building materials, know building and zoning codes and develop final construction documents. Artistic and drawing ability, mathematical and visual skills essential. Must be up to date in using computer-aided design systems to create building designs. Must have good communications skills to work with clients, other professionals and construction firms. Must have strong sensitivity to human and environmental needs while keeping budget in mind.

◆ **Salary:**

_1991_	_2000_
$39,946	**$61,596**

Inside Track: Good opportunities are projected for architects, and 21,000 new jobs will be created by the end of the century. Most of the jobs will be in small rather than large private architectural firms, especially those with overseas clients. The best opportunity for architects will be working for clients in Asia, particularly Japan, Korea and Indonesia. U.S. architects also are expected to do a great deal of business with nations in the European Common Market, where "old, quaint and crummy hotels need gutting and redoing to attract tourists," says Alan Lapidus, a New York architect.[4] A fast-growing area in the United States will be in designing and rehabilitating offices and manufacturing plants to conform with federal laws mandating easy access for disabled people.

The element present in every successful project is "client cooperation and participation," says Gigi McCabe-Miele, an architect.[5] Experience is the most important building block for architects. "Once you're registered in your own state and other states, you'll have no trouble working," says Gertrude Lempp Kerbis, president of her own architectural firm. "Start working in your own community with zoning and code planning people to establish a network of contacts. Start your own business by doing pro bono work, which pays off later, even if you're employed by someone else." There will be an explosion in 2000 of small architectural firms doing renovations of old buildings—a good way to launch your own practice. After years of experience, and with the necessary financial training and backing, architects become developers— where the big money is.

AUTOMOTIVE MECHANIC

Job Requirements: Must have two-year college education or associate degree in mechanics from community college or vocational school to repair and service automobiles with mechanical or electronic problems. Apprenticeship or hands-on job experience essential. Intense on-the-job training. Knowledge of electronics basic. Need good reading and mathematical skills. Background in physics, chemistry and English. Must have mechanical aptitude and ability to follow checklist of problems. Certification by the National Institute for Automotive Service Excellence helpful; must have two years' experience and pass written exam. Ability to concentrate and solve problems important. Physical strength and dexterity needed. Basic requirement: a "feel" for cars.

✦ **Salary:**

1991	*2000*
$26,460	**$36,000**

Inside Track: A good auto mechanic, hard to find in the 1980s, will be even more scarce in the 1990s and beyond. An estimated 126,000 more auto technicians will be needed by the end of the century because people will be purchasing new cars less frequently and will need more repairs on their older vehicles; because new antipollution devices will have to be installed as laws governing emissions continue to change; and because there will be more cars on the road.

Most of the new jobs will be in automotive repair shops and automobile dealerships as gasoline stations phase out repairs. Those with formal training will move ahead quickly into supervisory jobs. The increasing use of electronic, computerized equipment means those who master it will be the most successful. Automotive dealers and manufacturers give short training sessions at factory training centers. Make sure your employer sends you to as many as are offered. Certification, which must be renewed every five years, positions you for advancement. You may want to pick a specialty, such as automatic transmissions, air-conditioning, radiator or tune-up; the last area will have the most jobs. Entry-level salaries are low, but mechanics who are known to do a good job and continue to update their skills will get good pay increases. If you want to own your own business, get at least ten years' experience first and take courses in business administration. Update your computer skills and learn how to use bookkeeping programs.

The most successful auto mechanics are those who love cars the most—former hot-rodders who live to tell the tale. In order to move ahead in this field, you have to get in there and examine every inch of the vehicle. John L. Holdos, manager of service marketing for Mack Trucks in Allentown, Pennsylvania and a former automotive technician, knows every each of the 18-wheel, 80,000-pound heavy duty Mack truck. "I've been under it, in it and everything in between to repair and check it out," says Holdos, who used to tinker with cars as a teenager. "The truck is a huge piece of iron. The parts are heavy and the work is dirty. But when I see a Mack truck on the road, doing its job, there's a gleam in my eye from a bit of corporate and personal pride."[6]

CARPENTER

Job Requirements: Must be at least 17 years old and have intensive on-the-job and formal training to work on buildings, installation and maintenance. Graduate of trade school or vocational school, followed by three- to four-year apprenticeship program offered by Associated Builders and Contractors, Inc., Associated General Contractors, United Brotherhood of Carpenters and Joiners of America, Associated General Contractors or the National Association of Home Builders. Increasingly complex, electronic and computerized equipment make a high school diploma essential. Most know mathematics, mechanical drawing, elementary structural design, form building, rough framing, inside and outside finishing. Ability to read blueprints, use equipment and materials is essential. Good physical condition and strength needed for demanding jobs. Must be able to work as member of a team and communicate with supervisors and clients.

◆ **Salary:**

1991	*2000*
$23,152	**$34,650**[7]

Inside Track: Construction is one of the few blue-collar industries that will grow in the 21st century. The building industry is cyclical, but carpenters always are in demand: 180,000 more will be needed by 2000. "We in this country have developed the assumption that with a growing high-tech society, skilled craftspeople are no longer important, but just the opposite is true," says Harley Shaiken, labor economist at the University of California at San Diego. "They are pivotal."[8] Demand for carpenters—and to a lesser degree painters, paper hangers, floor coverers, dry wall installers, metal workers, glaziers and insulation workers—will be driven by the demand for new housing and industrial plants. Another fast-growing area will be in renovating existing buildings.

Getting into an apprenticeship program is key. In the past, the programs have been almost completely closed to women and minorities. This will change in the coming decade as the federal government more closely regulates apprenticeships and works to open them to everyone on an equal opportunity basis. The weather, geographical location and the economy are important factors in this field, but there will be jobs. Most carpenters work for a construction firm and also do jobs on the side, which usually adds up to a good income. Many U.S. construction firms are doing overseas projects. Though they usually hire local carpenters, they often bring along some of their own professionals to supervise. The goal of many carpenters is to start their own business. To do so, it's better to have all-around skills than a specialty. To move toward your own construction firm, "get a four-year college degree," advises Newell A. Johnson, veteran carpenter and vice president of Bert Williams Construction Company, a general contracting firm. Study drafting, architecture, management and business administration. "Learn a little bit about everything, especially how to handle people," says Johnson. "Contractors get not only the gravy, but the headaches, too."

FARM MANAGER

Job Requirements: Must have family farm or experience from programs offered by Future Farmers of America and 4-H. Also need strong educational background in science, business, management, finance and computer literacy. Degree from four-year college of agriculture with expertise in mathematics, dairy science, agriculture economics, horticulture, crops, soil and animal science. Accreditation from American Society of Farm Managers and Rural Appraisers. Must be up to date in latest farm technology, changing foreign agricultural policies and international exchange rates. Must understand U.S. commodities markets, distribution and pricing. Accounting and bookkeeping important, along with knowledge of latest software programs to run farm's recordkeeping and business analysis. Must have good supervisory and communications skills. Also must have strong commitment to work, determination and patience.

◆ **Salary:**

1991	*2000*
$18,742	**$30,000**

Inside Track: The trend toward fewer but larger farms means there will be fewer farmers, but the increasing complexity of farming will fuel the demand for highly trained and experienced farm managers in the next century. Managing a farm is hard work, and in the coming years the emphasis will be on financial and marketing skills as much as crop, livestock and scientific knowledge. The salaries look low, but housing, food and expenses are included as part of the job. Farm managers, who generally will not own the farms they operate, will have far more power and prestige than farmer-owners do.

The computer rather than the plow is the key to success in this field. You will use the computer to run the farm and to access the latest information on scientific agriculture, the commodities markets and national and international news. A global marketplace long has been a fact of life for U.S. farmers, and the expanding world market for agricultural products means the farm manager must know world trends, prices and pockets of need. It's important to be active in organizations such as the American Farm Bureau Federation, which distributes information and lobbies for farmers.

The most successful managers will be in demand to run several large farms or to manage the operations of large farm combines. Harold McQueen, a veteran farmer, can hardly wait to get back to his field each year, but he's less eager to face the reams of paperwork involved. "I'm working too hard to survive," says McQueen.[9] But only the hardest-working farmers with the most efficiently managed farms will survive, and they will have the brightest future.

INDUSTRIAL DESIGNER

Job Requirements: Must have a bachelor's degree in industrial design from four- or five-year accredited program to develop and design manufactured goods that are competitive with others on the market, attractive and easy to recycle. Degree in fine arts also acceptable. Must have artistic skills, business sense, ability to work as part of a team to relate products and things to people. Background in art, marketing, aesthetics, humanities, problem solving, manufacturing and materials. Computer literacy essential: Must be highly skilled in using computer-aided design and computer-aided manufacturing (CAD/CAM) software programs. Mechanical ability important. Work requires creativity, imagination, strong color sense, eye for detail and sensitivity to needs of the public. Knowledge of foreign languages helpful. Must be free spirit, yet able to accept direction and business restraints. Must have a portfolio of designs and successful products.

◆ **Salary:**

1991	*2000*
$26,823	**$45,000**
(starting)	(starting)

Inside Track: International competition for the best industrial designers and growing emphasis on the quality and visual appeal of manufactured goods will create significant job growth for industrial designers in 2000. The United States will rely on industrial designers to reestablish its manufacturing position in the world. Another factor: The Industrial Designers Society of America estimates that every dollar a company spends on industrial design results in an average increase in sales of $2,500. Graduates of the top industrial design schools will be on the fastest career track. Among the best schools are the Art Center College of Design, Pasadena; Cleveland Institute of Art; Cranbrook Academy of Art, Bloomfield Hills, Michigan; Illinois Institute of Technology, Chicago; Pratt Institute, Brooklyn; and Rhode Island School of Design, Providence. The fastest-growing design areas in the United States and worldwide, especially in Japan, will be in toys, furniture, medical instruments, cars and environmental products.

Industrial designers are artists, and those with a passion for design and concern about their fellow human beings will be most successful. "Industrial design crosses and blurs the boundaries of art and science, and industrial designers lend a human touch to an otherwise cold landscape," says Gerald B. Hirshberg, vice president of Nissan Design International in San Diego, a division of Japan's Nissan Motor Ltd.[10] The best career path is to start out with a large manufacturing firm and learn the business. Then move to a group of design consultants. The next step is to open your own firm. Industrial design is on the cutting edge of technology and leads to many other avenues, such as architecture, computer software, interior design, marketing and quality control. A proven theory to follow: Form follows function follows fashion follows emotion.

LANDSCAPE ARCHITECT

Job Requirements: Bachelor's degree in landscape architecture from four- or five-year accredited college to design and install functional, beautiful and environmentally sound flowers, shrubs, grass and trees. Master's degree preferred. Most states require licensing, based on results of uniform national examination. To be eligible for licensing, must have college degree and one to four years' experience in the field. Federal government does not require licensing. Background in surveying, landscape design and construction, computer science, structural design and city and regional planning. Must know plant and soil science, geology, design and color theory, meteorology, botany and drafting. Creativity and artistic ability essential. Must be able to work as a team with client, architect, developer and contractor. Able to use computer-aided design (CAD) system to draw detailed plans. Good communications skills, both written and oral. A true love of nature important in this rigorous job.

◆ **Salary:**

1991	*2000*
$23,152 to $28,665	**$35,000 to $42,600**[11]
(starting)	(starting)

Inside Track: Because of the projected increase in new construction and a rapidly growing interest in environmental planning and historic preservation, 5,500 additional landscape architects will be needed by 2000. Landscapers who learn quickly to work within their budgets will be in great demand. Areas of fastest growth will be historic landscape preservation, parks, playgrounds and shopping malls. Employers actively recruiting landscape architects will be government agencies, environmental groups and private developers. Landscaping for residential customers will be a growth area, but it is hard work and doesn't pay well. The best way to get in the field is to spend summers doing grunt work for a local landscaping firm. After you get your degree, get a job with a large landscaping firm that does a variety of work.

Most successful landscape architects own their own businesses. To prepare for that, make sure you have several years of work experience and take marketing and business administration courses. "If you plan to go on your own, first work for a design/building firm," says Peter Wodarz, landscape architect and owner of Milieu Design. "To be successful, you need a quality product that enhances the value of the property and has curb appeal. It's difficult to be both designer and contractor, but the advantage is you can implement your designs from start to finish."

OFFICE/BUSINESS MACHINE REPAIRER

Job Requirements: High school diploma plus at least one year technical training in electronics and electricity at vocational school or community college to repair business machines. Three to six months' training on the job. Additional training in electronics needed to repair computers. Must have background in mathematics, physics, computer programming, data processing equipment maintenance and electrical engineering. Need computer theory, computer math and circuitry theory for computerized equipment. Ability to communicate well with clients while making repairs in business offices and homes. Must be familiar with technical manuals and diagnostic programs for equipment. Up to date on technological changes and maintenance procedures. May be asked to train new workers or clients on machine's use. Outgoing personality helpful.

✦ **Salary:**

_1991_	_2000_
$25,809	**$37,565**

Inside Track: The U.S. Department of Labor projects faster than average growth for these technicians, with 44,000 new jobs being created by the end of the century. As more computers, faxes, printers and duplicating machines are used in homes and offices, demand will increase for repairers. Most jobs are with copier and computer manufacturers, but some large companies have repairers on staff.

It's important first to get work experience, preferably for a large company. To move ahead, you will need to update your technical skills continually by taking advanced courses or degrees. The next step up both professionally and in salary is the job of troubleshooter, helping other technicians for the company diagnose difficult problems, and from there on to management, where salaries often go as high as six figures. With advanced studies in electronics and computer science, you will be able to consult with engineers in designing equipment and developing maintenance procedures.

Sharon E. McCants-Ford, a senior customer service representative for Xerox Corporation, has always been handy, she says, and has good electronic and mechanical aptitudes. "In addition to having technical skills, you have to be people-oriented," says the technician, who goes from account to account repairing copiers. "You can't just walk in and fix a machine. You have to deal with the customer." She's upbeat about the future of her profession: "Machines will always need repairing," she says.[12]

OPERATIONS MANAGER/MANUFACTURING

Job Requirements: Responsible job for qualified person to run manufacturing operations. Must have bachelor's degree in business, engineering or liberal arts, followed by an MBA. Proven work experience as product line supervisor. Certification by American Production and Inventory Control Society. Intensive on-the-job training. Skilled in finance, technology and dealing with people. Orientation in quality of the product and quality control; sensitivity to needs of customer; exposure to global marketplace; awareness of the importance of human resources. Expert in qualitative methods, production, operations, international business, exchange rates, statistics and operations management. Leadership skills important. Must be able to work under pressure from chief executive, colleagues, employees, suppliers and customers. Up to date in latest computer technology for manufacturing, design and business procedures. A personable approach to employees is important.

✦ Salary:

1991	*2000*
$85,000	**$95,000**

Inside Track: Increased production of consumer and industrial products will add 39,000 jobs for industrial production managers by 2000—with good opportunities and excellent salaries going to their supervisors, the operations manager. A new generation of industry leaders can restore the nation's competitive edge in an international marketplace—if they can be found. Demand for top-notch operations executives increased during the recession of the early 1990s and is projected to grow even more in 2000. U.S. manufacturers are aggressive about expanding their shrunken industry, and only the best operations managers will be able to do that.

Success will depend on motivating workers. Those who institute participatory management and a team approach instead of a military command will be most successful in raising productivity, cutting costs and reducing turnover. "Manufacturers are looking for top operations executives," says Richard F. Teerlink, president and chief executive officer of Harley-Davidson. "We can find design engineers and marketing people, but just try to find manufacturing executives."[13] John N. Lauer, executive vice president and chief operations officer of B.F. Goodrich, says his firm "puts a large premium on technology. You also have to be an individual who excels in the context of the team—and the team has to win." American Pfauter, a firm that manufactures gear-producing machinery, has a hard time finding qualified operations executives. "We grow our own," says David W. Goodfellow, president. "We take engineers, send them to an MBA program during work hours, pay for it, invest in them—and wait three to five years for them to develop."

RADIO/TV SERVICE TECHNICIAN

Job Requirements: One to two years' electronic training at junior college, on the job, through correspondence schools or at private or vocational schools required to repair radios, television sets, stereos, VCRs, video cameras, compact disc players and home security systems. Must have background in mathematics, physics, schematic reading, electricity and electronics. Hands-on experience. Apprenticeship with International Brotherhood of Electrical Workers. Up to date in latest computer technology and equipment. Must know how to use voltmeter, signal generator, oscilloscope and frequency counter. Familiarity with manufacturers' service manuals and technical publications. Physical strength needed to repair heavy equipment; physical dexterity and good eye-hand coordination needed to manipulate small parts. Pleasant personality needed to deal with customers.

◆ **Salary:**

1991	*2000*
$17,867 to $25,525	**$24,000 to $35,000**

Inside Track: People love their home electronic equipment as much as they do their cars, and jobs for these service technicians are projected to grow by 5,500 by 2000. Though few people get radios repaired today, the expansion will be in other types of home equipment such as video games, compact disc players, VCRs, audio recorders and microwave ovens.

If you have mechanical ability and the right training, start out by working for a busy repair shop, manufacturing company or retail store. The ticket to success is continuing education in engineering, electronics and math. The next move up from an entry-level job is as supervisor or service manager of a repair shop. To become a troubleshooter and help other repairers solve difficult problems, you will need continuing courses in automatic controls, electronic engineering, television engineering and mathematics. Nearly 25 percent of electronic home equipment repairers own their own businesses, the best way to make money in this field. To do so, you will need to take business, management and marketing courses; keep up with changing technology; acquire a good reputation and have a large roster of satisfied customers.

TRUCK DRIVER

Job Requirements: Qualifications set by state and federal agencies. Must have a valid driver's license from your state and a good driving record. To drive trucks that carry 26,000 pounds—tractor-trailers and large trucks—must have state commercial driver's license. To get commercial license, must pass state written and driving exam. The U.S. Department of Transportation requires truck drivers in interstate commerce to be at least 21 years old, pass a physical exam, have good hearing and 20/40 vision with or without glasses. For some trucking firms, must be at least 25 years old, able to lift heavy objects and have three to five years' experience. All firms require drug and alcohol screening. Must be able to keep good records, have physical and mental endurance, be a courteous driver, remain constantly alert and be able to handle long, solo assignments. Must be up to date on latest safety procedures for the road and for the protection of products transported, a good representative for the company and able to plan own schedule.

◆ **Salary:**

<u>1991</u>	<u>2000</u>
$17,867 to $25,525	**$24,000 to $35,000**

Inside Track: If you have it in your home or office, a truck probably brought it. That will not change in the next century, when an additional 382,000 truck drivers will be needed. Truck drivers are one of the top four workers most in demand in this decade because of projected increases in the amount of freight transported by trucks. This is a job that is being upgraded as more technical skills are needed. You will start out as an extra driver, going on trips with experienced drivers. When assignments open up, you get one. If you do well, you will get better-paying runs and preferred schedules and working conditions.

The good money is in long distance hauls, which are the most demanding physically, emotionally and intellectually. The fastest-growing area is the transportation of fragile and complex electronic and computer equipment. Drivers who have the training to handle high-tech, perishable freight will be paid the best. Those with college degrees have the best future because they usually can move more easily into becoming independent operators. Owner-operators must be skilled in accounting, business, mathematics and maintenance.

Due to the growing national concern about drug abuse by truckers, drivers will have to undergo drug testing frequently. The route to success as a trucker is to augment your driving skills with the latest information on moving and delivering products. "It takes a lot of skill to pick up a 5,000-pound computer and deliver it to the top floor of a large office building," says Ronald B. Rudolph, president of Geo. W. Noffs Moving & Storage.

16

MEDIA AND THE ARTS

Actor/Director/Producer
Advertising and Marketing Account Supervisor
Arts Administrator
Commercial and Graphic Artists
Editor/Writer
Interior Designer
Photographer/Camera Operator
Public Relations Specialist
Radio/TV News Reporter
Reporter/Correspondent

In the coming instant-communications age, professionals in the arts and media will have many excellent and interesting jobs to choose from, jobs with good pay and a future. Technological changes will create new jobs that will require new skills to satisfy Americans' need for information and entertainment. Though some forms of print media will shrink, TV and cable will proliferate. Entertainment in the form of films, movies, videos and compact discs will become one of the major U.S. exports in a global marketplace. The field of media and the arts is for creative, artistic, energetic people with strong business skills.

ACTOR/DIRECTOR/PRODUCER

Job Requirements: Must have college degree and experience even for entry-level jobs in these three fields. Each of these jobs requires talent, creativity, determination and a deep love of entertaining. Must be able to work at a variety of jobs to stay in the field. Must pay your dues in years of hard work to get toehold in profession. Ability to take rejection and hang in for the long haul. Actors need formal training and a love of performing in public. Directors need training, experience, an aesthetic sense, creativity and financial acumen. Production managers need bachelor's degree or two years' on-the-set experience in motion picture or television production to enter assistant directors training program offered by Directors Guild of America and motion picture and television companies. A good reputation as a professional essential for all three. Actors need an interesting physical appearance; directors, ability to motivate others and good connections to get work; producers, strong marketing skills, ability to create a team and financial backers. Skill, perseverance and versatility basic for these extremely glamorous but tough professions in which salaries range from four figures at the bottom to six figures and more at the top.

◆ **Salary:**

1991	*2000*
Actor: $6,614	**$12,000**
to $100,000 +	**to $150,000 +**
Director: $38,587	**$70,000**
to $100,000 +	**to $200,000 +**
Producer: $66,150	**$95,000**
to $100,000 +	**to $200,000 +**

Inside Track: As the entertainment industry expands both nationally and internationally, some 24,000 new jobs will be created for professionals in theater, movie, commercial and cable television and video and audio productions. Fastest-growing opportunities will be in video and cable television productions, not only in entertainment, but in educational presentations for schools and colleges and for training films for businesses. Most jobs are in New York and Los Angeles. Actors and directors should get started in school and community productions. Actors should be listed with a casting agency such as Central Casting and join the Screen Actors Guild or other professional organizations. For actors and directors, one job leads to another, though there are often long dry spells between jobs. The rewards, both psychic and financial, are great for those on the top. Once actors get established, many become directors and, to have even more control, producers. Actors Ron Howard, Jack Nicholson, Robert Redford, Whoopi Goldberg, Demi Moore and Barbra Streisand are actor-producers.

By the 21st century, television will be more than a window on the world; it will be a door. "Future communications are going to become virtually instant," says Brian Rivette, marketing vice president of Call Interactive. "Not only will I have the ability to express my opinion, but I'll be able to learn more editorially from companies about what's happening and express myself to the media, all in an instant."[1] Interactive television will change the work done by actors, directors and TV producers as another element—the public as participants—becomes widespread. Cornell University's Department of Theatre Arts gives interactive theater training on managing a diverse workforce for Xerox Corporation, and these types of projects may be bread and butter in 2000 for actors, directors and producers.

Those artists who can survive the ups and downs of their profession and remain confident will be successful. "I've always felt that I thrive in chaos," says Marla Brown, producer of Arsenio Hall's five-night-a-week television show. "I think that the places I've done the best have been the most chaotic."[2] Her success, she says, comes from starting out with big rather than small production companies. "It's better to be an assistant on 'Good Morning America' or 'The Today Show,' even though at first you will have more responsibility with a small production company."

ADVERTISING AND MARKETING ACCOUNT SUPERVISOR

Job Requirements: Broad liberal arts background with degree in advertising, marketing or business to develop strategies to market products or services. Courses in sociology, psychology, accounting, English, philosophy, speech, journalism and business administration. Well-rounded experience in market research, marketing strategy, promotion, pricing, product development and distribution. Must have strong sales, marketing, creative and oral and written communications skills. Knowledge of foreign languages, cultures and markets for international trade. Ability to motivate and work with team. Mastery of computer and computer-aided graphics. Ability to inspire confidence in colleagues and clients. Must know basic copywriting; print and video production; network, cable and syndicated TV; sales presentation; brand and product research. Most important: experience, enthusiasm, imagination and energy.

✦ **Salary:**

1991	*2000*
$48,041	**$70,000**

Inside Track: Intensifying domestic and foreign competition in the production of consumer goods will lead to the creation of 105,000 new jobs by 2000 for marketing, advertising and public relations managers. The best opportunities are for those who have degrees in business administration or advertising from a good school and who are multicultural and multinational in outlook. If you're creative and communicate well, if you look at a product and immediately have ideas how to sell it, this is the field for you. As mass circulation print media—newspapers and magazines—and network TV erode as major markets, you will have to create new methods of delivering your clients' message in the next century. Most jobs are in New York on Madison Avenue, where some 13,000 commercials are made for television each year, and those in charge of producing them are paid well.

Start out with an internship and get experience in local and national advertising and marketing campaigns. Get a job with a firm or agency large enough to have a strong management training program, one that includes international marketing and the latest high-tech computer training. Get experience in copywriting and market research. Your creativity and financial knowledge will position you for promotion in the firm and will make you a prime candidate for job openings as account supervisor.

The areas projected to grow the fastest in this decade: consumer services, content analysis of consumer interviews, marketing to children, international financial marketing and marketing the industries of data processing and computers, business services, radio and television and motor vehicles. Internationally, opportunities for new accounts will expand in the European Community. Advertising in these countries is expected to increase by 10 percent or more annually. "Wacky humor is in . . . and boring products are out," the experts say. "Dare to be offensive or risk losing your viewers, listeners and readers."[3] Despite their aloofness from "commercialism," law firms, physicians, dentists and graduate schools will increasingly use marketing and advertising to attract and retain clients.

A fast-growing field will be brand management. Brands are the lifeblood of marketing and advertising supervisors, and every product has a manager. The companies that will thrive in 2000 are those whose brands connect with people, says Fred Posner, director of research and marketing for N.W. Ayer. "Companies will have to turn their brand name products, whether clothing, airlines or food, into a comfortable and reliable friend . . . something people will view as an oasis of clarity in a challenging and stressful world," Posner says.[4] Salaries for brand managers range from $70,000 to $100,000 and up. Most have MBAs. To get on this track, start out as an assistant in the marketing department of a consumer goods firm and learn its brands. Then, move from company to company or from agency to agency until you get the top slot. "Most brand managers are miniature chief executives who live or die by the brand they represent," says Miles L. McKie, managing director of Russell Reynolds Associates, an international executive search firm.[5]

ARTS ADMINISTRATOR

Job Requirements: Bachelor's degree in fine arts or liberal arts plus graduate work in management, finance or business to run arts programs as efficient businesses. MBA preferred. Expertise in financial and facility management, grant writing, computer programming, visual and performing arts, operational organization, marketing, development, public relations, communications, booking, scheduling and arts presentation. Advanced degree in arts administration preferred. Ability to deal with colleagues, employees, artists, business executives and volunteers. Flexibility and creativity in putting together programs that work.

✦ **Salary:**

1991	*2000*
$20,000	**$50,000**
(starting)	(starting)

Inside Track: Art is a big business in the United States and is projected to grow dramatically in the next decade locally, nationally and internationally. Arts management is a new profession that will expand in the future in view of reduced government funding to the arts. Agencies, centers and institutions will need to be well run in order to stay in business. Arts administrators will be in demand to make sure the groups get funded and are run on a financially sound basis. These professionals also will be expected to get exposure for artists and to expand the audience for arts. At the same time, national museums are expanding or renovating facilities and hiring new managers. Many who work for government, community and private arts groups handle million-dollar budgets. Though starting salaries are low, executives of major museums command six-figure salaries. The demands of the profession are extremely varied. John Hawarth, assistant commissioner of the New York City Department of Cultural Affairs, directed the automation of Big Apple arts organizations to speed subscription sales and box office transactions. "We've installed more than $1.5 million in computer systems," says Hawarth, who has an MBA and a background in the arts. He has a staff of 60 and a budget of $160 million.[6]

The area of arts administration that will grow fastest in the 21st century is in linking the business and artistic communities. Across America, city councils and businesses have discovered that the arts are good for the economy, especially for downtown revitalization. "We use the arts as an impetus to bring people downtown," says Dian Magie, executive director of the Tucson/Pima Arts Council in Arizona. "We work with owners of vacant storefronts to put art in their windows and with shopping malls to help attract and develop retail outlets." Robert L. Lynch of the National Assembly of Local Arts Agencies gives this straightforward advice: "If you want a job, go west, but there are jobs everywhere. You have to have a love for the arts. Just being a manager is not enough to cut it. You have to have a reason for working late every night, and it's not a field you get rich in."

COMMERCIAL AND GRAPHIC ARTISTS

Job Requirements: Must have undergraduate degree in fine arts and demonstrated ability to create artwork for print and electronic media. Some jobs available for those with two-year associate degree if work experience is varied and extensive. Technical skills in handmade, computer-generated and print graphics. Must have talent, confidence and ability to market work. Some background in business, especially marketing. Extensive portfolio demonstrating a range of ability and professionalism. Must be able to communicate ideas, emotions and thoughts visually in commercially profitable way.

◆ **Salary:**

1991	*2000*
$27,562	**$35,000**[7]

Inside Track: Employment of visual artists will grow by 58,000 by the year 2000 as the demand grows for commercial and graphic professionals to create art, illustrations and design for advertising agencies, publishing, business and multimedia organizations. The field has a glamorous image, but the work is demanding and stressful. In the information age of 2000, increasing emphasis will be on visual appeal in product design, advertising, marketing and television. Those who have the best artistic techniques and who can easily and skillfully use high-tech computers to design will be in demand. But no matter your training or background, your portfolio is your resume and calling card. This is a profession where having a specialty heightens your chances for success, especially if you work for an advertising agency, magazine, newspaper or television station. But most designers are freelance, where hours are your own but pressure is constant to acquire and retain clients. From the very beginning of your career, earn a good reputation by always meeting deadlines and turning in quality work. Computers have replaced such tools as pencils and paste to lay out and test designs, patterns and colors, so you will have to be on top of the latest computer technology. "Keep up with the trends in your field by reading trade magazines and as many publications as possible to see what's actually being used," says Judie Anderson, a successful illustrator. "Remember, you only get three seconds to catch the viewer's eye."

A hot area for commercial artists in 2000 will be animation, to satisfy a growing hunger by Americans, Europeans and Asians for animated cartoons such as "The Simpsons." The movie *Who Framed Roger Rabbit* generated a worldwide interest in animation, says Milt Vallas, vice president of Pacific Rim Productions. Then came Disney's *Duck Tales*, which, Vallas says, "bridged the gap between high-quality, full-length feature animation and television animation. Now, there is a huge demand for high-quality, animated TV shows."[8]

EDITOR/WRITER

Job Requirements: College degree in journalism or English. Internship important at publishing, communications or advertising firms. Master's degree an asset. Experience in writing and editing in college, in the community or as a stringer for larger publication. Perfect grammar and command of the English language. Computer literacy important: Writers must know word processing; editors must know how to use electronic equipment to edit, lay out and design pages and to transmit materials to printer. Both writers and editors need a well-rounded background and interest in history, politics, sociology, psychology, demographics, current trends and international affairs. Business expertise increasingly important. Must be able to gain confidence of sources and meet deadlines. Able to communicate well with colleagues and work as a team. Reputation for ethical behavior and integrity essential. Willingness to work long, hard hours and to go anywhere a story takes you. Must question all information given you and be able to do research, fact checking and copy editing. The most important requisites: undying curiosity about everything that's happening and pride in an attractive, interesting and effective product.

◆ **Salary:**

1991	*2000*
$35,059	**$50,000**[9]

Inside Track: Some 55,000 salaried writers and editors will be needed in publishing, communications and advertising. Intense competition for the best jobs will continue into the next century. The fastest-growing source of jobs will be corporations that need writers or editors to handle their internal and external publications. Editing and writing jobs also will proliferate at nonprofit organizations, whose publications attract and retain members, inspire donors and disseminate the group's message. Technical writing—explaining how a product or service works—will be another excellent area to work in. Jobs will open up in firms that offer on-line databases for scientific, medical and business subjects, and writers and editors will be needed to provide abstract articles for easy reading. Other good opportunities will be at specialty newspapers, magazines and technical publications. Financial writers and editors also will be in demand.

Publishing is a rapidly changing industry because of economic pressures and high-tech innovations. In the future, fewer people in the industry will be doing more work. Increasingly, editors and writers will be freelancers, working from their homes anywhere in the world, linked to their publishers by modems. Freelancers will have opportunities as contract workers in different media outlets that are increasingly reluctant to hire full-time employees and pay them benefits. Salaried professionals usually start at low wages—especially in book publishing. Earnings pick up after five years, though average salaries remain low. What drives the writers and editors who do not make a lot of money—though the successful ones do—is a love of the printed word, of telling a story, informing the public, bringing to life a person, place, event or idea. It takes that kind of commitment to be a success, because editing and writing are demanding fields where your ego is often up for grabs—and sometimes loses. Writers who are the most persistent will be the most successful; so will editors who can guide and encourage writers.

"Developing a specialty, along with high-level writing, reporting and computer skills are keys to success," says Jean Gaddy Wilson, who follows publishing trends and is executive director of New Directions for News at the University of Missouri. Most jobs, she says, will be "less than full-time because of inroads of automation." But those with experience and finely honed skills will get them.

INTERIOR DESIGNER

Job Requirements: Bachelor's or master's degree in interior design or in fine arts needed to plan and furnish interiors of private homes, buildings, commercial offices, restaurants, hotels and theaters. Must be skilled in computer-aided design (CAD). Must have formal credentials such as advanced diploma from two- or three-year professional interior design school. Courses in art, art history, principles of design, designing, sketching, textiles, drafting, sculpture, architecture and basic engineering. One to three years' on-the-job training. Must know how to work with clients to develop designs, drawings and specifications for interior construction, furnishings, lighting and finishes that please client and are affordable. Good artistic sense needed to coordinate colors, select furniture, floor coverings, curtains. Must know governmental building codes, including accessibility for the disabled. Expertise in plumbing, electricity, heating and air-conditioning essential. State licensing becoming more universal and can be stringent. Professional membership in groups such as Industrial Designers Society of America or American Society for Interior Designers a plus. Must have good business sense, ability to market yourself and inspire confidence. Creativity, strong color sense, eye for detail, sense of balance and proportion and aesthetic sense important.

◆ **Salary:**

1991	*2000*
$31,972 +	**$47,000 +**

Inside Track: Job opportunities will expand for interior designers in 2000, but only those who have exceptional talent, formal preparation and strong determination will thrive in this profession. The proliferation of state licensing, with requirements of master's degrees, internships and years of practice—some as long as eight years—upgrade this field dramatically, resulting in higher salaries and higher client fees. The way to move ahead is to work for an established firm and join a professional association to increase your visibility and contacts. With experience, you will be able to move up to chief designer, design department head, general supervisor and then to open your own firm. Design fashions change rapidly, so keep up to date by continuing your education in trends and in new computer technology: It will be common practice in the 1990s to show your clients a variety of suggested designs by computer, changing an item here and there by pressing a button.

The way to make money is to open your own business, so make sure you have the requisite business management and marketing skills. You will also need a stable of furniture finishers, upholsterers, drapery specialists and painters you can depend on. To attract and retain clients and referrals, establish strong professional relationships and easy communication with your customers.

After maintaining the status quo in household furnishings for so long, interior design is ready to take a quantum leap into radical innovations. "Right now, there's very little encouragement to design anything new," says Kevin Walz, a New York interior designer. "I think this period of time is about being safe. We're at the end of a century, and the design that was produced at the beginning of the century is a lot more daring than it is now."[10] But dramatic breakthroughs are expected in the 21st century.

PHOTOGRAPHER/CAMERA OPERATOR

Job Requirements: Few formal requirements for this field outside of a high school education and creativity. College degree in journalism or communications helpful. Must know how to use cameras and attachments and have knowledge of lighting. Must be able to develop and edit own film if necessary. Experience in camera store or photo, movie or television studio helpful. On-the-job training needed to acquire technical expertise. Background in history of photography and operation of video, television and movie cameras. Must be up to date in latest electronic equipment, computerized databases and new technology such as digital still cameras and photo-compact disc systems. Must have good eyesight, artistic ability and manual dexterity. Must be patient, willing to take risks, able to handle detail work. Knowledge of mathematics, physics and chemistry important. Must be dependable and hard working; some business skills needed. Ability to empathize with subjects, strong curiosity and a fresh way of looking at things important.

◆ **Salary:**

1991	*2000*
$25,357	**$35,882**

Inside Track: There will be 20,000 new jobs for photographers and camera operators by 2000 as visual images gain importance in education, communications and entertainment nationally and internationally. Photojournalism will remain highly competitive, with jobs only for the best, but opportunities will be plentiful for camera operators in network, local and cable television and motion picture productions.

If you're interested in becoming a photographer, start as an intern or assistant in a photography studio that does fashion, commercial and portrait photography. For newspaper photographers, work for your local community paper and be a stringer for other publications until you have earned a reputation as a good and dependable professional. A fast-growing and lucrative field for photographers is biomedical photography. TV and movie camera operators also must start out as interns or assistants to pick up technical know-how. The best opportunities for camera operators are in cable television. Almost half of all photographers and camera operators are self-employed, so courses in business and marketing are essential for success. Your portfolio, credits and reputation are your most important assets. It's important to know copyright laws so your work is not stolen or duplicated without your permission.

High-tech equipment will radicalize photography: You will have to learn to transmit photos over wire services and to call up work by other photographers on a computerized database such as the Associated Press's

Electronic Darkroom. You will need to know how to crop, size and touch up photos electronically, and then send them to be printed through systems such as Scitex. Camera operators will find it more difficult to operate on a freelance basis, though you will be able to be part of pickup crews for special productions. With the knowledge you gain behind the camera, you can move up to director or producer—where the big money is. Both camera operators and photographers should be aware that the nature of their profession—the use of the camera itself— could change overnight. "Hybrid imaging systems in general and photo CD in particular are an end game," says Kay Whitmore, chief executive officer of Eastman Kodak Company. "They're the optimal solution for those who want high-quality photos in an electronic environment."[11]

PUBLIC RELATIONS SPECIALIST

Job Requirements: Bachelor's degree in journalism, communications, public relations, marketing or English to help organizations present goals, policies and news to the public. Must have served internship or have previous experience in television, broadcast or print media. On-the-job training provided by employers. Must be creative, articulate and energetic. Computer skills, including desktop publishing, a must. Must have finger on pulse of the public in order to communicate effectively. Being able to write well is a top requirement. For corporate public relations, background in company's business and in science, engineering or finance helpful. Educational background in organizational communication, advertising, political science, psychology and sociology. Need outgoing personality and confidence. Accreditation by Public Relations Society of America after five years' experience and passing mark on written and oral test. Important to be able to maintain good relationships and establish trust with media.

✦ **Salary:**

1991	*2000*
$31,972	**$50,000**

Inside Track: Communications is a growth industry in the instant-information age of 2000, and by that year, 14,000 additional jobs will be created for public relations (PR) specialists. Most of the demand will come from the business community, and it will be for well-educated and experienced professionals to present the corporation's best face to the public—especially in view of the projected public airing of environmental issues and suspected corporate polluters. But the shift will be away from in-house staff to outside agencies to handle public information, investor relations, public affairs, corporate communications, political campaigns and crisis management. "Public relations is a growth business but with caveats," says Joseph Epley, head of Epley Associates, a PR firm in Charlotte, North Carolina. "Many of the larger corporations have downsized their PR departments. . . . There has been a direct shift away from working in big cities and providing only publicity services. Small firms, like mine, which offer a total communications package, are growing in smaller markets. From a personal perspective, things look good."[12]

At corporations, PR staffs focus on community relations, internal relations, government services, speech writing and damage control. The latter is a lucrative area: Crisis management, helping large corporations deal with the public in emergency situations, is a specialty that will command six-figure salaries. Nonprofit organizations will be another major and satisfying employer of PR people. "When I've helped our activists make front-page news across the country on such issues as a national energy policy, global warming, protecting national forests and parks, I go home satisfied," says Paul Larmer, media representative for the Sierra Club, headquartered in San Francisco.[13]

Start out by writing for your school publication or for local radio or television stations. Develop a portfolio of published material, tapes, slide presentations and computer-created materials to help in finding a job. Large public relations firms have established training programs and a variety of accounts, so they are the best place to get needed experience. Pay your dues by learning to write appealing and informative press releases, to link your clients with members of the media for interviews and background information, and to use desktop publishing to print pamphlets, corporate reports and other material. Your next move might be to become an account executive at a smaller firm with a specialty that interests you. Somewhere down the line, you may want to start your own business, but first you must establish credibility in the field, have a strong marketing plan, financial backing and potential clients.

RADIO/TV NEWS REPORTER

Job Requirements: Bachelor's degree in journalism or technical school education. Must have experience in news gathering, broadcasting, production or research. Professional audition tapes, good appearance, effective delivery and appealing style important. Must be able to communicate easily and accurately, especially under stress. Pleasant voice, good timing, correct pronunciation and perfect English usage needed to instill confidence in viewers or listeners. Background in public speaking, drama, political science, sports and music helpful. Community involvement, willingness to relocate frequently and flexibility about work schedule important. Self-confidence a basic requisite.

◆ **Salary:**

1991	*2000*
$28,972	**$44,000**[14]
(starting)	(starting)

Inside Track: As new radio and TV stations are licensed and cable TV stations continue to proliferate, some 11,000 jobs will be created for on-air reporters—the people who present the news rather than gather it. For entry-level broadcasters, radio—especially FM stations—will provide the best opportunities because more radio than television stations hire beginners. This job is considered glamorous, and competition for it is keen, but broadcast reporters who are determined and persevere will be able to advance in their careers, and some will make it to the top slots that pay extraordinarily well.

To start out in radio, first get an internship; then apply for jobs in smaller communities, where turnover is high. From there, position yourself to move to a better-paying job in a larger community—and keep moving to cities with bigger audiences. For TV, the road is a bit rockier, but the rewards are greater in exposure and salary. Take any kind of job at any station just to get on the inside. Work as a production secretary or assistant, researcher or reporter. When you feel you know the industry from the inside—perhaps in a year or two—apply for a job as on-air announcer at a television station in a small community. Once there, gain experience, exposure, ratings and videotapes showing what you can do. Use that job as a base to build on and keep moving to larger stations in larger cities.

As a radio or TV broadcaster on a fast track, it's helpful to have a specialty, such as politics, news, sports, entertainment or weather. To move ahead, don't confine yourself to broadcasting the news: Do special reports and documentaries about issues that concern people the most. Most people in this field do not become top stars, but even those at lower levels are well paid and are considered celebrities. Keep in mind that station managers, your bosses, decide whom they want to have on air and for how long. You will be at the mercy of their decisions and what they perceive the public wants.

REPORTER/CORRESPONDENT

Job Requirements: Bachelor's degree in journalism or English, experience on college publication or as a stringer for community paper and newspaper internship needed for entry-level job to gather information and write articles for newspapers. Master's degree helpful. Skill in using computer to write and transmit stories. Background in politics, sociology, psychology and economics an asset. Must have "nose for news" to pursue stories of interest to public. Must also be objective and succinct in reporting. Concern about the public, commitment to getting the whole story, high ethical standards and a strong sense of fairness important. Able to handle stress and meet deadlines. Mobility and flexibility in work hours important. Basic requirement: excellent writing skills.

◆ **Salary:**

_1991_	_2000_
$16,537 to $60,637	**$30,000 to $100,000**[15]

Inside Track: While newspapers remain highly profitable, daily circulation has stagnated and staffs have been downsized. However, there will be 12,000 new full-time jobs created, most of them on newspapers in small towns and suburbs. There will be even more opportunities for freelance reporters and correspondents—the employment trend at most newspapers. Freelancers with newspaper experience or impressive internships at major papers will be hired by big city papers to cover local news and suburbs, supplementing the work of the staff, often on a one-year contract basis. The best freelancers will ultimately be hired as full-time employees, so starting out this way—despite the lack of benefits, expense accounts or job security—is beneficial.

Reporters like to report, and the more you do of it the better for your professional advancement. Go beyond your particular beat and write for various sections of the paper. Your versatility will bring you to the attention of the editors, and your value will be enhanced. Try to develop dependable sources so you will be the first to get the story. Above all, know the city you're in and where to verify information. Accuracy often makes the difference in how fast you move ahead. Check and recheck your work before transmitting it to your editor. The old advice—"If your mother says she loves you, check it out!"—is still sound. After a few years on general assignment, ask for a specific beat, such as the police, courts, education, City Hall, health, business or sports. Most papers will expand their financial coverage in the coming decade, so opportunities will be opening in the business section of newspapers. Try to switch beats frequently during your career to get a variety of experience.

Overseas assignments, which are diminishing as electronic communications replace on-site reporters, are plum jobs that go to correspondents who have proven themselves as professionals. Another step up the ladder is to become a columnist, which usually pays better than reporting assignments. Newspaper columnists write about whatever interests them, and some of them earn six-figure incomes. Top writers also often move into posts as editors and managers at newspapers. "Passion and tenacity, in equal doses, will make you a successful newspaper reporter or correspondent," says Jean Gaddy Wilson, executive director, New Directions for News at the University of Missouri.

17

SALES AND PERSONAL SERVICES

Cosmetologist
Insurance Salesperson
Retail Salesperson
Wholesale Sales Representative

This segment of the service industry will provide 75 percent of the job growth in the service-producing sector, according to federal projections. It is the field for people who enjoy dealing directly with clients and customers, who know how to sell but not oversell, who know how to give personal services yet remain professional. The mammoth field of retail trade alone will add the astounding sum of 2,486,000 new workers by the year 2000. Sales and personal services will have more job openings than any other industrial category—but just how good the job is, how much opportunity there is for advancement and how high the wages are will depend on your skills, education and experience.

COSMETOLOGIST

Job Requirements: All states require licensing, but qualifications vary from state to state to shampoo, cut and style hair. In general, must be at least 16 years old, graduate of state-licensed cosmetology school and pass physical exam. Courses ranging from 1,200 to 2,000 hours available at public high schools and private vocational schools. One- to two-year apprenticeship training also acceptable for licensing. Must pass state written and skills examination. Finger dexterity, sense of form and artistry and desire to help people look more attractive are basic. Some business skills needed. Must enjoy dealing with the public, be flexible about following clients' directions and keep up to date on latest fashions and beauty techniques. Willingness to work long hours, evenings and weekends, plus physical strength to stand for extended periods of time. Outgoing personality, ability to communicate with clients, to carry on casual conversations and to make client feel attractive and confident.

◆ **Salary:**

1991	*2000*
$13,325	**$18,000**[1]

Inside Track: The growing demand for cosmetologists—aging baby boomers and yuppies want to look good—will create 82,000 new jobs for cosmetologists by 2000. The best opportunities will be in part-time jobs, which have always been an attraction of the field. Small, independent beauty salons and boutiques will continue to have job opportunities for the most outstanding hairstylists, but the largest growth in employment will be at national and international hairstyling franchises featuring fast and inexpensive haircuts. Starting salaries are very low, mostly because the work is part-time, but you can increase your income by giving the best service and getting the best tips. Full-time workers with loyal clienteles can expect to average $50,000 plus tips. With experience and some business background, you will be able to move up into supervisory positions, managing one salon in a franchise, then becoming a regional manager, and then opening your own shop.

"Start out with a department store beauty salon because you will be eligible for benefits and the variety of customers gets you started the right way," advises Fred Piattoni, veteran hairstylist and executive director of the Chicago Cosmetology Association. Be ready for changes in techniques, fashions and equipment, he urges, and stay on top of the field through continuing education. He notes that "the coming shortage of hairdressers will make the field wide open for good, qualified cosmetologists."

INSURANCE SALESPERSON

Job Requirements: Some high school graduates hired and trained, but college graduates preferred to sell life, casualty and health insurance. Must have previous business experience, preferably in sales, and educational background in finance, mathematics, accounting, economics, business law, government and business administration. Courses needed in psychology, sociology, public speaking and sales techniques. Understanding of various financial products on the market. Computer literacy essential to keep track of customers, policies and latest information on insurance sales and regulations. Must be licensed by state. Continuing education mandatory in some states. Certification available in most specialties. Intensive on-the-job training. A warm and compassionate manner essential. Must be enthusiastic, outgoing, confident, disciplined, hard working, able to communicate well and able to inspire confidence.

◆ **Salary:**

1991	*2000*
$54,000	**$86,400**

Inside Track: The graying of America and rising incomes will create a larger pool of insurance customers—and more jobs for people to sell to them. Though the insurance industry is under close scrutiny and is regrouping, sales opportunities will increase by 58,000 jobs. The best jobs will be won by ambitious people who enjoy selling and who are experts in all areas of insurance, investments and financial services. In order to be competitive, you will have to continue your education by taking pertinent college courses and attending institutes, seminars and workshops sponsored by insurance organizations. Most jobs will be with brokerage firms that do not sell for a particular company but place policies for clients at various companies at a competitive price.

It's important to qualify for certification in your specialty, such as underwriter, financial consultant, health underwriter, insurance counselor, professional insurance agent, property casualty underwriter and liability underwriter. You will have to be adept in marketing yourself to build a strong, loyal following. And then you must stay in touch with your clients to make sure that you don't lose them. With experience and proven sales ability, your next step up is as sales manager, agency superintendent or as an executive in the company. Many good salespeople prefer to stay in sales because they can earn six-figure incomes from commissions. The fastest-growing insurance market will be selling to the women and minorities who will make up the diverse workforce of 2000.

Kathleen Chavira, an insurance agent and registered representative for the Prudential Insurance Company of America in Fresno, California, learned the profession in a special, hands-on career development training program at the firm that encourages women and minorities to be successful in insurance. "The sky's the limit—I can go as far as I want to go because the financial opportunities are there," says Chavira, who has a bachelor's degree from Stanford University, an MBA from the University of California at Los Angeles and experience in banking. The agent says women and Hispanics are the bulk of her sales. "Corporations have a responsibility to demonstrate their interest in women and minorities, not just because it's the right thing to do, but because it's good business."[2]

RETAIL SALESPERSON

Job Requirements: Must have at least a high school diploma. No experience necessary for entry-level job. Associate degree from community college, bachelor's degree from four-year institution and graduate degree in retail sales increasingly important for better jobs. College education essential for management jobs and training programs. Computer literacy required. Must have pleasant personality and appearance, knowledge of mathematics, sales techniques and marketing. Flexibility in work schedule, willingness to serve the public and ability to communicate important. Familiarity with security procedures. Must remember that the customer is always right.

◆ **Salary:**

1991	*2000*
$13,781 to $18,522	**$20,000 to $27,000**

Inside Track: Jobs in retail sales are expected to have a dramatic spurt in the 1990s, when 922,000 additional retail salespeople will be needed. Job prospects will be excellent for full-time, part-time and temporary workers. But getting a top job selling expensive merchandise at the highest commission will be very competitive. Most opportunities will be not in large department stores, but in specialty chains, mass merchandisers and discount stores. At entry level, retail sales is low paying, career advancement is slow, and benefits such as health insurance and pensions are scarce. But college graduates who start out in management jobs at stores and get exposure to various aspects of training will eventually be promoted and make good salaries. Salespeople with marketing skills, who know how to promote merchandise and attract customer interest, will move forward most quickly. Success in this occupation requires determination and long hours of work. In the early part of your career, you may have to support yourself and your family on very low wages, but the payoff comes when you finally move into positions of buyer, supervisor, branch manager, regional manager and, ultimately, corporate executive.

"There's a great concern about getting qualified people," said Jack Fraser, vice president of human resources and operations for the National Retail Federation, a trade association based in New York. "There's a shortage of entry-level sales associates. The lack of first-time workers and the increased number of fast-food service jobs will affect general merchandise stores. There are fewer people and more jobs."[3] Breck Ray, senior vice president of the executive search firm Paul R. Ray & Company, based in Fort Worth, says, "There will be jobs at entry level and for store managers. Specialty retail stores need district managers and regional managers. Unlike department stores, they have training programs for entry-level workers to move them up rapidly." Computer technology will change the way sales are made and recorded, stock records are kept and merchandise is ordered, so computer literacy is becoming an essential for large retail stores. You may be selling merchandise through a computer network to customers in their homes or helping customers visualize through computers what various styles will look like. Whatever the technical innovations, it will still be up to you to make the sale.

"The most important thing I get across when I train salespeople is to provide backup, service and consultation," says Dirk Beveridge, of Beveridge Business Systems, an international sales and marketing consulting firm. "Identify the needs of the customer. Don't just sell the product and get out. That's the old image of sales. It just doesn't work anymore."[4]

WHOLESALE SALES REPRESENTATIVE

Job Requirements: Undergraduate degree increasingly important, but previous sales experience and impressive sales record may substitute to market products to manufacturers, wholesale and retail establishments and government agencies. Skills needed vary by product and market, but basic requirements are ability to sell and thorough knowledge of market. To sell industrial products, must have degree in science or engineering plus experience. Intensive two-year training to learn production and distribution of product. Must be current in technological changes, new merchandise and changing needs of customers. Must be self-starter, goal-oriented, persuasive, dependable and able to work independently. Pleasant personality, problem-solving and mathematical skills, ability to take rejection and willingness to work long hours on the road essential. Background in international markets, culture and language important. Organizational, accounting, marketing and administration skills needed.

◆ **Salary:**

_1991_	_2000_
$27,364	**$40,000**

Inside Track: Manufacturers' and wholesale sales representatives will add 434,000 new jobs by 2000 when the economy is expected to expand and the demand for goods to increase worldwide. These professionals will be an integral factor in determining whether the United States regains its foothold as a chief supplier of goods both at home and abroad. Best opportunities in 2000 will be selling food products, motor vehicles and parts, hardware, plumbing, electrical and electronic goods worldwide. Representatives who know their products inside and out, understand the art of the deal, are willing to keep trying until a sale is made and then to follow up with technical support will be the most successful. Most firms pay salary plus commission. A few pay straight commission or salary only. In order to advance, to be a sales leader and to keep current in your field, attend trade shows and read professional publications.

Though computer technology will make it faster to present ideas to your customers throughout the world, going in person, spending time, establishing a one-to-one relationship will still be the best way to sell. Once you have a good sales record, demonstrate leadership ability and sell yourself to your bosses, you will be in line to advance to sales manager or other executive positions. Additional credentials, such as an MBA and continuing education courses in marketing and business, will help move you along more quickly. Making sure you are prepared to function in a global marketplace—to sell auto gears or computer software in Japan and Belgium as well as in Montana—will be your door of opportunity. In order to be a successful manufacturers' and wholesale sales representative in the 21st century, you will have to have world-class abilities. "Remember, you will be competing against Chinese, Russians, Poles, English, Brazilians and Kenyans," says Roger E. Levien, vice president of strategy for Xerox Corporation in Stamford, Connecticut. "You will have to do a better job and raise your skills."[5]

18

SCIENCE

Agricultural Scientist
Biological Scientist
Chemist
Environmental Scientist
Food Scientist
Physicist/Astronomer

The shortage of American scientists is approaching a crisis as the number of college students majoring in science continues to dwindle. The real crunch is expected to come in the year 2000, when some 50,000 jobs will open up for scientists. While supply is dwindling, demand is increasing, especially for scientists who specialize in genetic engineering, the environment and outer space. Anyone interested in the science professions will be in an ideal job situation: Scientists will be in short supply, and demand for these professionals will be great.

AGRICULTURAL SCIENTIST

Job Requirements: Bachelor's degree in agricultural science from accredited college for entry-level job to develop ways of improving quantity and quality of farm crops and livestock. Master's degree for sales, production management, inspection, regulatory and other nonresearch work. Doctorate for college teaching or research. Background in biology, chemistry, physics and engineering. Studies in environmental management increasingly important to apply biotechnology advances. Marketing and production experience for jobs in companies that produce food products or agricultural chemicals. Must be able to work independently and as team member and to communicate effectively.

◆ **Salary:**

1991	*2000*
$23,835	**$45,000**[1]
(starting)	(starting)

Inside Track: Good employment prospects are expected because the number of students majoring in agricultural science has decreased while the need for these professionals has grown: By 2000, an additional 5,200 jobs will be created. There is a mistaken belief that because the number of farmers is diminishing jobs for agricultural scientists also will disappear. But the opposite is true: Biotechnology is increasing the need for these specialists on a global basis, especially experts in applying recombinant DNA to agriculture. Most agricultural scientists work with biological scientists to manage research and development programs or marketing or production operations for companies that produce food products, agricultural chemicals, supplies and machinery. The fastest-growing area—and the most lucrative—will be in consulting to business firms and government agencies worldwide.

Breakthroughs in molecular biology will change the way agricultural scientists work in the 1990s and beyond. Genetic engineering will produce healthier crops and animals. Many of the new technologies will be controversial, such as injecting cows with the hormone bovine somatrophen to increase their milk production, or using ionizing radiation to process food. Growing concern about fertilizers and disposal of waste materials means you will have to be aware of your impact on the environment. Inventions in this profession will result in great financial benefits: Wool harvesting, for instance, without shearing—through the use of a natural protein—has an estimated $100 million global world market.[2]

Most agricultural scientists start out specializing in areas such as animal, dairy, poultry, agronomy, horticulture, soil analysis, entomology, agriculture or food. (See Food Scientist, this section.) To move ahead, a doctorate is necessary, says Allan Goecker, assistant dean of Purdue University's School of Agriculture. With a PhD, Dr. Goecker says, you will be qualified to conduct and manage research. "The most dramatic and fast-changing area in 2000 will be the genetic engineering of plants and animals." The scientists who will advance most rapidly into management and desirable research slots, he says, will be those with proven skills in business and resource management.

BIOLOGICAL SCIENTIST

Job Requirements: Bachelor's degree in biological science for entry-level job studying living organisms and their relationship to environment. Master's degree for applied research, management, sales and service. Doctorate for independent research, teaching and administrative posts. Background in biology, medicine, pharmacy, botany, zoology, physics, biochemistry, microbiology, physiology and agriculture. Must be highly trained in computer uses and methods, especially for cutting-edge biotechnological research and inventions. Ability to sell ideas, work independently and as part of a team. In addition to technical skills, most important quality: basic curiosity about everything.

◆ **Salary:**

_1991_	_2000_
$33,075	**$50,000**

Inside Track: The increased demand for genetic and biological research to discover new medical procedures and life-saving drugs and to preserve and clean up the environment will result in 15,000 jobs for biological scientists. Though these professionals traditionally work as aquatic biologists, biochemists, botanists, microbiologists, physicists and zoologists, the fastest-growing area will be in genetic and biotechnical research for food, medical and pharmaceutical manufacturing firms. Teaching is another growing area because of the emphasis in the United States on science education and the need for science teachers at all educational levels. Health-related areas are expected to experience a surge in employment opportunities.

About two-fifths of all biological scientists do research, and biotechnologists will be on the cutting edge of change in the most lucrative field: The market capitalization of the ten largest U.S. genetic engineering firms hit $12 billion in 1991. Among the genetic drugs developed are Interferon for hepatitis and cancer and Epogen to stimulate red blood production in AIDS patients.[3] The geographical areas with the most opportunities in biotechnology will be Bethesda (Maryland), Boston, Los Angeles, New York, San Diego and San Francisco. "The most rapidly growing jobs are for specialists in biotechnology," says Dr. John Kopchick, professor and head of the molecular biology division of Edison Animal Biotechnology Center at Ohio University. Those with bachelor's degrees, he says, will find plentiful employment as technologists in industry; those with master's degrees will be able to start out in research; those with doctorates will be able to lead research teams. "Genetic engineering and biotechnology are the hot options," Dr. Kopchick says. "There will be many good opportunities for scientists who follow the old hard work ethic in industry, government and universities."

Though dramatic biotech products will be developed more rapidly in the future, most biological scientists spend years bringing their projects to fruition. Since 1970, Dr. Timothy Tricas, a sensory neurobiologist at Washington University School of Medicine in St. Louis, has studied the electrosensory systems sharks use for courtship and reproduction. He hopes eventually that his research on the shark's production of certain hormones to locate mates will have "some relevance" to human-based receptor systems and to human fertility.[4]

CHEMIST

Job Requirements: Must be graduate of four-year chemistry program at accredited college or university for entry-level job to develop new chemical processes and products. Master's degree for research; doctorate for teaching at university level. Must have broad background in analytical, inorganic or physical chemistry and physics. Laboratory experience and independent research required. Competence in building lab apparatus and performing experiments. Computer literacy important to do research and analysis. Must be patient, dedicated, careful of details and self-motivating. Basic requirement: fascination with properties, composition and structure of matter and laws governing combination of elements and reactions of substances.

◆ **Salary:**

_1991_	_2000_
$33,000[5]	**$64,000**
(starting)	(starting)

Inside Track: There will be exceptional job opportunities in this field, with 13,000 positions created for chemists by 2000. The number of people earning degrees in chemistry is not enough to meet the projected demand. The fastest-growing areas will be pharmaceuticals, biotechnology and environmental protection. Entry-level workers usually start out analyzing or testing products for chemical, medical or pharmaceutical manufacturers. The next step up can be working in technical sales or as a technician in a research lab. Advanced degrees, continual updating of skills, attendance at conventions and seminars and familiarity with the latest literature are basic ingredients for career advancement. You can work toward a master's degree or PhD while employed; most employers will pay for graduate studies as an investment in your value to them.

An exciting new area of research is lunar chemistry. "The moon will be the logical place for research and development," says Dr. Larry Haskin, a geochemist. "Each cubic meter of lunar soil contains the chemical equivalent of lunch for two—two large cheese sandwiches, two 12-ounce sodas with sugar and two plums—with substantial nitrogen and carbon left over."[6] Another fast track will be the study of chlorofluorocarbons, the family of chemicals linked to damage to the earth's protective layer. And, as in other areas of science, genetic engineering will also be a growth field. Tobacco growers are looking for new uses for their products to replace the dying cigarette market, and chemists are exploring ways to turn tobacco plants into living chemical factories, producing such things as an AIDS drug, a human blood protein and an enzyme used in the food industry.[7]

"The best chemist is someone who loves chemistry. It's a demanding occupation, and unless you truly enjoy it, you're not going to make it," says Dr. Mary L. Good, internationally known chemist and senior vice president of Allied Signal. Terrance Russell of the American Chemical Society says that biotechnology, pharmaceutics and computer-aided chemistry are growth areas. Certification by the chemical society, Russell says, means better jobs and better salaries. He adds: "We're going to see a bidding war for chemistry professors in the next century."

ENVIRONMENTAL SCIENTIST

Job Requirements: Bachelor's degree in science or environmental studies from accredited college or university program for entry-level job as technician to help solve problems of environment, conservation, health and safety. Master's degree—particularly an MBA—for corporate management positions. Doctorate needed to research environmental problems. This broad scientific category includes disciplines such as hazardous and solid waste management, air and water quality, chemical engineering, geology, geophysics, conservation, meteorology, ecology, economics, chemical engineering, geology, botany, biology, sociology, zoology and anthropology. Background in toxology, hygienics, environmental law and safety. Must have laboratory and field experience. Ability to work with team and to do independent research. Must be highly ethical. Able to communicate with government and corporate officials at their level to convince them of need to make changes. Business background and expert knowledge of production and prevention costs essential. Patience in doing tedious, methodological research; courage of convictions important. Basic necessity: deep love and concern for the environment.

◆ **Salary:**

1991	*2000*
$39,060	**$68,200**
(starting)	(starting)

Inside Track: This is a new job category that encompasses many other scientific disciplines but is emerging as a strong professional field of its own. The anticipated rapid growth of this profession stems from public, government and corporate concern about the effects of hazardous waste, global warming, oil spills and fires, acid rain, deterioration of the ozone layer, toxic emissions, wildlife extinction, destruction of tropical rain forests and other environmental problems caused by humans. "Work in the environment is more than a job," says environmentalist Sanford Berry of Stowe, Vermont, editor of *Environmental*

Opportunities, a national employment letter. "It demands training, commitment, experience and passion."[8]

Though most environmental scientists start out in government jobs working for such agencies as the Environmental Protection Agency and the Occupational Safety and Health Administration, the "greening" of American business—its growing awareness of its legal and social obligation not to destroy the earth—makes the corporate sector a fast-growing area. Business and industry will need scientists who are expert in managing toxic waste disposal and lawyers who specialize in the environment. "Big companies are taking environmental regulations much more seriously than before because those with bad environmental records are likely to be disliked by customers," says Andrew Purkey, a graduate of John F. Kennedy School of Government at Harvard who works for a Washington, D.C., environmental and public policy consulting firm. His firm advises companies on compliance with federal environmental standards and regulations.[9]

Recycling is another fast-growing occupational area: Corporations and government agencies will hire scientists to manage waste, a $20 billion industry that is expected to grow because the nation's waste disposal companies are expanding rapidly. "There definitely will be an increase in jobs in our industry," says Kimberly D. Hedzik of the National Solid Waste Management Association in Washington. "Companies are acquiring other companies, building new facilities and hiring more people to staff them."[10] Employers will need engineers, chemists, waste control officers, operations supervisors, technicians, coordinators, planners, equipment sales personnel and operations and landfill managers. Anyone who comes up with an environmentally sound way to dispose of plastics will be a millionaire. But idealistic job seekers who want to clean up the environment should be cautious about working for waste management firms: They may be part of the problem. You have to ask, what happens to waste disposed of by so-called reputable firms?

At the research level, efforts to stop global warming and the further pollution of the waters through energy conservation and reforestation will create well-paying jobs for environmental scientists. An emerging consumer field will be environmental diagnostics, the development of kits ordinary citizens can use to test food, water or other substances for pesticide residues, food contaminants and industrial pollutants. The new technique, called "immunoassays," analyzes and measures the concentration of chemicals.[11]

Environmental concerns also are fueling demands for health scientists, and there aren't enough technically qualified people to fill the positions that will be available. Job openings will be in research and development, regulatory areas and occupational safety and health. The best job opportunities will be offered by nuclear power utilities, corporate radiation safety departments, the federal Department of Energy, consulting firms, radioactive and waste management sites and state regulatory agencies. Environmental hygienists will be in demand as consultants to business because of the projected increase in federally regulated materials, such as asbestos in building materials and lead in drinking water and paint. "The market for health scientists was wide open for me in 1990, and it will continue for future health scientists," says Tamara Edmonds, a graduate of Purdue University's School of Health Sciences. She is a health physicist who works on emergency preparedness for a nuclear power company.[12]

There will be 6,700 new jobs created for geologists and geophysicists who study the physical aspects and history of the earth. American owners of oil refineries will seek new sources of petroleum and will finance new explorations worldwide. Geologists will be in demand at companies involved in the recovery of petroleum and the extraction of coal. The race for clean fuel will propel jobs for geochemists who will be asked to step up research on finding less-polluting forms of unleaded gas. The international devastation caused by earthquakes has also increased demand for geologists to analyze earth stresses, formulate warning systems and design safe buildings for those areas of the world.

Environmental scientists must continue their education and keep up to date on the latest research and high-tech computerized equipment. To move ahead rapidly in this emerging profession, "you need good, old-fashioned training in the physical sciences such as chemistry, geology and biology," says Dr. Robert T. Moline, professor of geography at Gustavus Adolphus College in St. Peter, Minnesota. "You also have to read the deep ecology writers who have something to say to your soul."[13]

FOOD SCIENTIST

Job Requirements: Bachelor's degree in food science from four-year accredited college program to work with scientific and technological aspects of food and related products. Master's degree and doctorate needed for basic research to determine fundamental aspects of chemical, physical and biological nature of food. Background in chemistry, mathematics, physics, microbiology, nutrition, food analysis, biochemistry, food processing, calculus, organic chemistry, economics, biology and biometry. Need good communications skills to report findings and promote projects. Ability to work with team and to do independent research. Knowledge of global food production essential. Must combine strong technical skills, creativity, perseverance and good business sense with deep commitment to feeding people throughout the world in a nutritional and economical way.

✦ **Salary:**

_1991_	_2000_
$25,000	**$35,000**[14]
(starting)	(starting)

Inside Track: The sheer size and diversity of the food industry in the United States and the need for food professionals in developing countries will create unlimited job opportunities for these professionals in the 1990s. This important field of agricultural science attracts scientists concerned about eliminating world hunger and developing nutritional food and food products for healthy dieting by weight-conscious Americans.

Food science is a career of the future, though it is less known than other, more visible agricultural specialties. In sharp contrast to employment for farm workers, food science is a growing field for the 21st century because it combines high-tech advances with the public's concern about health and nutrition. Dr. Fergus Clysdale, professor of food science and nutrition at the University of Massachusetts in Amherst, says, "The U.S. Department of Agriculture has named food science as one of the critical employment needs areas over the next 15 years. People are going to eat less in the future, so we need to design foods that have a high nutrient and low calorie content. It's going to be cheaper in the long run to build the 'needs' into the food plants than to try to fortify the end product."[15] Creating low-calorie yet nutritious foods will be the assignment of food scientists—a far different job description from that of their nontechnical predecessors in agriculture, whose job is simply to grow food to feed as many people as possible.

Food scientists are typical of the biotechnology revolution that promises to change American agriculture in the next century. Food, from a chemical and physical standpoint, is the most complex of all natural products, and qualified food scientists, who analyze its quality and possible uses, will find jobs in product development, technical sales, quality assurance and food inspection or grading. There will be job opportunities with international agencies that fight famine, with government enforcement agencies and with small and midsize food processing companies.

As food science emerges as an independent profession, demand for technical workers in it will surge. "First and foremost, you have to be a scientist," says Dr. R. Glenn Brown, nutrition expert. That means, he says, you will have to have outstanding skills in chemistry, mathematics, physics, biochemistry and microbiology. Dr. Brown says the jobs with the best futures in 2000 will be at "medium-size companies that fill a specific niche, rather than large companies that are in a state of flux due to mergers and takeovers." Research scientists with strong business backgrounds are in a good position to head their own firms. "Think entrepreneurial," the food scientist says. "Take an idea and start your own business."

PHYSICIST/ASTRONOMER

Job Requirements: Bachelor's degree followed by master's in physics for entry-level jobs in practical application of basic principles governing structure and behavior of matter and energy. Doctorate essential for best jobs, including teaching, research and study of outer space. Must have background in mechanics, electromagnetism, optics, thermodynamics and atomic and molecular physics. Skilled in using lasers, cyclotrons, telescopes, mass spectrometers and high-tech computer equipment. Must understand gravity and nuclear energy. Experience in lab work. Must have specialty in elementary particular physics, nuclear physics, atomic and molecular physics, outer space, physics of condensed matter, optics, acoustics or health, plasma or fluids physics. Need inquisitive mind, extremely high intelligence, imagination, patience and ability to work on your own. Must be up to date on latest theories and rapidly changing computer technology.

◆ **Salary:**

_1991_	_2000_
$44,000	**$62,000**[16]
(starting)	(starting)

Inside Track: Job opportunities for physicists and astronomers (astronomy is a branch of physics) are projected to grow by 2,200. At the same time, enrollment of American students in these disciplines is low. The best openings will be for those with doctorates because of the pending retirement of many physics professors. Trained physicists will be offered well-paying, prestigious jobs in business, industry, academia and the government designing and performing experiments with the latest technology. The U.S. Department of Defense will continue to be a major employer and pay the highest salaries, but physicists will find growing job opportunities in nuclear energy, electronics, communications, medical instrumentation, navigation, space flight and aerospace technology. Beginning physicists often do routine work, supervised closely by experienced scientists. As you gain more experience and confidence, you will be given more challenging assignments and will be able to work independently.

One of the most rapidly expanding fields will be imaging science, which studies how images are formed, recorded and transmitted. Research results are applied to high-definition television, computer animation, copying machines, color reproduction, graphics and satellite photographs from space. Imaging physicists will be recruited to work in remote sensing, medical diagnostics and electronic printing.[17] Dr. Rodney Shaw, head of the Center for

Imaging Science at Rochester Institute of Technology, says that by the year 2000 at least 80 percent of the Fortune 500 companies will have imaging scientists on staff.

Astronomers will be doing research on the thousands of small, icy planets looping in orbit around the sun, billions of miles from earth, say scientists at the University of Colorado–Boulder's Center for Astrophysics and Space Astronomy. The best physicists in the world will be recruited to work on the superconducting supercollider, the new high-energy physics machine to be built in Texas by the end of the century. The state-of-the-art atom smasher will be at the cutting edge of research, and committed scientists will want to be a part of its team of experts. It will take one to two years of training to learn to operate the supercollider; then the real work of research will begin.[18] "We're always looking for geniuses and people skilled in accelerators," says Dr. Leon M. Lederman, Nobel Prize winner in physics and former director of Fermi National Accelerator Laboratory.

GLOSSARY

Birth dearth Refers to the fact that the number of Americans ages 18 to 24 years, the typical entry-level worker, is at an all-time low.

Cafeteria benefits Corporate benefit plans that allow employees to choose types of benefits and levels of coverage that suit their individual needs.

Career A chosen pursuit, lifework; progress in a profession.

Compressed time Working only at peak hours, such as from noon to 2 P.M. at a bank.

Computer literacy Basic knowledge and training in using computers and understanding how they work.

Dislocated or displaced worker Person who has lost a job and whose skills now are obsolete. For instance, those auto and steel workers who have been replaced by robots or whose factories are closed will not get their former jobs back. They have to be retrained.

Diversity, cultural diversity or diverse workforce Refers to projected changes in the composition of the labor force by the year 2000, in which white men will make up only 15 percent of all new hires. The workforce will be made up largely of women, minorities, immigrants, elderly, retired and disabled people.

Flexible hours or flextime Weekly work schedules in which workers, with approval of their supervisors, plan work hours that allow them to combine job and family responsibilities.

Glass ceiling A hypothetical but real barrier that keeps women from rising to the top of their professions because of sex discrimination.

Global marketplace or global economy A marketplace spread throughout the world that entwines the economies of all countries.

Goods-producing sector One of two industrial divisions of the economy. It includes manufacturing of durable goods such as metal products; nondurable goods including food, tobacco, apparel and other textile products; chemicals and allied products. The other sector is service producing. (See below.)

Graying of America Refers to the fact that by the year 2000, one out of three Americans will be 50 years or over, a result of the fact that the nation's 76 million baby boomers are middle-aged.

Headhunters Slang word for executive recruiters who work as consultants to public and private organizations to find qualified employees.

High-tech jobs Jobs that involve creating computer hardware, software and networks and other jobs involving new technology. Term refers to such jobs as computer analysts, programmers, electronic engineers, electronic data processing equipment operators and office machine repairers.

Low-tech jobs Jobs that involve using the equipment and systems created by high-tech personnel. (See above.) An employee who presses buttons to activate complicated computers is a low-tech worker.

Job A paid position in which you are employed.

Job bank A directory of available jobs collected by professional associations, state and private employment agencies and informal groups of job seekers.

Lateral move A job change in which a worker does not advance, but moves sideways. The move often brings more pay and diverse experience.

Occupational segregation Refers to the fact that most women work in only a handful of job categories, such as teaching, nursing, secretarial work and cosmetology, while men work in jobs across the board. The women's jobs are usually low-paying.

Old boy network The sharing of power and inside information by white men with other white men.

Outplacement agency An organization hired by corporations to counsel fired or laid-off employees in job-hunting techniques. Outplacement agencies do not find people jobs.

Profession An occupation or vocation requiring advanced study in a specialized field.

Service industry A subdivision of the service-producing sector (see below) that includes business services (e.g., lawyers, accountants, court reporters), health care and personal services, automotive services, legal and educational services and social services.

Service-producing sector The larger of two U.S. Department of Labor classifications of industrial divisions of the economy. It includes transportation, travel and hospitality, communications, utilities, wholesale and retail trade, finance, insurance, real estate, government and the service industry. The other sector is goods producing. (See above.)

Skilled worker An employee trained in a specific profession, such as in the building trades, technical jobs or in managerial and administrative work.

"Smart" or "expert" machines Computers programmed to do much of the work, respond to voice commands and link users instantly with sophisticated data from all over the world.

Stringer A journalist who works regularly but on a freelance basis for a specific news organization.

Turnover Describes the loss of employees who quit their jobs.

Unskilled worker An employee without training, such as a janitor, physical laborer, clerk, messenger or household worker.

NOTES

CHAPTER 1: THE NEW DEMOGRAPHICS

1. Statistics and projections are from the U.S. Department of Labor and the Bureau of Labor Statistics. Other background information is from the Hudson Institute's *Report on the Year 2000: Work and Workers for the 21st Century,* prepared for the U.S. Department of Labor, 1987.

2. Albert R. Karr, "Labor Letter: Affirmative Action Gains Favor as Way to Meet Labor Shortage," *The Wall Street Journal,* Nov. 1, 1988.

3. "Opportunity 2000: Creative Affirmative Action Strategies for a Changing Workforce," *Occupational Outlook Quarterly,* U.S. Department of Labor, Fall 1989.

4. *Ibid.*

5. Carol Kleiman, "Looking Ahead: What Are the Workplace Issues of the 21st Century?," *The Chicago Tribune,* June 18, 1989.

6. Carol Kleiman, "No Fear of the Future at the Women's Bureau," *The Chicago Tribune,* Oct. 10, 1988.

7. Carol Kleiman, "Working Women's Advocate Sees Good Dialogue with Pres. Bush," *The Chicago Tribune,* Feb. 27, 1989.

8. Carol Kleiman, "The Leap Across: What's the Secret to Clearing the Job-Gender Gap?" *The Chicago Tribune,* Feb. 19, 1989.

9. Jane Bryant Quinn, "Demographics Shout: Older Workers Are Needed," *The Chicago Tribune,* Sept. 18, 1989.

10. "Job Banks Keep Retirees Active on Part-Time Basis," *The Chicago Tribune,* Oct. 1, 1989.

11. Carol Kleiman, "More Retirees Making Their Encores as Temps," *The Chicago Tribune,* May 14, 1989.

12. Carol Kleiman, "Disabled Press Their On-the-Job Abilities," *The Chicago Tribune,* Oct. 9, 1988.

13. "Labor Force 2000 Facts," Allstate Forum on Public Issues, April 20, 1989.

14. James E. Robbins, "Temps Meet the Challenge," in *Flashes,* a newsletter published by Stivers Temporary Personnel, March 1987.

15. Edward E. Gordon, Judith Ponticell and Ronald R. Morgan, "Back to Basics," *Training and Development Journal,* August 1989.

16. Helen Frank Bensimon, "New ASTD Study Identifies 16 Basic Workplace Skills," in a press release from the American Society for Training and Development, Oct. 25, 1988.

17. Robert Pear, "Congress Acts to Admit More Skilled Immigrants," *The New York Times,* Aug. 15, 1990.

18. Dianna Solis and Pauline Yoskihashi, "Immigration Bill Would Expand Access to U.S. by Easing Entry for Skilled Professionals, Investors," *The Wall Street Journal,* Nov. 15, 1990.

19. Gina Kolata, "Japanese Labs in U.S. Luring America's Computer Experts," *The New York Times,* Nov. 11, 1990.

20. "36,000 U.S. Workers Displaced," *The New York Times,* Nov. 25, 1990.

21. Carol Kleiman, "Global Economy Means More U.S. Jobs," *The Chicago Tribune,* Jan. 20, 1991.

CHAPTER 2: THE WORKPLACE OF THE 21ST CENTURY

1. Carol Kleiman, "Family Trends at Corporations," *The Chicago Tribune*, April 14, 1991.

2. Carol Kleiman, "Alternative Work Schedules," *The Chicago Tribune*, April 1, 1991.

3. Bruce Buursma, "4-Day Week Runs Behind Schedule," *The Chicago Tribune*, Sept. 2, 1990.

4. "Workstyles in the '90s, the Age of the Home Office," press release from the Electronics Industries Association, January 1991.

5. Deidre Fanning, "The Executive Life: Fleeing the Office and Its Distractions," *The New York Times*, Aug. 12, 1990.

6. Carol Kleiman, "Taking Baby Steps: Corporate Child Care is Coming, But at a Slow Pace," *The New York Daily News*, Aug. 12, 1990.

7. "Employee Benefits Vital to Recruitment, Retention, Survey Shows," press release from Employee Benefit Research Institute, Sept. 11, 1990.

8. Annette Ney Meade, "Business of Wellness," *The Chicago Tribune*, Jan. 27, 1991.

9. Jerry Vondas, "Looking at the Hot Jobs of the Future: Get an Education," Scripps Howard News Service, July 19, 1988.

10. Carol Kleiman, "Apprenticeships Get New Lease on Life in Service Jobs," *The Chicago Tribune*, Feb. 3, 1991.

11. Carol Kleiman, "Future Lies in Adaptation, Training," *The Chicago Tribune*, Jan. 1, 1989.

12. Carol Kleiman, "Tip for Job Hunters: Open Your Own Doors," *The Chicago Tribune*, Nov. 26, 1989.

13. "Projections 2000: The Growing Need for Education," *Occupational Outlook Quarterly*, U.S. Department of Labor, Fall 1987.

14. "Liberal Arts Majors No Longer Minor Players in Big Business," from *The Chicago Tribune* wires, Aug. 7, 1988.

15. Edie Gibson, "More Firms Lean to Liberal Arts," *The Chicago Tribune*, Jan. 1, 1989.

16. "The 1990s: A Decade of Change for Graduate Business Education," press release from HWH Public Relations, New York, Oct. 3, 1990.

17. Richard Phillips, "Sex Rears Its Ugly MBA," *The Chicago Tribune*, Oct. 3, 1989.

18. Michael Kiernan, "Jobs in the 1990s," *U.S. News & World Report*, Sept. 25, 1989.

19. Carol Kleiman, "Shortage of PhDs Goes Beyond Campus," *The Chicago Tribune*, Nov. 18, 1990.

20. Selwyn Feinstein, "Labor Letter," *The Wall Street Journal*, Oct. 3, 1989.

21. Jane Bryant Quinn, "Sleazy Trade Schools Bleed the Poor, Taxpayers," *The Chicago Tribune*, May 8, 1989.

CHAPTER 3: THE FASTEST-GROWING FIELDS

1. Elizabeth McGregor, "Emerging Careers," *Occupational Outlook Quarterly*, U.S. Department of Labor, Fall 1987.

2. "Projections 2000," *Occupational Outlook Quarterly*, U.S. Department of Labor, Fall 1987.

3. Valerie A. Personick, "Industry Output and Employment Through the End of the Century," *Monthly Labor Review*, September 1987.

4. Carol Kleiman, "Manufacturers Eye Assembling Top Execs," *The Chicago Tribune*, Sept. 30, 1990.

5. Ceel Pasternak, "HRM Update," *HRMagazine*, October 1990.

6. Carol Kleiman, "Demand Running High for Janitors," *The Chicago Tribune*, March 3, 1991.

7. *The Federal Government, the Nation's Largest Employer*, U.S. Office of Personnel Management, Office of Public Affairs, 1990.

8. "Projections 2000," *Occupational Outlook Quarterly*, U.S. Department of Labor, Fall 1987.

9. Carol Kleiman, "Federal Government Still Needs a Lot of Good People," *The Chicago Tribune*, May 6, 1990.

10. Carol Kleiman, "Environmental Issues Fuel Growth in Job Possibilities," *The Chicago Tribune*, Aug. 20, 1989.

CHAPTER 4: FUTURISTIC JOBS

1. Jon Van, "Technology May Put Data Just a Femtosecond Away," *The Chicago Tribune*, Oct. 24, 1990.

2. Mitchell Locin, "Underpowered FCC Stepping into the Future," *The Chicago Tribune*, April 28, 1991.

3. Rory J. O'Connor, "Computers Opening the Window to New 'Realities,'" *The Chicago Tribune*, Dec. 26, 1990.

4. Barbara Brotman, "A Preview of Coming Attractions," *The Chicago Tribune*, Dec. 2, 1990.

5. *Ibid.*

6. Carol Kleiman, "Take a 21st Century Occupations Odyssey," *The Chicago Tribune*, April 14, 1991.

7. Norman Feingold's list appears in *Careers Tomorrow: The Outlook for Work in a Changing World*, published in 1991 by the World Future Society, Bethesda, Md. Additional job titles were given to me by Feingold in a telephone interview.

8. The rest of Chapter 4 is based on *The Chicago Tribune* column cited in note 6 above and on additional interviews with each of the sources.

CHAPTER 5: INSIDE TIPS FOR GETTING THE BEST JOB AND MOVING AHEAD

1. Carol Kleiman, "Tip for Job Hunters: Open Your Own Doors," *The Chicago Tribune*, Nov. 26, 1989.

2. Carol Kleiman, "Get Ready to Dig Deeper," *The Chicago Tribune*, Jan. 6, 1991.

3. "Careers, Ideals Remain," Associated Press News Wire, May 8, 1989.

4. Carol Kleiman, "Tip for Job Hunters: Open Your Own Doors," *The Chicago Tribune*, Nov. 26, 1989.

5. Michael Stanton, "Cooperative Education: Working Towards Your Future," *Occupational Outlook Quarterly*, Fall 1988.

6. Carol Kleiman, "Smart Job Seekers Do Homework at Library," *The Chicago Tribune*, Nov. 5, 1989.

7. Albert R. Karr, "Labor Letter: It's Who You Know," *The Wall Street Journal*, Oct. 16, 1990.

8. Carol Kleiman, "The Who's What of Employment Professionals," *The Chicago Tribune*, Jan. 6, 1991.

9. A good source for executive search firms, listed by specialties, is *The Career Makers: America's Top 100 Executive Recruiters*, by John Sibbald (New York: Harper & Row, 1990).

10. Carol Kleiman, "Unhappy? Try a Small Company," *The Chicago Tribune*, April 24, 1988.

11. "Sun-Belt Jobs are Growing," *Chicago Sun-Times*, Oct. 12, 1990.

12. Carol Kleiman, "Planning, Not Dreaming, Will Land That Foreign Job," *The Chicago Tribune*, Nov. 4, 1991.

13. Carol Kleiman, "Tip for Job Hunters: Open Your Own Doors," *The Chicago Tribune*, Nov. 26, 1989.

14. Carol Kleiman, "Old Information Arts Undergo a Resurgence," *The Chicago Tribune*, Sept. 23, 1991.

15. Carol Kleiman, "Employers Itemize Their Hiring Desires," *The Chicago Tribune*, March 25, 1990.

16. Carol Kleiman, "These Days You Can Score with a Lateral," *The Chicago Tribune*, May 5, 1991.

17. Carol Kleiman, "Survival in Corporate Jungle: Workshop Teaches Self-Defense in Office Conflicts," *The Chicago Tribune*, Nov. 20, 1989.

18. Carol Kleiman, "Till Workplace Do Us Part," *The Chicago Tribune*, June 17, 1990.

19. Carol Kleiman, "World of Difference for Tomorrow's CEO," *The Chicago Tribune*, Oct. 15, 1989.

CHAPTER 6: CHANGING JOBS, SWITCHING CAREERS OR STARTING YOUR OWN BUSINESS

1. Carol Kleiman, "If Your Job's a Cul-de-Sac, It's Time to Map a New Route," *The Chicago Tribune*, Oct. 1, 1989.

2. Amanda Bennett, "A White-Collar Guide to Job Security," *The Wall Street Journal*, Sept. 11, 1990.

3. Jaclyn Fierman, "Why Women Still Don't Hit the Top," *Fortune*, July 30, 1990.

4. Carol Kleiman, "Labor Chief Investigating Corporate 'Glass Ceilings,' " *The Chicago Tribune*, Oct. 4, 1990.

5. Carol Kleiman, "Women at the Top Tell Keys to Success and Survival," *The Chicago Tribune*, Nov. 5, 1990.

6. Carol Kleiman, "How Bad Is Fired? Answer Is in 'Why', " *The Chicago Tribune*, April 7, 1991.

7. Carol Kleiman, " 'You're Fired' Can Be First Step in a New Direction," *The Chicago Tribune*, Nov. 12, 1990.

8. Alan L. Otten, "People Patterns: Jobless People Recover Fast Psychologically," *The Wall Street Journal*, Sept. 5, 1989.

9. Gordon Monson, "Four or Five Jobs per Career," *Los Angeles Daily News*, June 20, 1989.

10. "Changing Jobs Not Always a Good Idea," press release from Philip G. Ryan Inc., public relations, 1989.

11. Albert Karr, "Labor Letter: Switching Can Pay," *The Wall Street Journal*, April 25, 1989.

12. Leslie Baladacci, "Prime Time for Job Switch," *Chicago Sun-Times*, Oct. 23, 1989.

13. "What Are You Good At? Ask 20 Friends," *The Chicago Tribune*, July 7, 1991.

14. Monroe W. Karin and Robert F. Black, "America's Boom Towns," *U.S. News & World Report*, Nov. 13, 1989.

15. "Nationwide Study Finds 77 Percent of Entrepreneurs Remain in Business After the First Three Years," press release from American Express Travel Related Services Company, Inc., Oct. 1989.

16. Frederick H. Lowe, "Gale Sayers Scores Touchdowns in Business," *North Star News & Analysis*, August 1989.

17. "Layoff Victims Tell of the Trials and Fulfillment," *The Wall Street Journal*, Sept. 11, 1990.

18. "Courting the Fairer Market: Women-Owned Businesses Growing Fast," *Small Business Directory*, July/Aug. 1991.

19. Carol Kleiman, "Women Find Way to Top by Forming Their Own Businesses," *The Chicago Tribune*, Feb. 13, 1989.

20. "Trend in Work with All the Comforts of Home," *The Chicago Tribune*, Jan. 1, 1989.

21. Jane Bryant Quinn, Washington Post Writers Group, "Pink Slip's a Call to Shore up Financially," *The Chicago Tribune*, Nov. 12, 1990.

CHAPTER 7: SECURING YOUR FUTURE

1. Amanda Vogt, "Vocabulary of Success: The List Runs from Motivation to Sacrifice," *The Chicago Tribune*, March 31, 1991.

2. Discussion of high-tech and low-tech jobs in the 21st century is excerpted from Carol Kleiman, "High-Tech vs. Low-Tech in 2000," *The Chicago Tribune*, Sept. 1, 1991.

CHAPTER 8: THE TOP JOBS

1. I am especially indebted to tables and interpretations in George T. Silvestri and John M. Lukasiewicz, *Projections 2000: A Look at Occupational Employment in the Year 2000*, Division of Occupational Outlook, U.S. Department of Labor, Bureau of Labor Statistics, September 1987. I also used information from "Occupational Projections and Training Data," *Occupational Outlook Handbook*, April 1990.

2. Many of the current salaries that are not from professionals in the field are based on 1988 figures from the U.S. Department of Labor, Bureau of Labor Statistics. I updated the federal salary listings by 5 percent a year, based on average salary increases for the years from 1988 to 1991.

3. *The Future World of Work: Looking Toward the Year 2000*, a study by United Way of America, January 1989.

4. Bennett Harrison and Barry Bluestone, *The Great U-Turn: Corporate Restructuring and the Polarization of America* (New York: Basic Books, 1989).

5. *Working in America: A Chart Book*, U.S. Department of Labor, 1987.

CHAPTER 9: BUSINESS AND FINANCIAL SERVICES

1. Northwestern University, *1991 Lindquist-Endicott Report.*
2. David Birkenstein, attorney and certified public accountant.
3. C. Paul Johnson, chairman and CEO, First Colonial Bank Corp.
4. Bank Marketing Association.
5. Securities Industry Association.
6. Cathy Mrozek, court reporter and owner, Mrozek Associates, court reporting.
7. Northwestern University, *1991 Lindquist-Endicott Report.*
8. International Association for Financial Planning.
9. Securities Industry Association.
10. Carol Kleiman, "Wall St. Offers Jobs at Top and Bottom," *The Chicago Tribune*, Sept. 16, 1990.
11. Abbott, Langer & Associates.
12. Carol Kleiman, "The Latest Frontier for Lawyers," *The Chicago Tribune*, May 26, 1990.
13. Robb Lonan, "New Technology Sends Law Firms Recruiting Scientists To Be Partners," *The New York Times*, March 22, 1991.
14. Abbott, Langer & Associates.
15. Carol Kleiman, "Paralegals Take Law's Work into Own Hands," *The Chicago Tribune*, Jan. 14, 1990.
16. Steve Kerch, "U.S. Brokers Already on European Map," *The Chicago Tribune*, Jan. 6, 1991.

CHAPTER 10: EDUCATION, GOVERNMENT AND SOCIAL SERVICES

1. National Policy Board for Educational Administration.
2. Jon Van, "International Affairs Library Is Trading Paper for Laser Discs," *The Chicago Tribune*, March 17, 1991.

3. Northwestern University, *1991 Lindquist-Endicott Report.*

4. Carol Kleiman, "Industries Counting More on Statistics," *The Chicago Tribune,* Feb. 25, 1990.

5. Carol Kleiman, "Personal Woes Top Drugs as Job Problem," *The Chicago Tribune,* July 8, 1990.

6. Carol Kleiman, "Anti-Greed Attitudes Boosting Social Work," *The Chicago Tribune,* May 20, 1990.

7. American Federation of Teachers.

8. American Association of University Professors.

9. Carol Kleiman, "Shortage of PhDs Goes Beyond Campus," *The Chicago Tribune,* Nov. 18, 1990.

CHAPTER 11: ENGINEERING AND COMPUTER TECHNOLOGY

1. *Occupational Outlook Quarterly,* U.S. Department of Labor, Spring 1990.

2. Northwestern University, *1991 Lindquist-Endicott Report.*

3. Nicholas Basta, "Hot-Tech Hits," *Graduating Engineer,* December 1990.

4. College Placement Council.

5. DeVry Institute of Technology.

6. Illinois Institute of Technology.

7. Northwestern University, *1991 Lindquist-Endicott Report.*

8. Nicholas Basta, "Hot-Tech Hits," *Graduating Engineer,* December 1990.

9. Illinois Institute of Technology.

10. Moraine Valley Community College.

CHAPTER 12: HEALTH CARE PROFESSIONS

1. Dr. Paul Pladziewicz, Chicago Institute of Technology.

2. Mount Sinai Hospital and Medical Center.

3. Carol Kleiman, "How a Home Care Service Becomes and Remains a Healthy Firm," *The Chicago Tribune*, Sept. 10, 1990.

4. Suzanne Carleton, "New Promotional Strategy Targets Second Career Market," *OT Week*, May 17, 1990.

5. Carol Kleiman, "Physical Therapy Field Growing Fast," *The Chicago Tribune*, April 3, 1988.

6. Daniel A. Haney, "Some Doctors Ask: Are Physicians Too Greedy?" Associated Press, Sept. 24, 1990.

7. American Association of Physician Assistants.

8. Elisabeth Rosenthal, "That Person in the White Smock Is Not a Doctor," *The New York Times*, Jan. 10, 1991.

9. Roger Allan, "Radiology Careers Combine Health Care and Technology to Meet Critical Need," Summit on Manpower, 1991.

10. Metropolitan Healthcare Council.

11. Allan Johnson, "In Demand: Pros Tell Why They Chose Nursing," *The Chicago Tribune*, Jan. 27, 1991.

12. Carol Kleiman, "Shortage of Nurses Getting Worse," *The Chicago Tribune*, May 8, 1991.

13. Lester E. Fisher, director, Lincoln Park Zoo.

CHAPTER 13: HOSPITALITY INDUSTRY

1. Carol Kleiman, "Apprenticeships Get New Lease on Life in Service Jobs," *The Chicago Tribune*, Feb. 3, 1991.

2. Carol Kleiman, "Flight Attendants Win Fight over Weight Rules," *The Chicago Tribune*, March 3, 1991.

3. Future Aviation Professionals.

4. *Ibid.*

5. Carol Kleiman, "Graying of Airline Cockpits Means There Are More Jobs to Land," *The Chicago Tribune*, April 2, 1989.

6. Evelyn Echols, Echols International Travel and Hotel Schools.

7. Tom Beldon, "Firms Seem to Be Looking for a Few Good, Big Travel Agencies," Knight-Ridder Newspapers, April 21, 1991.

8. Carol Kleiman, "First Job with Future—Call It Entry-Level," *The Chicago Tribune*, March 31, 1991.

CHAPTER 14: MANAGEMENT AND OFFICE PERSONNEL

1. Carol Kleiman, "Firms Find That, with Retraining, Older Is Better," *The Chicago Tribune*, Feb. 4, 1990.

2. National Association of Personnel Consultants.

3. Carol Kleiman, "Study Links Spate of Job Bias Lawsuits to Unemployment," *The Chicago Tribune*, April 21, 1991.

4. *Ibid.*

5. Women Employed.

6. Pat Widder, "Take a Memo: Secretaries Want Bonuses, Not Bonbons," *The Chicago Tribune*, April 24, 1991.

CHAPTER 15: MANUFACTURING, REPAIR, CONSTRUCTION, AGRICULTURE AND TRANSPORTATION

1. Future Aviation Professionals.

2. Maudlyne Ihejirika, "City, Airline Join to Get Job Training off Ground," *Chicago Sun-Times*, Aug. 17, 1991.

3. Carol Kleiman, "Service Managers Thrive in Slump," *The Chicago Tribune*, Feb. 17, 1991.

4. Pamela Sebastian, "Labor Letter: Architects Go Global," *The Wall Street Journal*, Sept. 27, 1990.

5. Amanda Vogt, "Designs on Living: Architect Helps Homeowners Build Their Dreams," *The Chicago Tribune*, Nov. 9, 1990.

6. Carol Kleiman, "Service Managers Thrive in Slump," *The Chicago Tribune*, Feb. 17, 1991.

7. Newell A. Johnson, vice president, Bert Williams Construction Company.

8. Jonathon Hicks, "For the Skilled, It's a Seller's Market," *The New York Times*, June 5, 1988.

9. Stephen Franklin, "Farm Conservatism Weathering Upbeat Atmosphere," *The Chicago Tribune*, April 14, 1991.

10. Carol Kleiman, "Industrial Designers Plan New Future," *The Chicago Tribune*, June 16, 1991.

11. Peter Wodarz, owner, Milieu Design Landscaping.

12. Carol Kleiman, "Lucky Breaks for Repair Profession: Computer, Copier Machine Fields Are Fertile Grounds," *The Chicago Tribune*, Feb. 14, 1988.

13. Carol Kleiman, "Manufacturers Eye Assembling Top Execs," *The Chicago Tribune*, Sept. 30, 1990.

CHAPTER 16: MEDIA AND THE ARTS

1. Kenneth R. Clark, "Interactive TV Giving Viewers Their Prime Time," *The Chicago Tribune*, March 17, 1991.

2. Leigh Behrens, "Producing Arsenio," *The Chicago Tribune*, May 15, 1990.

3. Randall Rothenburg, "Advertising's Antic Upstarts," *The New York Times*, March 31, 1991.

4. Pat Widder, "Marketers in '90s Face a Brand Name Dilemma," *The Chicago Tribune*, Aug. 27, 1990.

5. Carol Kleiman, "Every Product Has Its Manager," *The Chicago Tribune*, March 17, 1991.

6. Information on arts administration is excerpted from Carol Kleiman, "Arts Painting a Picture of Management Opportunity," *The Chicago Tribune*, July 22, 1990.

7. Judie Anderson, associate editor, graphics, *The Chicago Tribune*.

8. Barbara Basler, "Peter Pan, Garfield and Bart—All Have Asian Roots," *The New York Times*, Dec. 2, 1990.

9. Jean Gaddy Wilson, University of Missouri School of Journalism.

10. Patricia Leigh Brown, "Design in the '90s," *The Chicago Tribune*, March 24, 1991.

11. Jon Van, "Kodak Relying on Marriage of Film, CDs," *The Chicago Tribune*, May 9, 1991.

12. Carol Kleiman, "PR People Spurn Pessimism on Job," *The Chicago Tribune*, Dec. 9, 1990.

13. Carol Kleiman, "Non-Profits Offer Careers for People with a Cause," *The Chicago Tribune*, May 12, 1991.

14. National Association of Broadcasters.

15. Jean Gaddy Wilson, University of Missouri School of Journalism.

CHAPTER 17: SALES AND PERSONAL SERVICES

1. Fred Piattoni, Chicago Cosmetology Association.

2. Carol Kleiman, "Insurance Firms Diversifying Staffs for Sound Business Reasons," *The Chicago Tribune*, April 8, 1991.

3. Carol Kleiman, "Retail Jobs Still Abundant Despite Industry Shakeups," *The Chicago Tribune*, Aug. 12, 1990.

4. Norma Libman, "First Person: Salesmanship Training," *The Chicago Tribune*, March 24, 1991.

5. Carol Kleiman, "Globalism Will Have Mixed Effect on Jobs," *The Chicago Tribune*, Jan. 20, 1991.

CHAPTER 18: SCIENCE

1. Dr. Allan Goecker, Purdue University School of Agriculture.

2. George Gunset, "Pitman-Moore: The Mouse That Roars in Animal Health," *The Chicago Tribune*, May 13, 1991.

3. David Walsh, "Biotech Companies Bloom as New Genetic Products Hit Market," *The Chicago Tribune*, April 7, 1991.

4. Kleila Carlsen, "Romancing the Ray: Fishes' Mating Rituals Prove Electrifying," press release from Washington University School of Medicine, May 1991.

5. Northwestern University, *1991 Lindquist-Endicott Report*.

6. "Its Waning Days Over, the Moon Makes a Comeback," press release, Washington University in St. Louis, May 1991.

7. Jerry E. Bishop, "Tobacco Plants Become Assembly Lines for Scientists Producing New Chemicals," *The Wall Street Journal*, May 14, 1991.

8. Carol Kleiman, "Environmental Issues Fuel Growth in Job Possibilities," *The Chicago Tribune*, Aug. 20, 1989.

9. John Arundel, "Environmental Field is Green with Growth in Employment," *The Chicago Tribune*, Jan. 16, 1991.

10. Carol Kleiman, "One Person's Trash is Other's Opportunity," *The Chicago Tribune*, June 24, 1990.

11. Marian Uhlman, "A Natural Market for At-Home Tests," *The Chicago Tribune*, Feb. 4, 1991.

12. Kathleen O'Neil, "Job Picture is Bright for Health Scientists," Purdue University press release, March 1991.

13. Carol Kleiman, "Environmental Issues Fuel Growth in Job Possibilities," *The Chicago Tribune*, Aug. 20, 1989.

14. Dr. R. Glenn Brown, University of Massachusetts at Amherst. Salaries for bachelor's degree only.

15. Dr. Clysdale is quoted in a press release from Dobiskey Associates, a media relations firm in Keene, N.H., Jan. 3, 1989.

16. Dr. R. Glenn Brown, University of Massachusetts at Amherst. Salaries for bachelor's degree only.

17. Elizabeth M. Fowler, "Vast Growth in Imaging is Forecast," *The New York Times*, Jan. 7, 1991.

18. Jon Van, "Funding Cut Baffles Fermilab," *The Chicago Tribune*, May 21, 1991.

BIBLIOGRAPHY

America's Changing Workforce. Nuventures Consultants, 1989.

Bard, Ray, and Susan K. Elliott. *National Directory of Corporate Training Programs.* Doubleday, 1989.

Beatty, Richard. *The Complete Job Search Book.* Wiley, 1991.

Boyett, Joseph, and Henry Conn. *Workplace: The Revolution Reshaping American Business.* Dutton, 1990.

Burek, Koek and Novallo. *Encyclopedia of Associations.* Gale Publishing, 1990.

Careers Tomorrow. World Future Society, 1990.

CEIP Fund. *The Complete Guide to Environmental Careers.* Island Press, 1990.

Cohen, Lilly, and Dennis Young. *Careers for Dreamers and Doers: A Guide to Management Careers in the Nonprofit Sector.* The Foundation Center, 1991.

Dictionary of Occupational Titles, 4th ed., rev., 2 vols. U.S. Department of Labor, 1991.

Feingold, Norman, and Maxine Atwater. *New Emerging Careers.* Garrett Park Press, 1990.

Ferguson, Trudi, and Joan Dunphy. *Answers to the Mommy Track: How Wives and Mothers in Business Reach the Top and Balance Their Lives.* New Horizons Press, 1991.

Geoghegan, Thomas. *Which Side Are You On? Trying to Be for Labor When It's Flat on Its Back.* Farrar, Strauss & Giroux, 1991.

Harkavy, Michael. *101 Careers: A Guide to the Fastest-Growing Opportunities.* Wiley, 1990.

Harrison, Bennett, and Barry Bluestone. *The Great U-Turn: Corporate Restructuring and the Polarizing of America.* Basic Books, 1989.

Heuer, Albert. *Moving up the Corporate Ladder: All You Need to Know to Make the Climb.* Small Business Press, 1990.

Hoover, Gary, et al. *Hoover's Handbook of World Business.* Reference Press, 1992.

Hyatt, Carole. *Shifting Gears.* Simon & Schuster, 1991.

Kanter, Donald, and Philip Mirvis. *The Cynical American: Living and Working in an Age of Discontent and Disillusion.* Jossey-Bass, 1991.

Kanter, Rosabeth Moss. *When Giants Learn to Dance: Mastering the Challenges of Strategy.* Simon & Schuster, 1989.

Krantz, Les. *The Jobs-Rated Almanac.* World Almanac, 1990.

Norback, Craig. *VGM's Careers Encyclopedia.* VGM Career Horizons, 1991.

Occupational Outlook Handbook, 1990–91. U.S. Department of Labor, Bureau of Labor Statistics.

Opportunity 2000: Creative Affirmative Action Strategies for a Changing Workforce. Hudson Institute, for the U.S. Department of Labor, 1988.

Sibbald, John. *The Career Makers: America's Top 100 Executive Recruiters.* Harper & Row, 1991.

Silvestri, George, and John Lukasiewicz. *Projections 2000: A Look at Occupational Employment in the Year 2000.* Division of Occupational Outlook, U.S. Department of Labor, Bureau of Labor Statistics, September 1987.

Swanson, Barbara. *Careers in Health Care.* VGM Career Horizons, 1990.

Sweeney, John, and Karen Nussbaum. *Solutions for the New Work Force: Policies for a New Social Contract.* Seven Locks Press, 1990.

Tepper, Ron. *Power Resumes.* Wiley, 1990.

Watanuki, Kumiko. *Business and Career Planning Workbook.* Vantage Press, 1990.

Wegmann, Chapman and Johnson. *Work in the New Economy.* American Association for Counseling and Development, 1990.

Workforce America: Managing Employee Diversity as a Vital Resource. Business One/Irwin, 1990.

Workforce 2000: Work and Workers for the 21st Century. Hudson Institute, for the U.S. Department of Labor, 1987.

Working in America: A Chart Book. U.S. Department of Labor, 1987.

Woy, Patricia. *Small Businesses That Grow and Grow and Grow.* Betterway Publications, 1990.

Wright, John, and Edward Dwyer. *The American Almanac of Jobs and Salaries.* Avon, 1990.

INDEX